Hiking Trails

of the
Joyce Kilmer–Slickrock
& Citico Creek
Wildernesses

Tim Homan

Hiking Trails

of the
Joyce Kilmer–Slickrock
& Citico Creek
Wildernesses

2nd Edition

PEACHTREE
ATLANTA

Published by
PEACHTREE PUBLISHERS, LTD.
494 Armour Circle NE
Atlanta, Georgia 30324

Text ©1990, 1998 by Tim Homan
Photographs ©1998 by David Acton Brown, Pete Schrantz, William Houghton, Page Luttrell
Cover photograph ©1998

Cover photograph by William Houghton

Interior illustrations by Carol L. Gubbins Hahn
Book design by Loraine M. Balcsik
Book composition by Robin Sherman

Manufactured in the United States of America

10 9 8 7 6 5 4 3 2 1
Second Edition

Library of Congress Cataloging-in-Publication Data
  Homan, Tim.
      Hiking Trails of Joyce Kilmer–Slickrock and Citico Creek Wildernesses / Tim Homan. — 2nd ed.
          p. cm.
      Rev. ed. of: Hiking Trails of Joyce Kilmer–Slickrock and Citico Creek Wilderness areas.

      ISBN 1-56145-033-2

      1. Hiking—Tennessee—Citico Creek Wilderness—Guidebooks. 2. Hiking—Joyce Kilmer–Slickrock Wilderness (N.C. and Tenn.)—Guidebooks. 3. Citico Creek Wilderness—Guidebooks.
   4. Joyce Kilmer–Slickrock Wilderness (N.C. and Tenn.)—Guidebooks.
   I. Homan, Tim. Hiking Trails of Joyce Kilmer–Slickrock and Citico Creek Wilderness areas.
   II. Title.

   GV199.42.T22C585 1998
   917.56'97—DC21   98-9326
                                               CIP

Cover photo: Unicoi Mountains
Photo credits: pages 33 and 165 by David Acton Brown; pages 55 and 189 by Peter Schrantz; page 129 by William Houghton; page 81 by Page Luttrell

Maps by XNR Productions, Middleton, WI

Acknowledgments

I WISH TO EXTEND SPECIAL THANKS to the following people for their help:

■ David Acton Brown, Andy Furlow, and Page Luttrell for hiking with me;

■ James Burchfield and Steve Rickerson, both formerly with the Cheoah Ranger District in the Nantahala National Forest, and Bill Cheeks, formerly with the Tellico Ranger District in the Cherokee National Forest, for their time and information;

■ Laney Cutshaw with the Cheoah Ranger District in the Nantahala National Forest and Mary Jane Burnette with the Tellico Ranger District in the Cherokee National Forest for answering questions concerning changing conditions in the wilderness;

■ Vicky Holifield for her editing and patience;

■ Carol Hahn for her illustrations and David Acton Brown, William Houghton, Page Luttrell, and Pete Schrantz for their photographs;

■ My parents, John and Irene, for their support.

■ My deepest and most heartfelt thanks go to my wife, Page Luttrell, for her typing, editing, patience, insight, and hard work.

—*Tim Homan*

Contents

Part I—Joyce Kilmer–Slickrock Wilderness

Part II—Citico Creek Wilderness

Preface

The First Edition

During the late winter and spring of 1988, I attempted to walk all of the trails included in this guide twice. On the first go-around, I rolled a measuring wheel—a big orange, incessantly clicking, spoked-wheel mechanism that resembles a unicycle. By using this apparatus I was able to record distances in feet, such as 57,152 feet for the Fodderstack Trail, then convert the large numbers to the nearest tenth of a mile. If a measurement fell exactly between tenths, 2.75 miles for example, the figure was rounded upward to the nearest tenth.

During the second trip on each trail, I took compass headings, more notes on plants and difficulty ratings, and generally took pleasure in walking without the wheel. I was nearing completion of the second cycle when I was struck down (actually sat down is more apt) by a protozoan pest—*Giardia lamblia*—in mid-June. Recovered, I finished up the second hike to all trails except Horse Cove and Pine Ridge, which I saw no reason to hike a second time, in the spring of 1989.

I wanted to hike each trail twice because I thought that if I saw more, learned more, it would help make this a better guide, and because I like to hike almost as much as anything else. Last and perhaps foremost, the longer I stayed in the woods, the longer I could forestall the inevitable torturous stint of sitting and writing.

The emphasis on spring is intended and planned. Relatively few people hike in July or January. And most people are already familiar with the aster gardens and brilliant foliage and berries of fall. News of autumn's peak is broadcast on the radio and television and is fairly obvious to anyone driving by.

But spring is different. Over the years, numerous hikers have asked me, "Where are all the wildflowers?" Invariably, the flowers had already finished blooming a month or two before. The real question is when and where are all the wildflowers. I have tried, as best I could, to answer that question.

My emphasis on spring wildflowers is also an attempt to help spread usage over more months of the year, to help prevent the May 15 through October 15 crunch. Except at the highest elevations, the ephemeral blossoms of early spring usually peak during late March and April before many campgrounds open. The weather during this time of the year is unpredictable, but often pleasant. And in my experience the trails are lightly traveled during this time, especially on weekdays. In fact, when I hiked on the Citico Creek side of the wilderness day after day during the week, I found myself hoping for other hikers.

The Second Edition

This revision had to wait until my publisher ran low on books and until the skyway, the new highway between Tellico Plains, Tennessee, and Robbinsville, North Carolina, was completed. Fortunately, both occurred at about the same time. During the decade since the first edition, there have been numerous changes, large and small, within and close to the Joyce Kilmer–Slickrock and Citico Creek Wildernesses. Outside the wilderness, signage to approach roads has improved and the skyway has increased the ease and speed of travel from one wilderness to the other.

At the wilderness edge, Wolf Laurel Trail has been completely rerouted and shortened. The Cold Spring Gap Trailhead has been abandoned and moved southward to Beech Gap. This move made Fodderstack Trail 1.8 miles longer, made Cold Spring Gap an interior trail, and made South Fork Citico's southeastern end inaccessible to motorized vehicles. This move also changed distances and directions to nearby interior trails, such as Brush Mountain. As in any network, one change brings many others.

Within the wilderness itself, the Forest Service changed a horse-trail designation and rerouted Big Fat and Hangover Lead South

Trails. In addition to purging Horse Cove Trail from this guide,* I have added Windy Gap. The greatest changes within the wilderness, however, were wrought by the wind. A late winter blizzard whipped through the mountains in 1993. Two years later, a still powerful Hurricane Opal ripped through the fully leaved hardwoods, uprooting and breaking thousands of trees. Many of these windthrows are still there, blocking the way with downed boles of varying thickness and height. The Forest Service is looking for a few good men and women who don't mind hard work to help clear the wilderness trails.

The completion of the skyway necessitated major changes in the directions. In an attempt to avoid repetition, to familiarize hikers with important junctions, and to avoid constant, out-of-section cross-referencing, we decided to provide the directions in tiers, each tier moving closer to the trailhead. For those who prefer topo sheets, or want them in addition to the wilderness map, the names of the topographic quadrangles—1:24,000 scale—have been added to the headers for each trail (See page 227 for address).

After six straight years of poking around the memorial forest in the 1990s, I realized that some of the flowering dates were wrong—too early for most years. The spring that I spent hiking the combined wilderness, 1988, was exceptionally early. Adjustments to the dates have been made.

While not particularly important, one change is at least noteworthy. The lunker trees along the two loops in the memorial forest are still slowly increasing their girth. The two thickest yellow poplars are now officially humongous—giants of the once great eastern forest. Over the past ten years these two trees have surpassed 20 feet in circumference at DBH (diameter at breast height): 4½ feet from the ground, measured from the high side if the ground is sloped. Enjoy the mountains.

* The first edition of this guide described Horse Cove Trail, which begins at the upper end of Horse Cove Campground. By the late 1980s the Forest Service had already designated this former road a low-maintenance trail. By the mid-1990s it had officially become a no-maintenance trail. The upper forks, now overgrown with saplings and briers, are tough going, and the upper section of the main trail is rapidly approaching the same condition. In the spring of 1998 only the lowermost mile could still be easily walked—but even that segment has old bridges that are now rotting and becoming increasingly dangerous. For these reasons—lack of maintenance and dangerous bridges—Horse Cove Trail has been deleted from this edition.

Wilderness complements and completes civilization. I might say that the existence of wilderness is also a complement to civilization. Any society that feels itself too poor to afford the preservation of wilderness is not worthy of the name of civilization.

—*Edward Abbey*
Down the River *(1982)*

The Combined Wilderness

THE CONTIGUOUS WILDERNESS, Joyce Kilmer–Slickrock and Citico Creek, encompasses 32,904 acres.* This substantial acreage ranks it as the second largest national forest wilderness, or combined wilderness, in the South. (Another combined wilderness, the Cohutta–Big Frog in Georgia and Tennessee, is largest.)

Even though this area is far from the size of a western wilderness, it offers the flexibility of numerous options and room enough to roam. This guide details a network of thirty trails totaling 123 miles, all but 4 or 5 miles of which are within the wilderness. You can day-hike a short trail in and right back out, or you can backpack a long circuitous route, with loops off of loops, and walk for a week or more without retracing your steps.

The wild green yonder of the eastern wilderness expands and contracts with you and your decisions. If you walk the widest trail to the most popular waterfall on a warm weekend, the wilderness—any wilderness—shrinks and becomes overcrowded. If you drop into a hollow that hasn't felt human footprints in years and become the first person to lay eyes on a bear-clawed tree, the wilderness looms larger, regains that special majesty of all wild and lonely places. The more solitude you want, the more solitude the wilderness has for you. The more wildness you want—the wilder and more adventurous you are—the wilder the wilderness will become.

Citico Creek History

Even the sketchiest accounts of this rugged region must surely start with the land, which was so recently rich with incredible forests and abundant wildlife including buffalo, elk, mountain lion, and

* Forest Service personnel recalculated the size of the Joyce Kilmer–Slickrock Wilderness. It is now on record as 17,394 acres instead of the former figure—17,013 acres. This increase raises the two-wilderness total to 33,285 acres.

wolf. And of course the people, the Cherokee, who lived amidst this Appalachian splendor. The date of the Cherokee's arrival in the southern mountains can only be approximated by anthropologists, but history clearly details the days when all but a few of their people were forcibly evicted. The year was 1838. What Washington euphemized as "The Removal," the Cherokee called the Trail of Tears.

As soon as the Cherokee were booted out, white settlers began to farm the river bottoms, primarily along the Tellico and Little Tennessee. Prior to the Civil War the land now within the wilderness was owned by wealthy plantation holders and used as a hunting ground. After the war a series of northern proprietors, including a U.S. senator, held title to the Citico.

Babcock Land and Timber Company bought the tract and began logging in the early 1920s. In the summer of 1925, a major fire burned over half the area now included in the preserve. The Babcock fire destroyed buildings, bridges, even railroad ties partially buried in the ground. The small amount of unburned timber that remained at the higher elevations did not warrant rebuilding the rail system, so Babcock discontinued its operation south of Pine Ridge. Cutting continued north of Pine Ridge until 1929.

Because the fire stopped the logging, scattered pockets of virgin forest still survive. A 200-acre parcel between Glenn Gap and the headwaters of Indian Valley Branch and a 180-acre stand surrounding the waterfall on Falls Branch are the largest sites. Much of the highcountry in the southeastern corner of the wilderness, while not strictly virgin because a few valuable species were taken, still has a large percentage of old-growth trees.

Settlement unrelated to the logging industry was light and sporadic, occurring primarily between 1880 and 1930. Few families attempted to homestead the steep terrain away from the western edge of today's wilderness. Most who tried their luck farmed what flatland they could find beside streams and used the main Unicoi ridge, where the Fodderstack Trail now runs, as summer pasture.

The U.S. Forest Service acquired the land from Babcock in 1935. Since that time, management policy has allowed nature to heal the portion of the forest that was both cut and burned. Approximately 11 percent of the acreage now within the wilderness was timbered from 1935 to 1975.

The Eastern Wilderness Act of 1975, the same legislation that established Joyce Kilmer–Slickrock, designated Citico Creek as a wilderness study area. After years of debate and controversy, the 1984 Tennessee Wilderness Act finally authorized the 15,891-acre Citico Creek Wilderness. This steep-sloped area, where elevations range from 1,400 feet to 5,160 feet on Bob Stratton Bald's western shoulder, is located in the northwestern corner of the Unicoi Mountains, one of many interconnecting chains that make up the wide, southern half of the Blue Ridge physiographic province. Citico Creek is situated entirely within the Cherokee National Forest in eastern Monroe County, Tennessee.

With the exception of one or two rivulets along Sassafras Ridge, the area's entire dendritic watershed system drains into Citico Creek, a Little Tennessee tributary. Citico is the anglicized word for the Cherokee's *Sitiku*—their name for the stream and the former town at the mouth of the creek. The word for the watercourse and town can no longer be translated. Perhaps it meant rugged land ribbed with ridges and veined with rushing streams.

The main Unicoi crest serves as Citico Creek's eastern boundary, the one it shares with Joyce Kilmer–Slickrock. Long spurs finger westward away from the dividing ridge. Secondary spurs and spurs splitting away from them further fold and wrinkle the country into roughs. Between all these spurs run sharp-sided streams, still slicing bluffs and drilling swirlholes.

And winding through all this mountainous terrain is a network of fourteen trails totaling 56 miles. (While Stiffknee's Farr Gap Trailhead is located on the Citico Creek side of the combined wilderness, the trail actually descends into the Joyce Kilmer–Slickrock Wilderness.) Most of these trails, including the two designated as horse routes, follow ridges, upper slopes, or streams. Many are lightly used; several of the remote interior footpaths are scarcely used. Between trails there are square miles of unfrequented woods where you can find as much solitude as you want—or can stand.

Slickrock Creek History

The early history of Slickrock Creek is essentially the same as that of its neighboring basin to the west, Citico Creek, except that man-made flood, not fire, stopped the logging. The remote country surrounding this quintessential mountain stream remained primeval forest—a long north-facing cove full of big trees, scarcely touched—into the twentieth century. In the entire watershed there was only one small farmstead, located beside Nichols Cove Branch.

Babcock Land and Timber Company bought the Slickrock basin and began timbering in 1915. After seven years of heavy logging, Babcock's rail system along the Little Tennessee River was flooded by the construction of Calderwood Lake, forcing the company to abandon its operation. By that time, however, approximately 70 percent of the drainage area had been cut clean or close to it.

Sources often state that the southern, upper-elevation end of the Slickrock valley, the 30 percent that wasn't cut clear, is a solid block of virgin timber. Given the definition of virgin, the evidence of rail spurs and skid roads, and the current composition and size of tree species in the area, this simply doesn't seem plausible. Babcock's knowledge of the dam's completion schedule allowed ample time to search the upper slopes for the best boles of the most valuable trees, especially the black cherry.

While no doubt there are small, scattered pockets of virgin forest, the greater part of this highcountry would most accurately be categorized as old-growth forest. In fact, many sites have so many large old-growth trees—Carolina silverbell, yellow buckeye, beech, hemlock, red and sugar maple—that the appearance is one of virgin wood. The presence of high-quality sugar maple in certain stands suggests that Babcock didn't have quite enough time to lumber all that it would have liked. A band of old-growth hemlock, unwanted trees, tracks east-west across the upper watershed. A particularly impressive stand of these conifers occurs from Glenn Gap down to and along Glenn Gap Branch.

The Slickrock Creek valley is a lumpy, lopsided rectangle, short sides at north and south. Its line-of-sight dimensions are slightly over 3 miles wide at its northern margin, slightly over 2 miles wide at its southern rim, and approximately 6 miles long from south to north. Except at its mouth, where the creek cascades into the Little Tennessee River (Calderwood Lake), the drainage is completely enclosed by ridges, most high and well-defined. The main Unicoi

Mountain crest serves as Slickrock's western boundary, the one it shares with Citico Creek. Its southern wall—the Slickrock–Little Santeetlah divide, the highest crest in the combined wilderness—stretches from Bob Stratton Bald to the Haoe. The eastern edge is a long, major spur named Hangover Lead. Across the north side of the frame runs a low, irregular ridgeline.

The Slickrock basin has the highest and lowest elevations within the entire Joyce Kilmer–Slickrock/Citico Creek Wilderness. Here the land rises from 1,086 feet at Calderwood Lake to at least 5,360 feet atop Bob Stratton Bald's crowning outcrops. An elevation gain of this magnitude, almost 4,300 feet over 6 miles, is extremely rare in eastern North America outside of the Southern Appalachians.

In 1936 the U.S. Forest Service purchased the Slickrock basin from Babcock. In that same year, the Forest Service submitted a proposal that would have included Slickrock in a large backcountry tract—the Citico-Cheoah Primitive Area. Nothing ever came of the plan, at least not at that time or with that name. Management policy has allowed the land to heal and the forest to regenerate. There has been no cutting in the watershed since Babcock withdrew in 1922.

The Eastern Wilderness Act of 1975 established Slickrock as the larger portion of a 14,033-acre, two-basin wilderness—Joyce Kilmer–Slickrock. The Slickrock Creek valley encompasses 10,193 acres; of those, 3,881 acres ascend into Tennessee's Cherokee National Forest. The remainder of Slickrock and all of the Little Santeetlah drainage (Joyce Kilmer Memorial Forest) lie within North Carolina's Nantahala National Forest in Graham County.

The 1984 North Carolina Wilderness Act added 2,980 acres to the Joyce Kilmer–Slickrock Wilderness. This extension, also within the Nantahala National Forest, raised the acreage to 17,013.

Joyce Kilmer–Slickrock has a system of sixteen trails totaling 67 miles, counting the various alternates, spurs, and connectors. (Stiffknee was placed in the Citico Creek Wilderness section because its Farr Gap Trailhead is located on the Citico Creek side of the combined wilderness. The trail itself, however, descends into the Joyce Kilmer–Slickrock Wilderness.) Most of that mileage follows streams or the perimeter ridges of the Slickrock–Little Santeetlah drainages.

Every trail has one end or the other near a ridge or stream. Horse travel is not permitted within the Joyce Kilmer–Slickrock Wilderness.

Little Santeetlah Creek History

Babcock Land and Timber Company owned the Little Santeetlah basin at one time, but never logged it. Other timber companies also held deed to the basin, but they did not log it either. In fact, no one has ever logged it, and hopefully, no one ever will. Today this virgin vestige has been a 3,840-acre memorial forest for over 60 years. In 1975 the Little Santeetlah Creek watershed—the Joyce Kilmer Memorial Forest—was incorporated within the congressionally designated Joyce Kilmer–Slickrock Wilderness.

The memorial forest has one of those small-world, fairy-tale histories. The plot combines two sets of totally disconnected circumstances, occurring on different continents and in different regions of our country. This convoluted story ties many dissimilar elements—a poet, a New Jersey oak, a popular poem, an insistent bravery, a German bullet shot on French soil, a New York VFW post, the U.S. government, the U.S. Forest Service, timber companies, lake constructions, and a bankruptcy—to the preservation of a small Southern Appalachian basin.

Alfred Joyce Kilmer was born on December 6, 1886, in New Brunswick, New Jersey. Coming from a well-educated family, he attended Rutgers College (1904–1906) and Columbia University (A.B., 1908). It was during his student years at Rutgers that Kilmer composed his most famous poem, "Trees," in homage to a venerable white oak that graced the campus grounds. After marriage and various jobs in education and journalism, the young poet accepted employment with the *New York Times* as an editor and reviewer. He continued to write and publish his poetry while producing literary essays and reviews for the *Times*. His greatest success as a poet came in 1914, the year World War I began, when "Trees" was published in his second book of poetry.

Although now chiefly remembered for one widely popular poem, Joyce Kilmer was an accomplished and respected journalist. His reviews and essays won critical acclaim; his poetry did not. In fact, Kilmer's verses were viewed at the time as overly simplistic and sentimental. But the simplicity and universality of his themes, while not appreciated by the critics, found a niche in public opinion. His poem, "Trees," became a schoolhouse favorite—a teacher's standard introduction of poetry to young minds.

When the United States entered World War I in the spring of 1917, Kilmer volunteered to fight and enlisted in the New York National Guard. He was placed in an officers training camp, a cushy assignment, because of his educational background and journalist status. But Kilmer would countenance no coddling. Anxious to see action before the war ended, he enlisted as a private and was later transferred to the 165th regiment of the Rainbow Division, where he quickly rose to the rank of sergeant.

The 165th regiment was sent to France in October 1917. Initially, the journalist turned soldier was given the job of senior statistician, a post designed to keep him close to regimental headquarters. Again dissatisfied with his soft assignment, he insisted on being sent to the front and obtained a transfer to an intelligence unit near the fighting.

On July 30, 1918, Joyce Kilmer volunteered—probably demanded—to take part in a reconnaissance mission to locate enemy machine gun emplacements. That was his last request. On that day a bullet to the head killed him at age 31. His fellow troops buried him near the Ourcq River in France, and the French government posthumously awarded him the Croix de Guerre for bravery in action.

Kilmer's beloved poem and the memory of his short, brave life lived on. In 1934, the Bozeman Bulger Post, a New York chapter of the Veterans of Foreign Wars, petitioned the federal government to establish a fitting memorial to the fallen soldier-poet. The federal government granted the request and instructed the U.S. Forest Service to begin a search for a tract of virgin trees within the once vast deciduous forests of the eastern United States.

Locating a publicly owned virgin grove during the mid-1930s was a difficult task. The Forest Service was established primarily to clean up the mess left by the cut-and-run timber barons who left millions of scarred, burned, and eroded acres scattered across the eastern half of our country. The main purpose of the Forest Service was to restore watersheds and return the land to productivity. Because of their mission, nearly every large tract acquired by the

Forest Service in the eastern United States has the same history. Timber companies bought the land cheaply, logged the living daylights out of it, then gladly sold their sproutlands to the Forest Service rather than pay taxes on them.

Remote and rugged Southern Appalachia—a land renowned for its huge trees—was the last large profitable region to be industrially logged in the eastern United States. By the time the Nantahala National Forest was created in 1920, most of the forest in western North Carolina had been or was about to be cut. By the beginning of 1935, the Forest Service knew of only one remaining excellent site for the memorial within their Southern Appalachian purchase boundaries. That site was the Little Santeetlah basin, nestled in North Carolina's portion of the Unicoi Mountains near the Tennessee line.

Little Santeetlah's forest had survived purely by fortuitous happenstance—luck, the kind Joyce Kilmer would have wanted. One timber company after another held title to this relatively small basin as part of much larger tracts. And one by one, over a period of more than 40 years, all of the watersheds surrounding the Little Santeetlah were logged. But each time the timbermen turned toward the huge yellow poplars and chestnuts in Poplar Cove something deterred them. Twice the construction of lakes, Calderwood then Santeetlah, flooded the rail system. In the early 1930s another logging company was in the process of building splash dams to float the trees out, when it went bankrupt, probably from something unrelated to the Little Santeetlah operation. One of the outfits did manage to cut the lowermost half-mile, up to where the picnic area is now.

Spurred by the request of the Bozeman Bulger veterans, the Forest Service purchased the Little Santeetlah watershed from Gennett Lumber Company in 1935. The subsequent dedication of the Joyce Kilmer Memorial Forest was held on the eighteenth anniversary of his death, July 30, 1936. Numerous officials traveled the newly finished dirt road to attend the ceremony. Among those present were regional Forest Service supervisors, representatives from the *New York Times*, search committee members, and Bozeman Bulger Post veterans. E.A. Sherman, assistant chief of the U.S. Forest Service, delivered the dedication address and read a letter from President

Franklin D. Roosevelt. Roosevelt's eloquent words expressed the purpose and sentiments of the memorial:

> It is particularly fitting that a poet who will always be remembered for the tribute he embodied in "Trees" should find this living monument. Thus his beloved memory is forever honored and one of nature's masterpieces set aside to be preserved for the enjoyment of generations yet unborn.

When you walk past the centuries-old hemlocks and immense yellow poplars, whisper a thanks to the man, Alfred Joyce Kilmer, whose poem and bravery inspired their preservation. And while you're whispering beneath this virgin canopy of big trees, thank the Bozeman Bulger veterans for their idea and the Forest Service for riding to the rescue.

Wild Boar

There are three large mammals—white-tailed deer, black bear, and wild boar—roaming the wilderness. Of those three, the wild boar is certainly the most common and conspicuous. Its signs— tracks, scat, wallows, and rooting—are impossible to miss. Although wild boar have adapted amazingly well, they are not native to the United States. They came to the Southern Appalachians from the Ural Mountains of Russia in the early 1900s. The history of how they arrived is an interesting story.

The narrative begins in 1908, the year Whiting Manufacturing Company, a British firm, bought an extensive tract of land in western North Carolina near the Tennessee border. In lieu of his commission percentage, George Gordon Moore, the financial agent for the purchase, was allowed to establish a European-style shooting preserve on 1,600 acres surrounding Hooper Bald in southern Graham County. In 1912 the animals—fourteen wild boar and small numbers of buffalo, elk, mule deer, American black bear, and Russian brown bear—were hauled by oxen teams to the bald.

The operation had major problems from the beginning. The bald was too remote for most would-be clients, and the animals kept escaping. By 1920 Moore, who had lost interest and money in the business, had moved away. And he had left the entire shooting gallery in the care of Garland "Cotton" McGuire, a local man who had been his foreman. Without capital or clients, McGuire did what he could to protect the animals and property.

By the early 1920s the boar, which had been breaking out in small numbers all along, were said to total between sixty and one hundred within their fence. Written accounts and local stories differ as to exactly how the remainder of the boars bolted from their 600-acre, chestnut-rail enclosure. But one way or another, they wound up on the outside of the hunting preserve. When Champion Paper and Fiber Company bought the land in 1926, the European wild boar (*Sus scrofa*) was already breeding very successfully in the wild. As for the other animals, none of them established lasting populations.

Before these exotics were accidently introduced, there were already free-ranging domestic hogs (also *Sus scrofa*), known as "ridge-runners," throughout much of the settled regions of the southern mountains. At first the local people tried to eradicate the "rooshi-ans," as they called them, because the wild swine mated with their semiferal hogs, creating an undesirable crossbreed that wouldn't fatten and wouldn't come home.

Running domestic hogs on the free range became unprofitable after the chestnut blight in the 1930s. Over the decades wild boar, in varying degrees of hybridism, have multiplied and steadily increased their range. Today, they are highly prized big game to hunters, but are vacuum-cleaning, roto-rooting pests to biologists in the Great Smoky Mountains National Park.

Although they now have a mixed lineage, the wild boar within the wilderness have retained most of their original characteristics. They have a heavy, bristly coat which varies in color from dark reddish brown to black. Compared to domestic swine, wild boar are longer legged, higher and more heavily muscled at the shoulder, and narrower in the hindquarters. A mane of bristles running along the back of the neck gives the animal a humped appearance. The mane stands up when the boar is excited.

The larger, solitary males reach weights from 300 pounds to slightly over 400 pounds. In areas where they are heavily hunted, such as the Joyce Kilmer–Slickrock Wilderness, they rarely live long enough to attain their maximum size. The females are smaller. Both sexes have intimidating tusks.

Despite their fierce appearance and fighting ability, wild boar are not a threat to your safety, provided you do not harass or antagonize them. The female considers your presence near her boarlets as harassment. In the very unlikely event that you should happen upon some of the yellow-striped young, don't raise your camera and move closer for a shot; move quickly away from them. These big-tusked hogs are most emphatically a threat to any dog that chases them or their young.

I would like to change an old woodsman's adage. The saying went something like this: When a pine needle falls in the forest, the hawk sees it, the bear smells it, and the deer hears it hit the ground. The updated version of this adage should be: When a pine needle falls in the forest, the hawk sees it, the bear smells it, the deer hears it hit the ground, and the boar eats it.

The Skyway

The Cherohala-Overhill Skyway, a long time in the making, was officially dedicated in October of 1996. The name of the skyway on the North Carolina side, Cherohala, comes from a combination of the two national forests—Cherokee and Nantahala. Tennessee's section of the skyway was named for the former Cherokee settlements known as the Overhill Towns. This road, which resembles the Blue Ridge Parkway, has been federally designated as a National Scenic Byway.

This skyway is undoubtedly one of the highest (if not the highest) paved through roads in the eastern United States. Its highest signed elevation is 5,390 feet. (In the Great Smoky Mountains National Park, US 441 climbs to an elevation of 5,046 feet at Newfound Gap. Maine's highest peak, the mythical Mount Katahdin, rises to 5,267 feet, and New York's highest mountain, Mount Marcy in the famed Adirondacks, is 5,344 feet.) This serpentine road remains above 4,000 feet for nearly 14 miles and above 5,000 feet for close to 4 miles. Clouds frequently drag their bellies across the byway, obscuring all views and enveloping the mountaintops with blowing gray.

The completion of the skyway has greatly increased the ease and speed of travel between Robbinsville, North Carolina, and Tellico

Plains, Tennessee. Because it bypasses dirt-gravel FS 81, the skyway has made it easier, faster, and safer for hikers to travel from the Joyce Kilmer–Slickrock Wilderness to the Citico Creek Wilderness. All this speed and ease, however, came with a high monetary cost and a long-standing controversy.

The skyway sliced through one of the largest solid blocks of national forest ownership east of the Mississippi. Much of the forest has only been cut once, scattered pockets were high-graded (selectively cut for valuable timber), and some never cut at all. For years, for decades really, the road was "that damn road" to many of the area's hikers. It seemed as if every peak's southward vista included that damn road, scarring and gouging its route through the highest lonesome around. But our viewpoint was only one among many.

Perhaps it cost too much, and perhaps it should never have been built. But it is now finished, a fact, and promises to bring change and tourist dollars to the local communities. The movers and shakers, planners and builders, did a good job; the rock walls and overlooks are solid and built for beauty and endurance. Travelers can enjoy picnic areas, plenty of trails, nearby balds, and magnificent views of the over-a-mile-high Unicoi Mountains. And the Southern Appalachian forest still stands rich and strong, often covering everything but the sky.

The skyway was built with visions of easily accessible natural beauty, backcountry recreation, the mountaineer's hemmed-in yearning for easy travel, and tourist dollars. Build it and they will come. The road received much publicity upon its opening. And people are coming, spending money, and enjoying the skyway as planned. Change is coming too. The die is cast. The completion of the skyway crowned tourism and recreation king and queen.

The skyway now offers an opportunity for its former opponents and proponents to share the same vision, at least for this time and this place. This National Scenic Byway cost taxpayers over 100 million dollars. This expenditure has earned them the right to see unscarred vistas and natural forests from the overlooks they paid for. Most people who drive all the way from Atlanta, Charlotte, or Nashville don't want to see clear-cuts from the overlooks along a National Scenic Byway; they can see those closer to home.

All of the public land along the skyway, as far as the eye can easily see, should be kept as pristine as possible. Thousands of acres to either side of the road should receive some sort of official designation, set in stone as strong as the highway itself. This designation—Scenic Area, Backcountry Area, or National Recreation Area—should allow the continuation of all of the legal recreational pursuits, from birdwatching to boar hunting, that are now permitted. It should also protect the forests and the viewsheds from future logging and road building. But most of all, these mountains should become part of Wallace Stegner's "geography of hope." Their wildness and grandeur should be left unimpaired for the future generations who will sorely need them.

Things to Know Before You Go

Hiking in the wilderness brings many rewards—the pleasures of
venturing into a virgin forest along a clean, clear stream, the thrill of
a magnificent view into wild and undisturbed lands, the feeling of
solitude and peace on a windswept bald—but this kind of hiking also
presents challenges. Trails within wilderness have a different standard
of maintenance from nonwilderness trails. Wilderness trails are
blazed less frequently and maintained less rigorously than nonwilderness trails. Hikers who are used to well-maintained, smooth treadways with frequent blazing need to be aware of what to expect on
wilderness trails.

Signs and Blazes

The Joyce Kilmer–Slickrock side of the wilderness has signs at all
trailheads and signs at all interior trail junctions. But it has no blazes
whatsoever, at least none painted by the Forest Service. Vandalism of
signs, including bear damage, is a recurring problem. If the sign is
gone, use the post as your sign. If the post is gone, use the hole as
your sign. But most of all use your head. Don't expect right-angle,
red-line intersections as on the wilderness map, and don't expect all
of the signs to be up all of the time.

The Citico Creek side of the wilderness has signs at all trailheads,
but no signs at interior junctions. More frequently marked near
junctions and potentially confusing turns, the trails are irregularly
guided by cut-bark blazes.

Stream Crossings

The area covered by this guide is wilderness, and with very few
exceptions, there are no guy wires or bridges to help you cross
streams. This is as it should be. Stream crossings are simply part of
wilderness hiking, a good, challenging part.

I will use two terms—cross and ford—to describe all unbridged
stream crossings. When a trail crosses a branch or creek, I mean

that, under more or less normal water levels, a person of reasonable coordination and wit (using a hiking stick) can cross dry-shod. When a trail fords a creek, it means wading and balancing on the stream bottom or submerged rocks. And perhaps getting wetter than you wanted.

Dividing the crossings into wet and dry, ford and cross, should help you know what to expect, what to plan for. However, more or less normal water levels fluctuate widely. There are no guarantees. Many winter and spring fords typically become summer and fall crossings. In most years after heavy rains, especially in winter and early spring, the longer side streams such as Nichols Cove Branch, Little Slickrock Creek, and Eagle Branch will rise above their step-across rocks. And after one or more heavy rains, especially in winter and early spring before leaf-out, the lower, downstream fords on Slickrock and South Fork Citico Creeks can become very tricky or too treacherous to attempt. Again, this is as it should be. Without the potential of challenge or danger, there is no wilderness.

Deadfalls

As of early spring 1998, three trails within the Joyce Kilmer–Slickrock Wilderness—Haoe Lead, Deep Creek, and Stratton Bald—and five trails within the Citico Creek Wilderness—Brush Mountain, Pine Ridge, South Fork Citico, North Fork Citico, and the southern-most end of Fodderstack—have numerous, trail-blocking deadfalls. The combined wilderness received a severe pounding in the 1990s: a late winter blizzard in 1993, Hurricane Opal in the summer of 1995, and a severe ice storm in the winter of 1997. A tornado also touched down in the southeastern corner of the Citico Creek Wilderness in the summer of 1997. Especially hard hit were the old, wide-crowned oaks that caught the full force of wind on the high ridges.

Wilderness trails are by regulation maintained to a more primitive standard than nonwilderness trails. This standard includes an acceptable number of deadfalls per mile. Under normal circumstances, the trails can be kept passable. After blizzards and hurricanes, however, when the number of deadfalls becomes unacceptable, when trails most need maintenance, the prohibition against chain saws in wilderness makes clearing the way very slow and strenuous. The Forest Service intends to work on these eight trails, a few perhaps as early as the summer of 1998. Their time, personnel, and money, however, are limited. Each ranger district maintains only a certain number of miles of wilderness trails per year. This means that some of these trails, especially in the Citico Creek Wilderness, will still be in rough shape after the year 2000.

The Forest Service greatly needs volunteers (one ranger used the word "desperately") to help them clear the deadfalls, or at least make the thick ones easier to cross. The work is hard, but it offers you the opportunity to put your muscle where your heart is: a reward in itself. Addresses and phone numbers are provided on page 227 in the back of this guide.

Because of all the paths leading left and right around the blow-downs, hikers occasionally have trouble remaining on the trail. On a seldomly used and frequently turning trail such as Brush Mountain, where the route is somewhat faint and unpredictable to start with, this can be a real problem. The physical effort required when you are bushwhacking through a nearly impassable portion of trail, frequently catching your backpack on branches, is no fun. If you are concerned about trail conditions, call the appropriate ranger district for current information.

Camping Areas

There are National Forest campgrounds to either side of the combined wilderness. On the North Carolina side, the Nantahala National Forest has three campgrounds—Cheoah Point, Rattler Ford, and Horse Cove—near the Joyce Kilmer–Slickrock Wilderness. Rattler Ford, a group campground that requires a reservation, opens from early to mid-April and closes at the end of October. Horse Cove and Cheoah Point open in mid-April and close at the end of October. These dates are subject to change and can vary from year to year, depending on the possibility of freezing weather and potential water pipe damage. Horse Cove's lower loop remains open, without water, during the colder months.

On the Tennessee side, the Cherokee National Forest has many campgrounds relatively close to the Citico Creek Wilderness. The closest one is Indian Boundary which opens April 1st and closes after the last Sunday in September. (Again, these general times can vary from year to year.) Indian Boundary's overflow area remains open, without water, during the colder months. In addition to Indian Boundary, there are at least five more campgrounds, some of which stay open all year, up the Tellico River past the Tellico Ranger Station. The prominently signed, paved road (it also leads to Bald River Falls and Green Cove) that leads to these campgrounds begins to the right of TN 165 East, approximately 5.0 miles from the town of Tellico Plains.

Camping is not allowed in the Cherokee and Nantahala National Forests within 300 feet of the Cherohala Skyway (NC 143) and the Overhill Skyway (TN 165). Camping is not allowed in the Citico Creek corridor except at designated sites.

Hunting Seasons

Hunting is a legal and popular pastime within the wilderness, even within Joyce Kilmer Memorial Forest. Various overlapping seasons occur throughout much of autumn and early winter. There is also a spring season for turkey. To further complicate matters for hikers and hunters, the two states—Tennessee and North Carolina—have different hunting seasons and laws.

As a hiker, you should be particularly aware of the bear/boar season. This split season—October 13 to November 22 and December 15 to January 1 in a recent year (subject to change from year to year)—brings many hunters and their hunting dogs to the Joyce Kilmer–Slickrock side of the combined wilderness. If you decide to hike during this time of year, please don't take your dog or dogs. A pack of hog dogs, especially the pit bulls, can and will rip your pooch apart. You'll be helpless and horrified; the pit bulls will show no remorse whatsoever, and your dog will be dead.

The entire Citico Creek Wilderness is part of the Tellico Bear Reserve. Within this reserve, bear cannot legally be hunted at any time of the year, and boar and deer cannot be legally hunted with dogs. The only hunting dogs allowed in the Citico Creek Wilderness are those that point upland game birds. Please realize that a pack in hot pursuit might ignore signs and boundary lines.

Weather

I started hiking the trails included in this guide in early March and, from time to time, met and talked with groups of backpackers. Invariably, the second or third thing people from the North said was, "We didn't realize it got so cold down here." I would usually try to hide my grin. Once, in the middle of a sleet storm up high near Bob Stratton Bald, I came upon a young man from Michigan sitting on a rock, shivering under his poncho. After we talked awhile, he confessed his poor planning. He had not bothered to pack any pants; he was wearing shorts in the driving sleet and wind at 5,200 feet.

Just as Southerners mistakenly think northern heat is a laugh, Northerners think southern cold is a joke. And generally speaking southern cold is a joke by northern standards except in the Southern Appalachians, where the higher mountains can be every bit as cold as Ohio or Pennsylvania.

When hiking in the southern mountains, keep the following factors in mind:

■ **Elevation.** To a measureable extent, the higher the mountains, the more they create their own weather. As you climb a mountain, average wind speed and annual precipitation increase as temperature decreases—2 to 3 degrees for every 1,000-foot rise in elevation.

■ **Shade.** High mountains create their own cloud cover and shade their own north slopes. When winter camping, it is important to remember that sunlight doesn't shine on many lower north slopes until after 10 A.M.

■ **Precipitation.** Tellico Plains averages 50 inches of precipitation per year; Robbinsville, 56 inches. The higher elevations of the wilderness, above 4,000 feet, average approximately 70 inches of precipitation per year. March is the wettest month—October is the driest. Assume that it might rain no matter what the weather forecast is for the nearby large cities of Knoxville, Chattanooga, and Asheville.

■ **Frost.** The last killing frost of spring is normally in early May, and the first killing frost of fall is usually in late September. In June, July and August, prepare for overnight lows in the 50s. During most of May and September prepare for overnight lows in the 40s. During the rest of the year prepare for overnight lows down to freezing and below freezing.

■ **Unpredictability.** October and November, March and April, are the transition months. During these months the weather may be mild and sunny for two or three days, then it may suddenly snow in the highcountry.

■ **Temperature.** During the average winter, ordinarily in January and February, but occasionally in late December or early March, the temperature drops to 5 to 15 degrees below zero several times at the higher altitudes of the wilderness. A real cold snap, the kind that blows through every 3 to 5 years, can send the mercury down to 20 to 30 degrees below zero on top of Bob Stratton Bald. That is without considering the wind chill factor.

■ **Wind.** Winter winds, sweeping across exposed ridges and funneling through gaps, are fierce. Steady 10 to 20 mile per hour winds are common. Branch-cracking gusts of 30 to 40 miles per hour are not unusual on the higher ridges.

How To Use This Guide

THIS GUIDEBOOK COVERS THIRTY TRAILS in or near the Joyce Kilmer–Slickrock and Citico Creek Wildernesses. The trails are grouped into trailhead sections; a list of trails, general directions, and a basic map highlighting trails for the section are provided at the beginning of each chapter. (See page 227 for addresses to order topo sheets and detailed wilderness maps.)

Trail Descriptions

A concise, at-a-glance summary of essential trail information is provided at the beginning of each trail description. You can quickly refer to the foot trail (or horse and foot trail) number as it is listed on the map, the trail's length, and its difficulty rating, often both for day-hiking and for backpacking. Also provided here are the starting and ending points of the trail, a list of junctions with other trails, topographic quadrangles, and a brief listing of some of the trail's outstanding features.

Following this information listing you will find a complete description of the trail, usually in the direction most frequently hiked, with special attention given to the type of terrain, stream crossings, trail intersections, and what you will see along the trail. At the conclusion of the trail description there is a section featuring some of the flora and fauna you may encounter while hiking.

Finally, the directions or references are given that will lead you to the exact trailhead or—if there is more than one path at a trailhead—to the specific trail.

When using this guidebook, keep in mind that conditions on wilderness trails are constantly changing and trails are occasionally rerouted. To be sure of current conditions, contact the appropriate Forest Service office before planning a hike. (See page 227 for addresses and phone numbers.)

Trail Ratings

Difficulty ratings are inherently subjective. The most useful systems, however, are those that achieve consistency by limiting this subjectivity to a single source. To this end, I have walked and rated all of the trails described in this guide. Even if you do not agree with my ratings, I hope that you will find them consistent and, after a trip or two, useful.

The trail ratings employed in this book were based on the usual criteria: the amount of elevation change, the way the elevation change is accomplished, a trail's difficulty compared to others within the wilderness, the length of the trail, and the strain on my legs and lungs during the hike. In general, to reflect the cumulative effect of the grade, the longer trails were rated as slightly more difficult than shorter trails with the same number of feet gained or lost per mile. Uneven footing, stream crossings, and fords were not taken into account; they are simply part of wilderness travel.

This rating system is also based on two assumptions. The first is that this scheme, or any other for that matter, does not apply to hikers at either end of the fitness spectrum—those in excellent condition and those in poor condition. People who are able to run long distances with little trouble already know that ratings are meaningless for them. Conversely, people who become out of breath after a flight or two of stairs would find difficulty classifications equally inaccurate, although much harder to ignore.

The other assumption is that a very high percentage of the people who walk or want to walk in this wilderness exercise, at least occasionally. After all, if you don't partake in at least one of the many types of cardiovascular exercise, why would you want to, or attempt to, hike a wilderness trail ranked more difficult than easy. Thus, this approach is designed to accommodate those people who exercise, at least sporadically, and who fall somewhere in that broad, general category between slightly below fair shape and slightly better than good shape.

Three categories of difficulty are used in this guide: Easy, Moderate, and Strenuous. As you will notice, many trails have been assigned two designations. These split designations are used to help span fitness levels when trail difficulty falls between obvious gradations. For instance, a trail may be rated "Dayhiking In: Moderate to Strenuous." A person in good condition would find this trail to be about moderate. A hiker in fair shape would probably rate the trail moderate to strenuous, and a person in poor fettle would probably consider it strenuous.

The decision to walk a certain trail is a commonsense personal judgment. When planning a trip, you should be aware of the trail's difficulty, not intimidated by it; you should think of it as advice, not a warning. If you keep the mileage low, walk at a leisurely pace, and take frequent rest stops, you will often be surprised at what you can accomplish. If you want to walk a trail, and think you can, give it a try.

Regional Directions and Maps

THIS GUIDE EMPLOYS A THREE-TIERED directional system. First, directions from the three main jumping-off points to the three most important intersections near the trailheads—as well as directions from each intersection to the others—are provided here. Next, directions from the three intersections to the trailheads, or to other prominent intersections closer to the trailheads, are given at the beginning of the trailhead sections. Finally, you will find at the end of each trail description the directions or references that direct hikers to the exact trailhead or—if there is more than one path at a trailhead—to the specific trail.

This three-tiered approach allows hikers, depending upon their level of familiarity with the area, to start the directions where they want, to wade through only what is necessary. It also eliminates having to read the same long directions over and over again. Some repetition and some overlap between the tiers are inevitable, but hopefully hikers planning a trip will find the detailed directions more helpful than tedious.

There are three primary jumping-off points surrounding the combined wilderness: Tellico Plains, Tennessee, to the southwest; Robbinsville, North Carolina, to the southeast; and the US 129 bridge over Calderwood Lake to the northeast in North Carolina. It is also possible to reach the Citico Creek Wilderness from the northwest following a succession of state, county, and Forest Service roads. Traveling from this direction, however requires a long, occasionally rough, dirt-road drive. Because very few hikers approach the wilderness from this direction and because TN 165 is such a good, easily described route from the west, no directions have been provided from the northwest.

Two of the three most important intersections close to the combined wilderness—the NC 143–FS 81 (Forest Service road)–SR 1127 (state road) junction and the four-way intersection at the

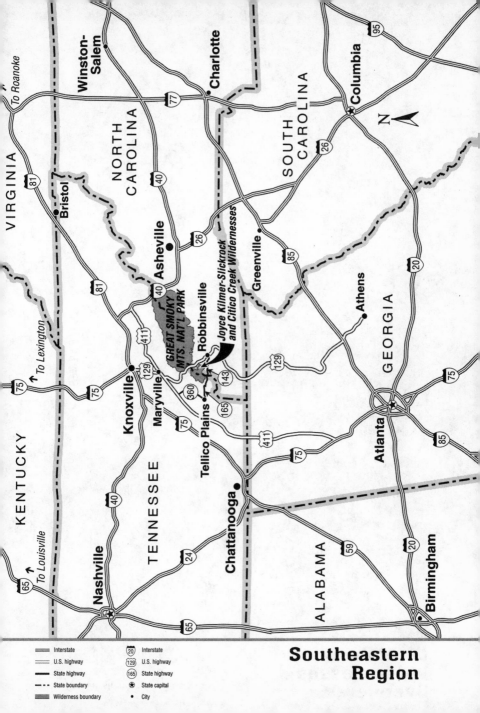

To Roanoke

VIRGINIA

To Lexington →

To Louisville ↑

KENTUCKY

Bristol

NORTH CAROLINA

Winston-Salem

Charlotte

77

40

26

Asheville

40

411

Knoxville

129

Maryville

75

360

Tellico Plains

165

143

Robbinsville

GREAT SMOKY MTS. NAT'L PARK

Joyce Kilmer-Slickrock and Citico Creek Wildernesses

129

Greenville

85

SOUTH CAROLINA

Columbia

95

26

20

Athens

GEORGIA

75

Atlanta

85

411

75

TENNESSEE

Nashville

40

24

Chattanooga

65

65

59

ALABAMA

20

Birmingham

81

81

75

75

Southeastern Region

Legend	
═══ Interstate	⑳ Interstate
─── U.S. highway	⑫⑨ U.S. highway
─── State highway	⑯⑤ State highway
─·─ State boundary	✪ State capital
▬ Wilderness boundary	• City

N

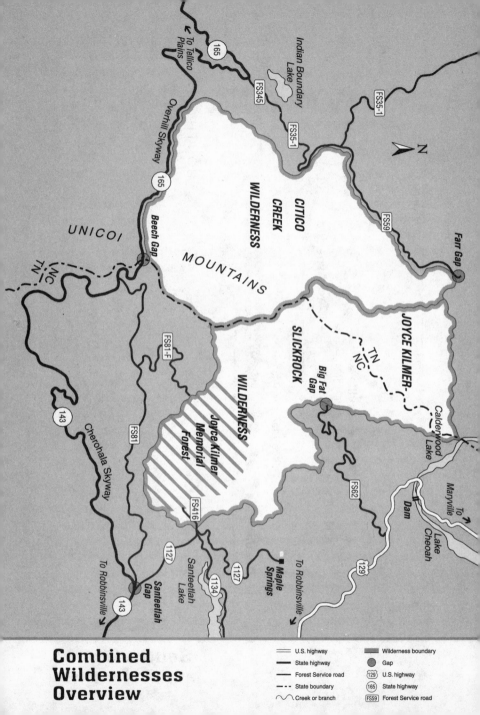

To Tellico Plains

165

Indian Boundary Lake

FS345

FS35-1

FS35-1

Overhill Skyway

165

UNICOI

Beech Gap

CITICO CREEK WILDERNESS

MOUNTAINS

FS59

Farr Gap

TN NC

FS81-F

FS81

JOYCE KILMER-

SLICKROCK

TN NC

Big Fat Gap

Calderwood Lake

143

Cherohala Skyway

WILDERNESS

Joyce Kilmer Memorial Forest

FS62

To Maryville

Dam

Lake Cheoah

To Robbinsville

FS416

1127

Santeetlah Lake

1127

Maple Springs

129

1134

To Robbinsville

143

Santeetlah Gap

To Robbinsville

Combined Wildernesses Overview

═══ U.S. highway	▓▓ Wilderness boundary
━━ State highway	● Gap
── Forest Service road	129 U.S. highway
─·─ State boundary	165 State highway
⌒⌒ Creek or branch	FS59 Forest Service road

entrance of FS 416—are near Robbinsville and the bridge over Calderwood Lake. The other, the TN 165–FS 345 junction, is near Tellico Plains.

Approach from the southwest. To reach the TN 165–FS 345 junction, follow TN 165 East (Overhill Skyway) slightly more than 13.0 miles from its intersection with TN 360 on the east side of Tellico Plains. The prominently signed, paved approach road to the popular Indian Boundary Recreation Area is FS 345. A left turn (northeast) onto FS 345 leads to all the trailheads in both the Citico Creek and Doublecamp Creek Trailheads sections. Continue straight ahead on TN 165 East to reach all the trailheads in the Sassafras Ridge Trailheads section.

If you continue straight ahead from the Indian Boundary junction on TN 165 East, then NC 143 East, you will come to the NC 143–FS 81–SR 1127 intersection at Santeetlah Gap after a little more than 27.0 miles. This junction, which has signs for Joyce Kilmer and Robbinsville, has an information kiosk at a paved, pull-off parking area to the left of NC 143. The paved entrance to FS 81 is downhill from the back of the kiosk.

To continue the tour of important intersections, turn left onto SR 1127 (Wagon Train Road) and proceed downhill to the northwest approximately 2.2 miles to the four-way intersection at the entrance of the Joyce Kilmer approach road, FS 416.

Approach from the southeast. The second major jumping-off point is Robbinsville, North Carolina. From the US 129–NC 143 intersection approximately 1.0 mile north of Robbinsville, turn left (assuming you are traveling US 129 North) with NC 143 West at the prominent Joyce Kilmer sign. Continue on NC 143 West for approximately 3.4 miles before turning right (another Joyce Kilmer sign) with NC 143 West at the T-intersection. After this turn, proceed straight ahead on NC 143 West slightly less than 7.0 miles to the NC 143–FS 81–SR 1127 intersection at Santeetlah Gap. Follow NC 143 West as it curves sharply to the left in Santeetlah Gap, which is marked with signs for Joyce Kilmer and Robbinsville. There is a pull-off parking area with an information kiosk to the outside of the curve.

Continuing on NC 143 West (becomes TN 165 at the state line) from Santeetlah Gap, you will arrive at the TN 165–FS 345 junction after slightly more than 27.0 miles.

If you leave NC 143 at the gap and head downhill to the northwest on SR 1127 (Wagon Train Road), you will come to the four-way intersection at the entrance of the Joyce Kilmer approach road, FS 416, after approximately 2.2 miles. All the trailheads in the Joyce Kilmer Forest Trailheads section, except Wolf Laurel, are near this four-way intersection.

Approach from the northeast. The final jumping-off point— where US 129 crosses the bridge over Calderwood Lake on the Graham County line—is located just northeast of the wilderness. Travel US 129 South (pass the Slickrock Creek Trailhead at Calderwood Lake and pass the Big Fat Gap approach road, FS 62) approximately 7.3 miles beyond the bridge over Calderwood Lake, then turn right onto Joyce Kilmer Road at the prominent Horse Cove Campground– Joyce Kilmer sign. Remain on this road (turn right with the road sign and cross the bridge at the first junction; follow the paved road approximately 2.5 miles until it changes to dirt-gravel, and pass through Horse Cove Campground near the end of the road) until you reach the four-way intersection after approximately 6.0 miles.

This route is referred to as the dirt-road shortcut in this guide.* It is the quickest way for southbound travelers on US 129 to reach the Joyce Kilmer Memorial Forest. This route also provides the quickest access from the Joyce Kilmer area to the Big Fat Gap and Slickrock Creek Trailheads and vice versa.

The Joyce Kilmer approach road, FS 416, is straight ahead through the intersection. Haoe Lead Trailhead is to the right, uphill, toward Maple Springs Observation Point. A left turn onto SR 1127 leads uphill (past the Stratton Bald Trailhead) approximately 2.2 miles to the NC 143–FS 81–SR 1127 intersection. A right turn on NC 143 West leads you onto and over the skyway, to the TN 165–FS 345 junction on the Tennessee side of the wilderness.

---

* This road is scheduled to be paved during the summer of 1998.

Joyce Kilmer–Slickrock Wilderness

We do not go to the green woods and crystal waters to rough it, we go to smooth it. We get it rough enough at home; in towns and cities; in shops, offices, stores, banks—anywhere that we may be placed—with the necessity of being on time and up to our work; of providing for the dependent ones; of keeping up, catching up, or getting left.

"Nessmuk"
Woodcraft and Camping

Slickrock Creek Trailhead

Wildcat Falls

Trails

Slickrock Creek
Ike Branch
Yellowhammer Gap

Slickrock Creek Trailhead
Directions and Map

THE SLICKROCK CREEK TRAILHEAD is on the west side of US 129 at the southern end of the bridge over Calderwood Lake, which is the boundary between North Carolina's Graham and Swain Counties.

Approach from the south. Take US 129 North slightly less than 14.5 miles beyond where NC 143 West turns left toward Joyce Kilmer Memorial Forest. This three-way intersection is approximately 1.0 mile north of Robbinsville, North Carolina. As you near the trailhead, US 129 parallels the Cheoah River (Cheoah means otter in Cherokee), passes the signed turn for Big Fat Gap, then finally crosses the Cheoah River at the community of Tapoco (name derived from Tallassee Power Company). After crossing the Cheoah, continue approximately 0.4 mile to the single-track road (paved entrance) to the left of the highway immediately before it crosses the bridge over Calderwood Lake. That road is the beginning of the trail. There is pull-off parking along and slightly in from the highway at the trailhead. The trailhead bulletin board, which is labelled as Tapoco Trailhead, is 0.1 mile down the narrow road.

Approach from the north. From the US 129–Foothills Parkway junction in Tennessee, travel US 129 South across the bridge over Calderwood Lake, then immediately turn off the highway to the right.

Approach from the southwest. If you are already near the Joyce Kilmer Memorial Forest, or if you are traveling from the southwest, from Tennessee on the Overhill-Cherohala Skyway, take the dirt-road shortcut through Horse Cove Campground. Once you reach US 129, turn left and proceed northward approximately 7.5 miles to the trailhead to the left immediately before the bridge. (See page 30 for the shortcut directions from Joyce Kilmer Memorial Forest to US 129.)

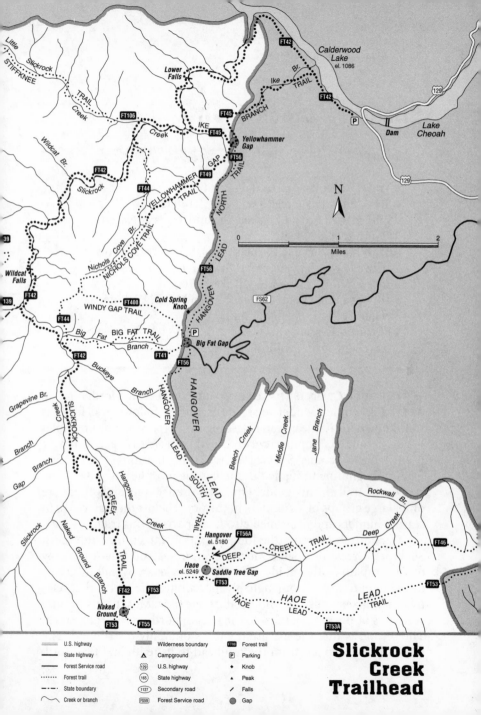

Slickrock Creek Trailhead

Slickrock Creek Trail

Foot Trail 42: 13.3 miles

- ■ **Trail Difficulty** See trail description
- ■ **Start** Slickrock Creek Trailhead, 1,160 feet
- ■ **End** Haoe Lead and Naked Ground Trails at Naked Ground, 4,860 feet
- ■ **Trail Junctions** Ike Branch (two), Stiffknee, Nichols Cove (two), Big Stack Gap Branch, Big Fat (see trail description), Haoe Lead, Naked Ground
- ■ **Topographic Quadrangles** Tapoco NC-TN, Whiteoak Flats TN-NC (small amount)
- ■ **Features** Cascades and waterfalls; old-growth forest; excellent spring wildflower display

S LICKROCK CREEK IS THE LONGEST AND WETTEST (ten fords) trail in the combined wilderness. The stream it follows and fords is well-known for its clear water, cascades, waterfalls, swimming holes —and people. Its popularity combined with its easy access have a predictable outcome: Slickrock Creek's northernmost 8.0 miles, from its beginning to Big Fat Branch, is the most heavily hiked long section of trail in this guide. On hot summer weekends there are often large groups of swimmers in the pools below the waterfalls. In season, hunters and fishermen also tread parts of this trail.

In addition to being the longest trail in the entire wilderness, Slickrock Creek also gains more elevation—3,700 feet—than any other footpath in this guide. Two factors make an overall difficulty rating impractical, if not laughably inaccurate. The first is that relatively few hikers walk the whole trail at one time. Most people traipse segments of the path parallel to the stream north of Big Fat Branch. The second is that the elevation gain is unevenly distributed. The route's first 8.0 miles, from the trailhead to its tenth and final ford, average a very gentle gradient of 105 feet of elevation gain per mile. Despite its occasional dips and rises, this long section is easy to moderate walked in either direction, dayhiking or backpacking.

In contrast the trail's last 5.3 miles, from the tenth ford to Naked Ground, ascend 535 feet per mile. Near its end, this stretch has a few short, rocky surges that are the steepest pitches in the combined wilderness. This portion of the walkway is, overall, moderate to strenuous for dayhikers and strenuous for backpackers.

Slickrock Creek, which originates outside of the wilderness, starts at the lowest elevation of any trail in this guide. This description begins at the trailhead bulletin board, 0.1 mile down the old road from US 129. The opening segment follows the road to the northwest, parallel to the shoreline of Calderwood Lake. Rock outcrops and boulders protrude from the upslope. Growing between the boulders is a diverse, second-growth forest—tall and straight and predominantly deciduous. For now at least, the 100-foot-high white ashes are keeping up with the yellow poplars.

At 0.6 mile the treadway arrives at the first of its many junctions. Ike Branch Trail angles up and to the left. Continuing straight ahead, the well-constructed trail crosses over Ike Branch on a log bridge, then undulates easily on the steep slope high above the lake. The rock outcrops are part of the bluff carved by the Little Tennessee, the river that was dammed to make the lake.

There are a few yellowwoods, a scarce tree of scattered and localized occurrence, on the downslope along this stretch. Its fragrant flowers, with their typical pea-family shape, hang in white, wisteria-like clusters, occasionally over a foot long. The yellowwoods throughout a given area bloom together, during the first half of May, at irregular intervals of 2 to 5 years.

Slickrock Creek Trail enters the wilderness in the middle of a descending, horseshoe bend at mile 1.6. Once inside the boundary, the walkway swings to the south, then steadily works its way down below bluffs to Slickrock Creek. Here, where the treadway picks up the old logging railroad bed at approximately 1,160 feet, is the lowest trailside elevation within the two-state wilderness.

Almost as soon as it reaches stream level, the footpath rises up and away from the water before coming right back down to it. This is part of the pattern. For the next 8 miles, the trail parallels winding Slickrock Creek up its basin to the south. It often leads up and away or out and away from the stream, then returns. Despite these repeated rovings, the route frequently remains right on the bank with scarcely a branch between you and the rushing water.

At mile 2.8 where the wide walkway becomes pinched, and where the railroad once crossed over on a bridge, the track fords Slickrock Creek (east side to west side, North Carolina to Tennessee) for the first of ten times. The Cherokee word for this watercourse means "slick rock." As was so often the case, early settlers simply translated the Native American name. The Cherokee were right; the rocks are slippery.

Three-tenths mile beyond the first ford, you arrive at a particularly high cascade that drops, perhaps 15 feet altogether, over two wide ledges. This cascade is labeled as Lower Falls on the topo map. While this falls is small by Southern Appalachian standards, its plunge pool is remarkable by any standard. A slightly flattened circle, wider than long, this catch pool is one of the largest I have ever seen on a creek-sized stream. Lower Falls pool is the dark green color of a good, over-your-head–deep, goose-pimple–cold swimming hole.

The railroad grade treadway runs past fords and junctions in rapid succession above Lower Falls. The second ford is at mile 3.6. Two-tenths mile upstream from that ford, Slickrock Creek comes to its second connection with Ike Branch at a campsite and sign. The route fords for the third time at mile 4.0. Three-tenths mile after this ford, Stiffknee Trail ends at its usually signed junction immediately before the main trail rock-steps across Little Slickrock Creek. Slightly more than 50 yards beyond where it regains the eastern bank after the fourth ford, the track passes its first meeting with Nichols Cove Trail at mile 4.5.

Shortly after crossing Nichols Cove Branch, the course closely parallels the creek below occasional bluffs or rocky cut-banks. In places the corduroy ripples of the old railroad ties are still evident. Here the walking, down and upstream from the fifth ford at mile 4.9, leads beside a series of cascades.

Since this trail is so long and there is not space enough to mention every shoaling run, every bedroom-sized boulder, every pool, every bank-to-bank ledge, I will simply state that this fast-footed creek is the embodiment of mountain water, which is to say that it abounds with the innately pleasing power and grace and beauty of a green stream flowing white through gray rock. All of this color and motion is flanked with forest and covered with sky and clouds, enhanced by the play of sun quiver and shadow on the moving mirror, and the unwavering sound of water wearing down rock. In the old days people categorized water as salt or sweet. This water is sweet.

The forest along Slickrock Creek was cut clean for miles up its watershed during the South's hell-for-leather logging days, in this case from 1915 to 1922. Today, the riverine and lower-slope forest is diverse, predominantly deciduous, and entirely second-growth. As you can see, the trees have grown up, competing for the canopy, rather than out. Yellow poplar, white ash, sweetgum, and an occasional sycamore and white pine are already at or above 100 feet in height.

Where it looks like the path might or should cross the stream, it skirts the rough, rocky footing on the west bank instead. The sixth ford, marked by an old bridge buttress, is at mile 6.3; the next ford is 0.4 mile farther. At mile 7.0 you come to Wildcat Falls—a series of four high cascades, sluicing raceways, and short free falls, cutting back into a series of stubborn ledges. The lowermost two chutes pour 20 feet into the larger of the two dividing catch pools.

A short distance beyond the falls, the wide treadway makes its eighth ford, then fords again at mile 7.4. Big Stack Gap Branch Trail ties into Slickrock Creek Trail at a campsite and sign immediately across the ninth ford. If you can't find this connection, you may have followed the fishermen's path too far up the bank before fording.

Most of the next 0.6 mile is easy walking through a floodplain forest out of sight of the stream. This is the only stretch of trail in the entire wilderness where the umbrella magnolia is conspicuously common. This deciduous magnolia, distinguished from the much more abundant Fraser magnolia by its uneared leaf base, has the largest leaves and flowers of any tree in the wilderness.

Approximately 100 yards after the route returns to the rocky creekside, it reaches its tenth and final ford at 8.0 miles and an elevation of approximately 2,010 feet. This ford has traditionally been marked by a short-posted sign on the western bank. Once across, you will quickly arrive, by one path or another, at Slickrock Creek's southern junction with Nichols Cove. This interior trail angles into and ends at Slickrock Creek just as the main trail gains higher ground. If you want to exit the wilderness by way of Big Fat Trail, turn left (northeast) onto the end of Nichols Cove and walk the well-worn treadway 0.1 mile to the Nichols Cove–Big Fat connection close beside Big Fat Branch.

Slickrock Creek Trail proceeds southward up the watershed on the east side of the stream. The hiking, rising easily between dips to tributaries, is usually on railroad grade and out of good sight of the brook. At mile 8.3 the track rock-hops Buckeye Branch; 0.7 mile farther it crosses Hangover Creek on a jumble of small boulders. As coolness and moisture increase with elevation, the trees become noticeably thicker than along the lower creek.

The route turns sharply left, up and away from its creek, at approximately 2,640 feet at mile 9.7. Where the trail turns, an overgrown fisherman's path continues straight ahead on the railroad bed. This path, labeled as 42A on wilderness maps, is the abandoned beginning of an aborted extension of Slickrock Creek to Cherry Log Gap. This overgrown stretch has never been maintained.

Over the years the sign that has marked this turn has had a few carved PG-13 phrases alluding to the climb ahead. Above the turn, where the treadway no longer parallels Slickrock Creek, the ascent to Naked Ground begins. This final segment gains 2,220 feet in 3.6 miles. If you walk slowly, this lightly traveled section is not as bad as entering the infernal regions, as the sign implies. The overwhelming majority of the grades are between easy and moderate. The short surges—the rocky scrambles that gain 40 to 60 feet of elevation on what seems like a 45-degree pitch—are challenging and memorable, especially during or right after rain.

The trail follows a logging spur to a fork of Hangover Creek before switchbacking up and away from the branch at mile 10.4. From here the footpath rises steadily by switchback to the crest of a spur ridge, and the first of the steep climbs. The track remains on or near the rocky keel for a few tenths of a mile, then half-circles through an impressive old-growth forest on a northwest-facing slope. At first the forest is dominated by both hemlock and Carolina silverbell. Many of the hemlocks are 9 to 12 feet in circumference and well over 100 feet in height, and many of the dark-barked silverbells are 6 to 8¹/₂ feet around and 80 feet tall.

Farther up the slope, this respite of easy walking passes beside large red and sugar maples, some 9 to 12 feet in circumference. Most of the upper Slickrock basin above the clear-cut was high-graded—selectively cut for valuable species. Timbering in the basin came to a halt when Calderwood Lake flooded the railroad system. Thus, as the lake neared completion, the loggers were forced to hurry, leaving the old-growth sugar maple. They did, however, manage to drag out the virgin black cherry.

The treadway winds back up to the crest and continues to climb on or near its narrow spine. Here, where the bare rock backbone of the steep-sided ridge frequently pokes out, and where picturesque, old-growth hemlocks stand in the full force of the wind, the land has that rugged look of out-West country.

The path ascends a ledged pitch with root holds at mile 11.9. At mile 12.5 the walking tunnels into a heath bald (the one plainly visible from the Hangover) composed primarily of Catawba rhododendron. Three-tenths of a mile into the tangle, the right fork leads a very short distance to an open view of the Haoe and the rocky heath bald atop the Hangover.

The final 0.4 mile, out of the rhododendron and into hardwoods, angles to the west away from the ridgeline. Seventy-five yards before Naked Ground, a side path bends back to the right to a last-water spring. Slickrock Creek Trail ends at Naked Ground—a gap that is a major trail intersection and an overused camping area. Haoe Lead passes through the gap; Naked Ground Trail ends at its south side, opposite Slickrock Creek.

Slickrock is the widest and deepest creek in the wilderness. Its fords can become dangerous following heavy rainfall during any season. The water level is normally highest in winter and early spring before leaf-out. Throughout this time of the year, the lower fords often remain midthigh to crotch deep for weeks. With normal spring precipitation, the stream flows fairly full until leaf-out reaches the highest ridges in late May. During summer and fall, except after thunderstorms, the fords usually present no problems for adults, other than slipping and getting wet. Several of the upper fords may be crossed dry-shod during drought.

Use good judgment. Remember that this and other steep-sided mountain streams rise very quickly after a heavy rain. If the creek becomes dangerous, abandon the route, work your way to a side trail, and get out of there, rather than risk a flooded ford.

Nature Notes

Slickrock Creek's two most spectacular spring wildflower displays occur at opposite ends of the route—roughly 12.0 miles, 3,300 feet of elevation, and two months apart. The initial area is on the rocky northeast-facing slope at the beginning of the trail. Here, on the incredibly lush hillside above Calderwood Lake, spring first unfolds within the area covered by this book. A warm spell in late winter may bring the hepaticas to bloom in early March. This tract, which rivals Poplar Cove in sheer numbers of ground-carpeting wildflowers, peaks in diversity from March 20 through April 10. (See Ike Branch, the following trail, for a more detailed description.)

The second show starts when the heath bald blossoms along the narrow ridge near the top end of the path. Although the bald is practically a monoculture of the Catawba rhododendron, this particular flowering species has blooms that are big and showy and, in a good year, abundant. This evergreen shrub ordinarily peaks sometime in late May or early June.

The pocket of old-growth forest starting at mile 11.2 has a higher concentration of mature Carolina silverbell than any other trail-traversed area in the combined wilderness. The silverbell was one of the moist-site species that loggers routinely left when they high-graded the woods above the end of the clear-cut. Thus today, at the higher elevations in the wilderness, from the end of the old clear-cuts to the tree's upper elevation limit at approximately 4,800 feet, burly, old-growth silverbells are common on moist slopes and ridges.

The Carolina silverbell is also known as snowdrop tree and mountain silverbell. Throughout most of its range, which is confined to the South, this silverbell is a shrub or small tree. But at the rainy, southern end of the Blue Ridge, it attains heights from 75 to 90 feet and girths from 7 to 9 feet. People can't quite believe that the tall, straight silverbell in the Southern Highlands is the same species as the stooped, understory silverbell in the Georgia Piedmont. Hence the name mountain silverbell.

This hardwood's alternate leaves—3 to 5 inches long, finely saw-toothed, and long pointed at the tip—are not particularly distinctive. The appearance of its bark, fruit, and flower, however, is unique in this wilderness. The bark on seedlings and saplings is longitudinally lined with light yellow streaks. These lines disappear while the tree is still fairly young. This trail's old-growth silverbells exhibit the typical bark of mature trees, which is dark blackish brown and divided into small, flaky squares. In the shady forest, splotches of their boles look black, so black they appear fire-scorched.

Carolina silverbell

Dangling in clusters beneath the branches, the countless bell-shaped blossoms wave back and forth in the spring winds. The flowers are white, four-lobed, and ½ to 1 inch long. The resulting chestnut-colored fruits have four broad, symmetrical wings running the length of the seedpod. Silverbells bloom along this trail, depending upon the altitude, from late April through most of May.

Directions

See the beginning of this section, page 34, for directions to the Slickrock Creek Trailhead.

Notes

Ike Branch Trail

Foot Trail 45: 2.2 miles

- ■ **Dayhiking** Easy to Moderate in either direction
- ■ **Backpacking** Moderate in either direction
- ■ **Interior Trail** Northeastern terminus on Slickrock Creek Trail, 1,320 feet; southwestern terminus on Slickrock Creek Trail at Slickrock Creek, 1,320 feet
- ■ **Trail Junctions** Slickrock Creek (two), Yellowhammer Gap, Hangover Lead North
- ■ **Topographic Quadrangle** Tapoco NC-TN
- ■ **Features** Old-growth trees; diverse second-growth forest; abundant spring wildflowers

THIS TRAIL IS DESCRIBED as it is most often walked, from northeast to southwest, from its first junction with Slickrock Creek Trail to its second. After walking the beginning 0.6 mile of Slickrock Creek, you will come to a signed fork; Slickrock Creek Trail continues straight ahead; Ike Branch Trail slants up and to the left.

The easily followed path climbs on the slope above its namesake stream for its first 0.3 mile. The hardest part of the upgrade, the middle part, is moderate to strenuous. Below this ascending stretch, Ike Branch slides into a steep ravine and quickly drops toward its end at Calderwood Lake—a beautiful mountain lake that drowned a more beautiful mountain river, the Little Tennessee.

Above the initial ascent, the treadway closely parallels and crosses the stream as it works its way up the watershed. Here Ike Branch is a gentle, mossy-rocked brook, 5 to 8 feet wide and often only a few inches deep. Near the second crossing the route travels through an open, parklike forest dominated by old-growth trees— hemlock, beech, and buckeye. This small area marks the homestead of a man whose nickname was Ike. He left, according to Forest Service sources, in the late 1890s or the early 1900s.

After the fifth and final crossing—a step over what's left of the stream—the footpath proceeds on easy grades up the dry notch of a hollow to a slight saddle on Hangover Lead. The trail enters the wilderness at 0.9 mile as it angles to the left across the saddle onto Hangover Lead's western slope. The next 0.6 mile half-loops out and around a low knob. There is no easier walking in the entire wilderness. Instead of continuing up and over the knob to the next gap, the trail builders took the long, easy way around. They closely followed the contour of the slope from gap to gap, both of which are about 1,800 feet in elevation. Before the trail crosses the shoulder of a pine-topped spur, there are winter views of mountains, Stiffknee Top and Little Fodderstack for the most part, to the west across the Slickrock Creek valley.

The treadway reaches a junction on the west side of Yellowhammer Gap at mile 1.5. (Early in 1940, CCC workers backpacked 8,000 brown trout to Slickrock Creek through this gap.) The trail to the left is the lower-elevation end of Hangover Lead North. From this first junction, the path descends 125 yards to a second one. The trail that proceeds straight ahead, uphill, is Yellowhammer Gap; Ike Branch turns sharply to the right (west) and down.

The remainder of the route descends steadily (easy or easy to moderate) near an unnamed tributary branch of Slickrock Creek. Here on the moist ravine slopes, the predominantly hardwood forest, tall and straight second-growth, is unusually diverse even by Southern Appalachian standards. Near its end the footpath dips to stream level, ducks down the stream a few feet, then continues on the same side without crossing. Ike Branch ties into Slickrock Creek Trail at a large campsite beside Slickrock Creek. Like all the other junctions in the Joyce Kilmer–Slickrock Wilderness, this one is usually marked with a sign.

The first 0.9 mile of this trail, botanically rich and picturesque, is outside the protected wilderness. The Forest Service, however, has a long-standing agreement with the community of Tapoco to protect its water supply, Yellowhammer Branch, from any disturbance. The small triangle of nonwilderness land from Yellowhammer Branch to the lake, which includes Ike Branch, has been traditionally included in this agreement. There has been no logging from the north slope of Caney Lead to the lake since 1936, when the Forest Service acquired the land.

Nature Notes

Ike Branch ranges through a maturing second-growth forest. Because of its low elevation, from 1,320 to 1,800 feet, and its numerous habitats, this trail has an unusually high number of tree species for its relatively short length. If you include the beginning segment of

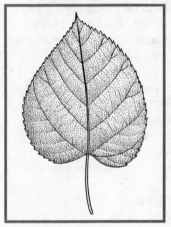

American basswood

Slickrock Creek Trail, you can see and perhaps identify more kinds of trees here than along any other 3.0-mile section of trail in the wilderness.

The tree with the large, heart-shaped leaf, the basswood, is common within its preferred habitat—hardwood cove, north slope, and stream bank—along this trail and throughout the wilderness, except at elevations above 4,500 feet. Recently there has been a botanical controversy concerning the basswood genus, *Tilia*. Current literature lumps all basswoods, including the former white basswood, into one species—the American basswood (*Tilia americana*)—with three recognized varieties.

Basswood is also known as linden, a name the German settlers transferred from a *Tilia* species in Europe, and as bee-tree, because honeybees swarm to its fragrant blossoms. The common name recognized by botanists and foresters comes from the fibers in the tree's inner bark, called bast, which Native Americans used to make rope.

The basswood is easily identified by its alternate leaves, which are sharply pointed, coarsely toothed, and usually 4 to 6 inches long and almost as wide. Bark on a maturing second-growth tree is light to medium gray. Patterns of slight furrows that rise straight up in broken lines split the bark into narrow ridges. A mature basswood can often be identified from a distance by its sapling ring—a circle of sprouts growing from the tree's base.

Usually 60 to 90 feet in height and 2 to 3 feet in diameter (these are southern mountain dimensions), the forest-grown basswood has a straight bole clear of branches to half its total height. Its maximum size, rarely achieved by an individual specimen, is 140 feet in height and 6 feet in diameter. An old-timer lives over 400 years.

The moist rocky slopes along the first 0.6 mile of Slickrock Creek Trail and the beginning 0.5 mile of Ike Branch have an incredible floral display in early spring. This area has one of the three richest botanical habitats (the other two are Poplar Cove Loop in Joyce Kilmer Memorial Forest and the first few miles of the Stratton Bald Trail) traversed by the trails included in this guide. Any of the three areas serves well as a primer for Southern Appalachian wildflowers.

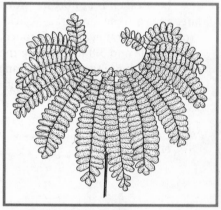

northern maidenhair fern

Spring's first wave of wildflowers blooms early at the low elevations near Calderwood Lake. For a two-week period, usually starting sometime from mid-March to later in the month, the ground beside Slickrock Creek Trail is carpeted with the color of spring beauty, hepatica, sessile and wakerobin trillium, bloodroot, rue anemone, Bishop's cap (miterwort), and several species of violets, including the easily identified long-spurred violet. By the end of April, however, when at least thirty kinds of flowers have already bloomed or are just about to finish, the show has moved on up the mountain. If you are too early for your favorites at Poplar Cove, you may want to try the beginning of Slickrock Creek.

The moist slopes on the way to and along Ike Branch Trail are also rich in fern species. One of the most common and conspicuously graceful is the northern maidenhair fern. The maidenhair's stems are glossy dark brown or black. Its main stem forks, and the two branches curve horizontally back toward each other until they form a horseshoe-shaped semicircle or sometimes a full circle. They vary in design; no two in a clump are quite alike. Those that bend into a full whorl have a delicate, double-circle symmetry.

The northern maidenhair is deciduous; it uncurls from its crosier by mid-April at this low elevation and withers from the first hard frost of fall.

Directions

Ike Branch is a short interior trail that has both of its ends connecting with the same trail—Slickrock Creek. Starting from the Slickrock Creek Trailhead near Tapoco, the two Ike Branch junctions are at 0.6 mile and 3.8 miles along the Slickrock Creek Trail. Both junctions, which are the first two along Slickrock Creek Trail, are usually marked with a sign. (See the beginning of this section, page 34, for directions to the Slickrock Creek Trailhead.)

Notes

Yellowhammer Gap Trail

Foot Trail 49: 1.7 miles

- **Dayhiking** Easy to Moderate in either direction
- **Backpacking** Moderate in either direction
- **Interior Trail** Northeastern terminus on Ike Branch
  Trail near Yellowhammer Gap, 1,720 feet; southwestern
  terminus on Nichols Cove Trail, 1,760 feet
- **Trail Junctions** Ike Branch, Nichols Cove
- **Topographic Quadrangle** Tapoco NC-TN
- **Features** Hardwood forest; winter views of Little
  Fodderstack Mountain

WALKING THIS TRAIL IS A LESSON in reading mountain land from a map. The interlacing patterns on the flat topographic sheet—the fingers of bunched lines pointing in opposite directions, running upslope from every stream and running downslope from every ridge, low flowing into high and high into low—are the typical contour configurations of Appalachian slopes. The wider, rounded fingers generally paralleling hollows and pointing toward the main streams are spurs: side ridges splaying out and down from the main ridges. The narrower, V-shaped fingers generally paralleling spurs and pointing toward the main ridges are hollows: side coves splaying out and up from the main coves.

Those unfamiliar with Yellowhammer Gap's spur-slope-hollow terrain might be surprised at the number of ups and downs for a path with a 40-foot, end-to-end elevation differential. Although the trail is seldom level, there are no long, steep grades and the few moderate grades are short. Thanks to an excellent job of trail making, most of the rises and dips are easy or easy to moderate.

This easily followed interior trail can be walked as a connecting leg along many different loops originating from both Big Fat Gap and Slickrock Creek Trailheads. Combining segments of Slickrock Creek and Ike Branch Trails with Yellowhammer Gap makes a good dayhike or a leisurely in-and-out backpacking trip. The trail is somewhat easier to walk as it is described, from northeast to southwest, from Ike Branch Trail to Nichols Cove Trail.

Early on, Yellowhammer Gap disposes of its hardest ascent—a switchbacking, progressively harder climb to the crest of the first spur. Along the way a big quartzite boulder, upslope to the left, gives you a good reason to rest a moment or two. After crossing the shoulder of the spur, the walking is easy on a slope that affords winter views of Little Fodderstack Mountain, nearly 3 miles distant across the Slickrock Creek valley.

From the first spur to near its southwestern end, the treadway follows the familiar pattern of most well-constructed slope trails: it ascends to and tops a spur, descends to and winds around the heads of one or more hollows, then rises to the next spur. The hollows are steep sided, notched at the bottom of the V. The only reasonable way to traverse this cut-up country is to half-circle around the heads (upper ends) of these hollows, more or less following the contour of the slope.

At 0.8 mile the route varies from the pattern. Here, instead of winding around a hollow, the path drops moderately into the hollow before continuing along the slope. On the way down you will pass a large, lone white pine, noticeably responsible for hundreds of sapling pines up and down the hollow.

After topping the final spur, the trail follows the wide walkway of a former sled road down to the gently sloping land in Nichols cove. This land, as the piled rocks, rusting buckets, and rotting bottom timbers of a corn crib testify, was once settled.

Yellowhammer Gap ends at its junction with Nichols Cove Trail. This junction is usually marked with a sign and always marked with a cemetery—a small, circular, rock-lined plot with two stark gravestones, one each for the twin sisters who died seven days after their birth in 1914. Nichols Cove Trail makes a 90-degree turn at the cemetery. Straight ahead, it leads to the southwest, toward its connections with Big Fat and Slickrock Creek Trails. To the right, it crosses its namesake branch after 0.1 mile, then parallels the stream to the north, toward its other junction with Slickrock Creek Trail.

Nature Notes

This trail passes under the canopy of a predominantly decidu-ous hardwood forest—oak-pine on the spur tops, low-elevation cove hardwoods in the hollows, and a mixture of the two types on the slopes between. The evergreens—eastern hemlock, American holly, pitch and white pine—are minor components. Yellow poplar is the dominant tree in the northwest-facing hollows and on the for-merly cultivated land in the cove. Tall, mature white oaks and pig-nut hickories are much more nu-merous here, below 2,000 feet, than they are at higher elevations.

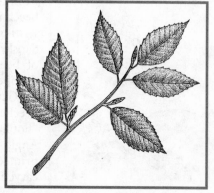

American beech

Near its Nichols Cove end the track ventures beside a half dozen or so old-timer beeches. These old-growth trees—remnants of the virgin forest before logging—escaped with their skins because they were deemed useless. The set-tlers didn't want them for fire-wood (you can't split green beech), and the loggers didn't want them for lumber. Lucky for the trees and lucky for us. Large beeches, 8 to 10 feet in circumference, 175 to 250 years old, scarce over most of Southern Appalachia, add beauty and diversity to this wilderness.

Classified as a northern hardwood, the American beech is char-acterized by its smooth, smoke-gray bark, which remains unwrin-kled even in old age, and by its saw-toothed, sharp-pointed dark green leaves. A few other trees, primarily Fraser magnolia and yel-lowwood, may be mistaken for beech in winter. But if you see the gray bark and slender, reddish brown buds, sharp pointed and up to 1 inch long, there will be no mistake in identification. There is another way to distinguish a beech in winter. It is the only deciduous tree in the wilderness that regularly retains many of its withered leaves, light tan in color, through the winter and into spring.

Mature beeches on good sites average 60 to 80 feet in height and 2 to 4 feet in diameter at breast height (DBH), 4¹/₂ feet from the ground. Its maximum size is 150 feet in height and 6 feet in diameter. American beeches grow slowly even under the best of conditions. But like the hemlock, they grow slowly for a long time: they may attain an age of 300 to 400 years.

The beech offered a welcome look of stability and familiarity to the early colonists because our species does not differ significantly

downy rattlesnake plantain

from the beech of Europe. The European beech is closely linked with the history of writing. Historians write that the earliest Sanskrit characters were carved on strips of beech bark. This practice spread to Europe, where the earliest scribblings of the Germanic people were inscribed upon beechen tablets. In fact, our modern word "book" was derived from the ancient Anglo-Saxon word for beech. Gutenburg printed the first Bible from movable type carved from beech wood.

Yellowhammer is another older and more rural name for the northern flicker. This bird flicks up insects, primarily ants, with its long, flexible, sticky tongue.

Yellowhammer Gap has a fair early spring wildflower display, starting with rue anemone, hepatica, sessile trillium, and trout lily in late March or early April and ending with showy orchis and wakerobin in late April. Frequently found along this and most of the other trails in the wilderness is the downy rattlesnake plantain. A member of the orchid family, this distinctive plant was probably named for its resemblance to sloughed snakeskin. Both the Indians and their botany students, the early settlers, considered this orchid a cure for snakebite. And both cultures once believed that the physical appearance of a plant was a direct, divine hint of its highest human use, usually medicinal. Today, many of our common botanical names—liverwort, birthwort, spleenwort—still reflect the ideas of medieval Europe.

The downy rattlesnake plantain has a basal rosette of easily recognized, dark green leaves, 1 to 3¹/₂ inches long, reticulated with a lacework pattern of white veins. These attractive leaves remain prominent throughout the winter. The white flowers—small (¹/₄ inch) and numerous, not particularly showy for an orchid—occur on a cylindrical cluster that crowns a leafless, woolly stalk. The small clumps or colonies bloom in June and July.

Directions

Yellowhammer Gap is an interior trail that connects two other interior trails, Ike Branch and Nichols Cove. It is the only trail described in this guide that requires walking segments of two other trails to gain either of its ends. To reach Yellowhammer Gap's southwestern terminus from the Big Fat Gap Trailhead, walk Big Fat Trail to its end (1.5 miles), then turn right (north) onto Nichols Cove Trail and follow it for 1.6 miles to its gravestone junction with Yellowhammer Gap. At this junction, usually signed, Nichols Cove turns sharply to the left onto path, and Yellowhammer Gap continues straight ahead on the old road.

To reach Yellowhammer Gap's northeastern terminus from the Slickrock Creek Trailhead, walk Slickrock Creek Trail for 0.6 mile, then turn left (southwest) onto Ike Branch Trail and follow it for 1.6 miles to its junction with Yellowhammer Gap. At this junction, usually signed, Ike Branch turns sharply to the right and downhill; Yellowhammer Gap continues straight ahead, uphill. (See Big Fat, page 67, and Nichols Cove, page 74, in the Big Fat Gap Trailhead section and Slickrock Creek, page 36, and Ike Branch, page 44, in this section for further information.)

Notes

*L*ike winds and sunsets, wild things were taken for granted until progress began to do away with them. Now we face the question whether a still higher "standard of living" is worth its cost in things natural, wild, and free. For us of the minority, the opportunity to see geese is more important than television, and the chance to find a pasque-flower is a right as inalienable as free speech.

Aldo Leopold
A Sand County Almanac *(1947)*

Big Fat Gap Trailhead

hiker on Hangover

Trails

Hangover Lead North
Hangover Lead South
Big Fat
Windy Gap
Nichols Cove

Big Fat Gap Trailhead
Directions and Map

THE BIG FAT GAP APPROACH ROAD—FS 62, Slickrock Creek Road—heads west from the segment of US 129 stretching from Robbinsville, North Carolina, to Calderwood Lake near the North Carolina–Tennessee border.

Approach from the south. To reach FS 62 from the south take US 129 North approximately 12.5 miles beyond where NC 143 West turns left toward Joyce Kilmer Memorial Forest. This three-way intersection is approximately 1.0 mile north of Robbinsville. After traveling the 12.5 miles, turn left onto the bridge (the only bridge in the area) of a side road that crosses the Cheoah River. This road—usually marked with a Forest Service road sign or a sign for Big Fat Gap, or both—is FS 62. Follow this gravel and dirt road (curl to the right at the first junction) as it winds uphill for about 7.0 miles to its dead end at the corralled trailhead parking area.

Approach from the north. To reach Slickrock Creek Road from the north, from the US 129–Foothills Parkway junction in Tennessee travel US 129 South approximately 1.7 miles beyond the bridge over Calderwood Lake before turning right onto FS 62.

Approach from the southwest. If you are already near the Joyce Kilmer Memorial Forest area, or if you are traveling from the southwest (from Tennessee) on the Overhill-Cherohala Skyway, take the dirt-road shortcut through Horse Cove Campground. Once you reach US 129, turn left and proceed northward about 5.7 miles to the left turn onto FS 62. (See page 30 for the shortcut directions from Joyce Kilmer Memorial Forest to US 129.)

Forest Service 62 is usually a good route, suitable for conventional cars after its first grading in the early spring. This road is closed from late December through early March; the closing dates depend on the weather. If you're cutting it close, call the Forest Service so you won't be faced with a sudden change of plans.

Big Fat Gap
Trailhead

Legend:

═══	U.S. highway
────	State highway
────	Forest Service road
········	Forest trail
─··─··─	State boundary
─··─··─	Creek or branch
▬▬▬	Wilderness boundary
▲	Campground
〔129〕	U.S. highway
〔165〕	State highway
〔1127〕	Secondary road
〔FS59〕	Forest Service road
〔FT90〕	Forest trail
〔P〕	Parking
◆	Knob
▲	Peak
╱	Falls
⬤	Gap

Map labels:

STIFFKNEE, Little, TRAIL, Slickrock, Lower Falls, Creek, Calderwood Lake el. 1086, Ike Br., TRAIL, FT42, 129, Dam, Lake Cheoah

FT106, Creek, IKE, FT45, FT45, Yellowhammer Gap, FT56, GAP, BRANCH, P, 129

Wildcat Br., Slickrock, FT42, FT44, YELLOWHAMMER, TRAIL, FT49, NORTH, TRAIL

N

Nichols Cove Br., NICHOLS COVE TRAIL, FT56, LEAD, 0 1 2 Miles, FS62

Wildcat Falls, FT42, FT400, Cold Spring Knob, HANGOVER

WINDY GAP TRAIL, FT44, BIG FAT TRAIL, Big Fat Branch, FT41, P, Big Fat Gap, FS62

FT42, Buckeye Branch, FT56, HANGOVER, HANGOVER

Grapevine Br., SLICKROCK, LEAD, Beech Creek, Middle Creek, Jane Branch

Branch, Gap Branch, CREEK, Hangover, Creek, SOUTH, Rockwall Br.

Slickrock, Naked Ground Branch, TRAIL, TRAIL, Hangover el. 5180, FT56A, CREEK, TRAIL, Deep Creek, FT46

Haoe el. 5249, Saddle Tree Gap, DEEP, LEAD, FT53

FT42, FT53, HAOE, HAOE, LEAD, TRAIL, FT53

Naked Ground, LEAD

Hangover Lead North Trail

Foot Trail 56: 2.4 miles

- **Dayhiking In** Moderate
- **Dayhiking Out** Moderate to Strenuous
- **Backpacking In** Moderate to Strenuous
- **Backpacking Out** Strenuous
- **Start** Big Fat Gap Trailhead, 3,060 feet
- **End** Ike Branch Trail in Yellowhammer Gap, 1,780 feet
- **Trail Junctions** Hangover Lead South (at trailhead), Big Fat (at trailhead), Windy Gap (at trailhead), Ike Branch, Yellowhammer Gap (see trail description)
- **Topographic Quadrangle** Tapoco NC-TN
- **Features** Winter views of the Hangover and the Unicoi Mountains; late spring flowering shrub display

I F YOU DON'T PAY CAREFUL ATTENTION to the map, the Big Fat Gap Trailhead can be confusing. There are four paths but only three trails. One trail, Hangover Lead, has its only vehicular access near its midpoint at the gap. This access divides the trail into two paths leading away from the same place in opposite directions. Because of the possible confusion, and because few people walk its entire length at one time, this guide divides Hangover Lead into two sections— Hangover Lead North, which heads to Cold Spring Knob and Yellowhammer Gap; and Hangover Lead South, which heads to the Hangover and the Haoe.

This lightly used trail quickly curls onto the crest of its namesake ridge and climbs on the wide walkway of an old road. Behind you, clearly visible to the south when the leaves are off the trees, is the unmistakable thumbnail profile of the Hangover, 2 miles away and 2,000 feet up. The straight upridge grade through a second-growth oak-pine forest is moderate to strenuous. It helps you understand the name Big Fat Gap.

At 0.4 mile the route reaches the crown of Cold Spring Knob (3,500 feet), the trail's high point. From here, continuing northward along the wilderness boundary, the remainder of the trail descends on Hangover Lead's spine. The descent is sharp—1,720 feet in 2.0 miles. Most of this elevation loss comes in quick bursts. A series of straight downridge pitches alternates with respites of much easier grades, including some short uphills. Some of these pitches, usually from 0.1- to 0.2-mile long, are as steep as any other grades of similar length in the wilderness. On the way down the track narrows to path, then becomes more isolated and primitive. During the months when the hardwoods are bare, there are steady between-branch views of the main Unicoi Mountain ridgecrest to the west across the Slickrock Creek valley.

Forty yards from the end of the trail, you will notice several "Public Watershed" signs posted on the nonwilderness side of Yellowhammer Gap. Please heed their message and stay away from Tapoco's water supply. Hangover Lead North ends at its signed junction with Ike Branch Trail. To the left (southwest) from this junction, it is less than 0.1 mile to the Ike Branch–Yellowhammer Gap Trail junction.

There are occasional level areas on the ridge suitable for camping. The entire trail, however, is dry as a bone. But there is water along Ike Branch Trail no more than 0.2 mile from Hangover Lead North's end. Follow Ike Branch Trail to the right and down from its junction with Yellowhammer Gap Trail.

If you're fit, full of energy and challenge, and want to climb a mountain from bottom to top, here is a suggestion. Hike to the Hangover and the Haoe—from the north, along the Hangover Lead ridgecrest all the way to its upper-elevation end. Starting from the Slickrock Creek Trailhead, combine segments of Slickrock Creek and Ike Branch Trails with the entire Hangover Lead Trail, north and south of Big Fat Gap. This route is 7.5 miles long and gains approximately 4,100 feet to the high point of the Haoe. It will provide the determined hiker with numerous, rugged, straight-up-the-ridge grunts. It's a calf-buster, the full treatment.

Nature Notes

The forest along Hangover Lead North exhibits the usual slope-dependent differences. The ridgecrest from Big Fat Gap to the top of Cold Spring Knob faces south, making it sunnier and drier than the remainder of the ridgecrest, which faces north. As is often the case, more pines are mixed in with the hardwoods on south-facing exposures than on north-facing exposures on the same ridge. Mature pitch pines are common along Hangover Lead North's south-facing segment. Frequently found on less fertile, drier ridges and slopes below 4,500 feet, the pitch is a medium-sized tree, usually 55 to 80 feet tall in the Southern Highlands. Its needles—dark yellow-green and often twisted, 3 to 5 inches long, and three to the sheath—are diagnostic. Also charac-

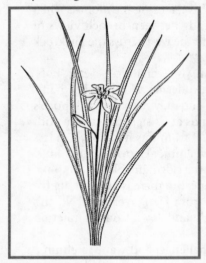

yellow star-grass

teristic are the tufts of needles that occasionally stick straight out of the tree's trunk, often head high or even lower.

The pitch pine's bark is highly variable and changes as the tree grows older. Most often it is furrowed into scaly ridges and is reddish brown at maturity. Mature pitch pines often have picturesque crowns of thick, contorted branches. By far the most common pine in the wilderness, the pitch seldom grows taller after the age of 90. Its maximum lifespan is 200 to 250 years.

The second-growth forest covering the ridge and upper slopes along the trail's north-facing segment is largely deciduous, dominated by oaks—white, black, southern red, northern red, chestnut, and scarlet—and hickories. The thickest trees are the occasional old-growth chestnut oaks, logger's culls, some 9 to 11 feet in circumference.

Hangover Lead North, like most low- to middle-elevation ridge trails, where a heavy understory of deciduous heath and a lack of moisture discourage herbaceous plant growth, has a poor early spring wildflower display. But like most ridge trails in the wilderness, Hangover Lead has a flowering shrub show during late spring. Three species of flowering shrubs—flame azalea, mountain laurel, sweet-shrub—blossom in May. The sweetshrub blooms earlier than the other two, which usually peak during the last half of May.

The late-spring wildflower you are most likely to notice on this trail, as well as on other ridge-running and dry-slope trails throughout the wilderness, is the yellow star-grass. As the name suggests, the delicate, bright yellow blossoms are star-shaped, six-petaled, and about 3/4 inch across. The long, thin, grasslike leaves complete an easy identification when seen in combination with the blooms. This perennial herb, which belongs to the same family as daffodils and jonquils, prefers open, sunny woods. It seems to take advantage of the extra opening created by a trail, for you will most often find it on or at the edge of a treadway. Yellow star-grass flowers from mid-May through mid-June, depending on the slope orientation and elevation (end of May and early June on Hangover Lead North).

Directions

Hangover Lead North shares the same trailhead with Hangover Lead South, Windy Gap, and Big Fat. Hangover Lead North begins through a gap in the railing directly across the road from the trailhead bulletin board. (See the beginning of this section, page 56, for traveling directions to the Big Fat Gap Trailhead.)

Notes

Hangover Lead South Trail

Foot Trail 56: 3.0 miles

- **Dayhiking In** Moderate to Strenuous
- **Dayhiking Out** Moderate
- **Backpacking In** Strenuous
- **Backpacking Out** Moderate to Strenuous
- **Start** Big Fat Gap Trailhead, 3,060 feet
- **End** Haoe Lead Trail on top of Haoe Mountain, 5,249 feet
- **Trail Junctions** Hangover Lead North (at trailhead), Big Fat (at trailhead), Windy Gap (at trailhead), Deep Creek (on side trail 56A to Hangover), Haoe Lead
- **Topographic Quadrangle** Tapoco NC-TN
- **Features** 360-degree panorama of wilderness; late spring flowering shrub display

THIS GUIDE DIVIDES Hangover Lead, which shares the Big Fat Gap Trailhead with Big Fat and Windy Gap Trails, into two sections—Hangover Lead South and Hangover Lead North. (See the first paragraph of Hangover Lead North, the preceding trail, for an explanation.)

The old, steep stretch of trail from Grassy Gap to the main ridge—the one that warranted the only strenuous to rugged rating in this guide—has been rerouted. Instead of continuing straight up the rocky pitch of the ridge through rhododendron and hemlock, the trail now slabs off the lead onto the western slope well below ridgeline. This rerouted section is 1.3 miles long, and added just over 0.2 mile to the total length of the trail. Although there are still occasional short, steep grades, most of the reroute is no harder than moderate. And while it is not as steep or scenic as the former path, the footing on the new segment, sometimes all rock and root, is every bit as rough.

Immediately rising from Big Fat Gap, the trail switchbacks steadily for 0.1 mile to the ridgecrest of Hangover Lead. On the way up, it passes a few old-growth oaks, the thickest a chestnut oak with a girth of approximately 13 feet (now dead and down). The route continues on the narrow ridge for a few tenths of a mile, veers to the right onto a rich north slope with tall black cherry, sweet birch, and Carolina silverbell, then slowly switches its way back up to the lead. Along the way, a left turn affords a good view of Bob Stratton Bald to the right and the Fodderstack ridgeline to the southwest and west. The easy-to-follow path dips to a slight gap at 0.7 mile.

Beyond this first gap, the next 0.7 mile gains elevation on or near the exact crest of Hangover Lead. The geographical term "lead," which appears infrequently on topographic maps, is just another word for a long, prominent spur ridge that leads to a high mountain, in this case the Hangover. Hangover Lead is the entire eastern rim of the Slickrock Creek basin. It is also the northeastern boundary of the Joyce Kilmer–Slickrock Wilderness, from Calderwood Lake southward past Big Fat Gap all the way to the knob before Grassy Gap.

The treadway descends gently to Grassy Gap (4,280 feet) at mile 1.5. This shallow gap is long and wide, and often nearly level from side to side. It is a surprisingly open, beautiful place, especially in spring, with glades of grass and moss beneath mature trees. The forest changes abruptly at Grassy Gap. For the first mile and a half the forest is predominantly second-growth hardwoods, dominated by red maple and three species of oak. But here at the gap, because of the elevation, the moisture of the north-facing ridge, and past logging practices, the forest becomes old-growth hemlock, beech, and Carolina silverbell, which blooms in mid-May.

Above the gap, the loggers selectively cut valuable species only. While the large trees that remain today may have been useless to the loggers, they are obviously valuable to the red squirrel. If you sit down for a few minutes in the gap, chances are good that an obsessively curious "mountain boomer," all twitch and chatter, won't be able to resist having a look at you.

The rerouted segment, which holds a generally southern course, starts at the high end of Grassy Gap. Instead of heading straight up the rugged picturesque ridge, the trail now slabs onto the lead's sunset slope. Here the treadway works its way up gradually (compared to the old route) through a forest of northern hardwoods and hemlock. Hobblebush, several species of wood fern, and wind-thrown deadfalls are common in the understory.

Following a double switchback, the footpath pops up to a narrow heath bald, dominated by rhododendron, on the exact crest of a spur off the lead at mile 2.5. The trail forks on the ridgetop. To the right, a dead-end side trail leads 80 yards down the western running spur to an open, rock outcrop overlook: a 360-degree panorama. Hangover Lead South continues to the left, up and over the spur. It then follows the upper southern slope of the spur quickly back into forest, mostly small beech and yellow birch. Three-tenths mile beyond the first junction, the route reaches the main ridge at a usually signed T-intersection.

To the left (northeast), Hangover Lead South side trail (56A) heads slightly more than 0.2 mile to the Hangover. Along the way (110 yards) the side trail passes the upper end of Deep Creek Trail. This usually signed junction is to the right opposite a rock outcrop. Turning left on the side trail to connect with Deep Creek represents a change. Prior to the rerouting, you had to turn right with the main trail to reach Deep Creek. Now, because the new section tops the ridge further to the south, you must turn left onto the side trail to join Deep Creek.

The remainder of the trail turns right and follows the ridgeline less than 0.2 mile to the top of the Haoe. The treadway enters the small, grassy clearing (not good camping) on the exact crown of the Haoe (5,249 feet) through a framed archway of rhododendron. Hangover Lead South ends at the clearing at its junction with the Haoe Lead Trail, which climbs its namesake mountain from the east, then turns and continues southwestward on the ridge toward Naked Ground and Bob Stratton Bald.

The side trail's second tenth mile is a straight, corridorlike cut through a heath bald dominated by Catawba rhododendron. The gradual upgrade dead-ends at the last protruding topknot of rock. Straight ahead, the ridge drops away in a free fall, then continues below the cliff. That topknot, the high point of the Hangover at approximately 5,180 feet, is just above and back from the edge of the cliff.

All around you, in an unbroken but short panorama, is the wilderness: Deep Creek's valley and Hangover Lead; the upper Slickrock Creek basin with its heath bald and long, fingering spurs; the rounded crown of the Haoe, the level wall of Bob Stratton Bald, and the main ridge of the Unicois. From northeast to southeast, mountains extend away in tumbling waves across western North Carolina, a land of high ridges and short horizons. To the northeast, the Smokies rise as a single unit—no roads, no cuts, just mountains and a completely canopied landscape (in contrast with the foreground of the view). The low ridgeline south of the Smokies is the crest of the Yellow Creek Mountains. The Cheoahs are the nearest mountains to the east. To the southeast, a dozen or so miles away, Joanna Bald is the prominent peak in the Snowbirds.

Nature Notes

If you spend some time on the Hangover, you will probably see or hear the *crunk* of one of Southern Appalachia's rarest birds: the common raven. Noticeably larger than the American crow, the raven's thick bill and wedge-shaped tail make it easy to identify. The raven, which is slowly increasing its range in the southern mountains, often soars and flies, alternately flapping and gliding like a hawk. Ravens are also fond of aerial displays. They power their way up high, tuck their wings, then drop in tumbling, looping dives.

There is no water on this trail. There is, however, a variable spring down the western (Slickrock Creek) slope from Saddle Tree Gap. Turn left onto the side trail, follow it to Saddle Tree Gap's overused camping area before Hangover's heath bald, then drop down to the left. The spring is not far, but it is variable; I have seen it flowing well and not at all. If you really need water, you can find it down the Deep Creek Trail within 0.5 mile.

This trail has a good flowering shrub display. Flame azalea, mountain laurel, sweetshrub, hobblebush, and Catawba rhododendron take turns blooming beginning in early May. Sweetshrub and hobblebush (also known as witchhobble) flower and fade first. The peak of color occurs in late May and early June, when the flame azalea, mountain laurel, and Catawba rhododendron bloom at nearly the same time. The flame azalea usually blossoms heaviest between May 15 and June 1. The Catawba rhododendron and mountain laurel are usually at their best in late May or early June. If you get lucky and hit it right, you might be able to see all three on the same trip.

Many people rank the Catawba rhododendron as the most beautiful flowering shrub in the Blue Ridge Mountains. It's easy to see why. The deep pink to rose-lavender flowers are striking. In years when flowering is heavy, these evergreen heaths have numerous branch-end clusters of blossoms, each cluster closely resembling a large, ready-made corsage. The dark magenta buds have an even richer color than the blooms.

When neither is in bloom it is often difficult to distinguish Catawba from rosebay rhododendron. Without going into taxonomic detail, there are two easy ways to differentiate these similar shrubs. The Catawba usually has leaves that are noticeably smaller (3 to 6 inches long) than those of the white to pale-pink flowering rosebay (4 to 10 inches long). And whereas the rosebay is most abundant on moist slopes and streamsides at the lower and middle elevations, the Catawba is most often found at higher elevations (above 3,800 feet) on upper slopes and narrow, rocky, thin-soiled ridges. The Catawba often occurs, as it does on this trail, in large stands in the understory of a thin ridgetop forest or in almost pure thickets that exclude trees—heath balds. The Catawba rhododendron is the dominant shrub of the Southern Appalachian heath balds. It is the shrub that people time their trips to see in the highcountry of the Great Smoky Mountains National Park.

Catawba rhododendron

Directions

Hangover Lead South shares the same trailhead with Hangover Lead North, Windy Gap, and Big Fat. Hangover Lead South heads uphill to the left of the trailhead bulletin board. (See the beginning of this section, page 56, for directions to the Big Fat Gap Trailhead.)

Big Fat Trail

- ■ **Dayhiking In** Easy to Moderate
- ■ **Dayhiking Out** Moderate
- ■ **Backpacking In** Moderate
- ■ **Backpacking Out** Moderate to Strenuous
- ■ **Start** Big Fat Gap Trailhead, 3,060 feet
- ■ **End** Nichols Cove Trail at Slickrock Creek, 2,000 feet
- ■ **Trail Junctions** Nichols Cove, Slickrock Creek (see trail description), Hangover Lead North and Hangover Lead South (at trailhead), Windy Gap (at trailhead)
- ■ **Topographic Quadrangle** Tapoco NC-TN
- ■ **Features** Winter views of Big Fodderstack; good spring wildflower display; second-growth forest dominated by large yellow poplars

B**IG FAT IS THE SHORTEST TRAIL** in the Joyce Kilmer–Slickrock Wilderness and the third shortest trail described in this guide. It is also the only route that provides quick, direct access into the middle of the Slickrock Creek basin. These two factors, its length and location, predictably account for another: Big Fat is heavily used by hunters, hikers, and fishermen. If you're searching for solitude, you may want to avoid Big Fat and the downstream section of Slickrock Creek during warm weekends.

To prevent further damage to an eroding trail, much of the lower end of Big Fat was rerouted from the north side of the branch to the south. This move took advantage of stable, old logging routes on the south side but only increased the trail's length by 0.1 mile.

The trail descends sharply on the wide treadway of a former jeep road into a diverse cove hardwood forest. Still dropping fast, the treadway quickly swings toward the center notch of the cove, then curls parallel to the beginning of Big Fat Branch. In winter you can see Big Fodderstack (4,346 feet) almost due west from the upper cove.

One hundred and twenty yards before the first crossing, there is an old, slowly moldering chestnut log to the left. At 0.5 mile the track crosses to the north side of the branch. Below this crossing, the downgrade becomes more gradual through a parklike grove of yellow poplar and hemlock. Three-tenths of a mile beyond the first crossing, where the old trail is blocked with branches (feel free to add to the disappearing pile), the rerouted segment begins. Instead of continuing along the north side of the branch, the path now curls down and to the left, crosses the branch, then follows an old logging route high above the stream.

At 1.2 miles the trail switchbacks down and to the right, descending a short distance to tie back into the original Big Fat beside the stream. The rest of the trail closely parallels the branch on a former railroad bed above its bank. This last section is gentle downhill walking through a streamside forest of sweet and yellow birch. The downslope to the stream is often crowded with fern fronds in season. Dense patches of New York fern commonly flank the trail.

Big Fat ends at its usually signed junction with Nichols Cove Trail near Slickrock Creek. To the left (southwest) Nichols Cove continues slightly less than 0.1 mile to its usually signed, south-end junction with Slickrock Creek Trail. (See Nichols Cove Trail, also in this section, for a description of Slickrock Creek Trail's route heading downstream and upstream, north and south, from this junction.)

If you want to walk Nichols Cove Trail to the north, turn right from the end of Big Fat onto Nichols Cove, cross Big Fat Branch, enter a large campsite, then look for the continuing treadway in the corner of the campsite diagonally opposite the confluence of the two streams.

Nature Notes

The forest along Big Fat Branch was cut, probably around 1918 or 1919, as the logging progressed up the Slickrock Creek watershed. In the moist upper cove, the second-growth hardwoods have regenerated impressively. The stand is dominated by tall, straight yellow poplars, many already 9 to 11 feet in circumference and 100 to 120 feet high, and still growing fast—so fast that they are noticeably taller and thicker within the same decade.

There are probably more large black locusts—a rapidly growing, relatively short-lived, early succession species—beside Big Fat than along any other trail in the wilderness. And there really aren't that many of these trees beside Big Fat. These broadleafs are often common shortly after the forest is disturbed by fire, disease, or logging. But since they are shade intolerant, black locusts become progres-

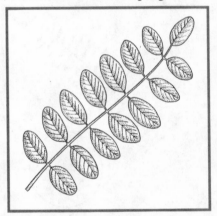

black locust

sively more scarce as the new forest continues to mature without further disturbance. Locusts that are overshadowed by taller trees die quickly. Those in Big Fat Cove are still alive because they are in the overstory, but most of them will be dead by the middle of the twenty-first century.

The rugged, easily recognized bark of the mature black locust is the most deeply furrowed—1 1/2 to 2 inches and more—of any small or medium-sized tree in the southern mountains. Gray to nearly black, the trunk is latticed like a hickory and as deeply grooved as an old chestnut oak. The long ridges fork and come together again—forming diamonds—all the while slightly twisting around the tree.

The black locust leaf, composed of 7 to 19 leaflets, is also distinctive. The leaflets—1 1/4 to 2 inches long and 1/2 to 3/4 inch wide—are smaller than the leaves or leaflets of any other trees that compete for the canopy in this wilderness. The whitish flowers, which hang in wisterialike clusters, usually bloom during the first half of May. You probably won't notice the blossoms high in the trees, but you might get a whiff of their fragrance.

Ferns are both abundant and diverse along Big Fat. One of the most prolific species along the lower part of the trail is also one of the easiest of all ferns to identify. The New York fern's pinnae (its leafy foliage) taper sharply to nearly nothing at either end. Simple as that. No hand lens or special books needed.

New York ferns are plentiful throughout this wilderness and the Southern Highlands. They frequently occur in dense monocultural beds that resemble well-tended gardens growing beneath widely spaced trees. The reason for this appearance is simple: these ferns use herbicide; they poison other plants.

Big Fat also has a good spring wildflower display. The season begins in late March and early April with sessile trillium, spring beauty, hepatica, rue anemone, trout lily, and squirrel corn among many others. The final burst—Vasey's trillium, foamflower, sweet cicely, mayapple—blooms from late April through mid-May.

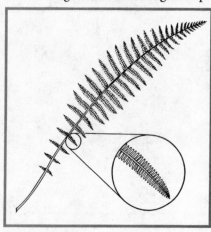

New York fern

Directions

Big Fat shares its namesake trailhead with Hangover Lead South, Hangover Lead North, and Windy Gap Trails. Big Fat is the wide descending path that starts behind the bulletin board. (See the beginning of this section, page 56, for directions to the Big Fat Gap Trailhead.)

Notes

Windy Gap Trail

Foot Trail 400: 1.6 miles

- ■ **Dayhiking In** Easy
- ■ **Dayhiking Out** Easy to Moderate
- ■ **Backpacking In** Easy to Moderate
- ■ **Backpacking Out** Moderate
- ■ **Start** Big Fat Gap Trailhead, 3,060 feet
- ■ **End** Nichols Cove Trail, 2,500 feet
- ■ **Trail Junctions** Nichols Cove, Hangover Lead North and Hangover Lead South (at trailhead), Big Fat (at trailhead)
- ■ **Topographic Quadrangle** Tapoco NC-TN
- ■ **Features** Views of the Hangover, Haoe, and Bob Stratton Bald to the south and Fodderstack to the west

THE FIRST EDITION OF THIS BOOK stated that the Forest Service had no plans to maintain this trail, and that it would be deleted from future maps. Obviously, there was a change of plans. Windy Gap has been well maintained; it is a good and easily walked trail, and it has remained on the most recent version of the wilderness map. Not only is Windy Gap a good trail, but this upper-slope and ridgetop path also provides numerous through-the-branch views of the Hangover and Haoe to the south. The descending, lower-elevation end of the route affords views of Bob Stratton Bald to the south and the Fodderstack ridgeline to the west.

Windy Gap is the least traveled trail originating from the Big Fat Gap Trailhead and among the least walked in the Joyce Kilmer–Slickrock Wilderness. It could use some more feet and Big Fat could use fewer feet. Instead of walking Big Fat in and out of the wilderness, try Windy Gap for the first or final leg. The Windy Gap–Nichols Cove–Big Fat loop is a short (3.8 miles), relatively easy dayhike. For a longer (6.6 miles), more challenging dayhike or an easy backpacking trip, walk the Windy Gap–Nichols Cove–Yellowhammer Gap–Hangover Lead North loop. Don't let Windy Gap's brushy beginning deter you. Once away from the light gap of the trailhead, it quickly becomes a forest path.

The footpath's first segment follows the easy grades of a former road on the southwestern slopes of Cold Spring Knob. Before wilderness designation in 1975, the roadbed was part of FS 62, the road that now ends at Big Fat Gap. The roadbed explains the young forest. Most of this first section passes through a predominantly hardwood, third-growth forest which has regenerated since it was cut in the early 1970s. An aggressive pioneer species on moist sites, the yellow poplar is especially abundant in the disturbed area. Occasional thick and crooked chestnut oaks, logger's culls, stand out amongst the tall, straight, thin yellow poplars.

At 0.6 mile, just beyond a wooden guardrail blocking a cliff, the trail changes from roadbed to path, from slope to ridgecrest, and from third-growth to second-growth forest. The remainder of the route follows this Cold Spring Knob spur downhill to the west through a dry, oak-pine forest. Pitch pines are common on the ridgetop and the upper, south-facing slopes.

Windy Gap starts the first of a series of short, steep descents alternating with easier downgrades at 0.9 mile. Most of the trail's 560-foot elevation loss occurs in its last 0.7 mile. This descending section also alternates between exact ridgeline and upper slope, usually the southern slope to the left.

Windy Gap ties into Nichols Cove at an obvious connection near that trail's high point. To the left (southwest) it is 0.7 mile to the Nichols Cove–Big Fat junction; to the right (north) it is 0.9 mile to the Nichols Cove–Yellowhammer Gap junction.

Nature Notes

A dense, low understory of heath shrubs often flanks the trail along its ridgeline and southern slope sections. Bearberry or bear huckleberry (*Gaylussacia ursina*) and deerberry (*Vaccinium stamineum*) are abundant. *Gaylussacia* is the genus name for huckleberries and *Vaccinium* is the genus name for blueberries. For those who care and have a hand lens, huckleberries can be distinguished from blueberries by the yellow resin dots on the undersides of their leaves. Berry-colored bear scat is common on the trail in late summer.

Directions

Four footpaths enter the forest from the Big Fat Gap Trailhead parking area. Windy Gap, usually marked with a carsonite sign, begins through the opening in the wooden railing at the far back end of the parking area. (See the beginning of this section, page 56, for directions to the Big Fat Gap Trailhead.)

Notes

Nichols Cove Trail

Foot Trail 44: 3.1 miles

- **Dayhiking (low to high)** Moderate
- **Dayhiking (high to low)** Easy to Moderate
- **Backpacking** Moderate in either direction
- **Interior Trail** Northern (low elevation) terminus on Slickrock Creek Trail at Slickrock Creek, 1,440 feet; southern (high elevation) terminus on Slickrock Creek Trail at Slickrock Creek, 2,020 feet
- **Trail Junctions** Slickrock Creek (two), Big Fat, Windy Gap, Yellowhammer Gap
- **Topographic Quadrangle** Tapoco NC-TN
- **Features** Winter views of Unicoi Mountains to the west and of the Hangover and Haoe to the southeast; Nichols Cove Branch

T**HE AREA WHERE** Big Fat, Nichols Cove, and Slickrock Creek Trails converge has caused confusion for years. Hikers have often thought, especially when the sign is down, that Big Fat Trail ties into Slickrock Creek Trail. It doesn't; it ends at Nichols Cove Trail, which ties into Slickrock Creek Trail nearby (as the Forest Service map shows). There has also been confusion about whether or not the southern end of Nichols Cove crosses Slickrock Creek: it doesn't. From the Nichols Cove–Big Fat junction (usually signed), Nichols Cove Trail continues to the southwest (left if you have walked down Big Fat) for slightly less than 0.1 mile to its south-end junction (usually signed) with Slickrock Creek Trail on the east side of the creek. If you want to hike Slickrock Creek Trail upstream toward Naked Ground to the south, continue straight ahead at the junction, staying on the east side of the stream. If you want to walk the Slickrock

Creek Trail to the north and downstream, turn right onto Slickrock Creek Trail, pass through an old worn camp and cross the creek. A low-stemmed sign on the opposite bank usually marks the crossing.

The details in the previous paragraph were included to help hikers if the signs are down. When the signs are up, and they usually are, there is no problem. In the the late 1980s, the Big Fat–Nichols Cove–Slickrock Creek area was overrun by too many confused feet. Thanks to a good job by the Cheoah Ranger District, this heavily used area has healed—compared to the late 1980s—and many of the bushwhack paths are disappearing. Please take extra care to remain on one of the three designated trails in this popular floodplain area.

This trail is described as it is most often walked, from south to north, from high to low, one climb then all downhill or level. The description starts at the Big Fat–Nichols Cove junction, 0.1 mile north from the southern end of Nichols Cove Trail. From the Big Fat–Nichols Cove junction, turn right onto Nichols Cove Trail, cross Big Fat Branch, enter a large campsite, then continue on the path leaving the campsite diagonally back from the confluence of the two streams.

The route quickly climbs (the hardest pitch is moderate to strenuous) through a dry oak-pine forest, gaining 400 feet of elevation to 0.4 mile, where it crosses a spur top. On the way up there are winter views of the gap-mountain-gap-mountain sine-wave–shaped ridgecrest of the Unicoi Mountains to the west and the camel-hump peaks of Hangover and Haoe, both over 5,000 feet high, to the southeast. From the first spur, the treadway gradually rises along slopes and over more spurs to the Windy Gap Trail junction, an obvious intersection usually marked with a sign and a small cairn at 0.7 mile. Beyond this connection Nichols Cove Trail heads downhill on top of a narrow pitch-pine ridge. There are more winter views from this ridge—Hangover Lead to the east and the long ridgeline leading to Little Fodderstack Mountain to the northwest.

At 0.9 mile the footpath veers to the right and down off the ridge, plunging 0.2 mile to the head of Nichols cove. Near the bottom of the moist north-facing cove, the trail abruptly enters a tall, straight, second-growth forest with a predominantly hardwood canopy and frequent shady thickets of hemlock in the understory. Some of the yellow poplars and occasional white pines are already over 110 feet tall.

A short, moderate descent that roughly parallels the beginning of Nichols Cove Branch is the last grade worth mentioning. The rest of the route is easy down or level. Where the terrain is gently sloping, the trail, following an old sled road, enters an area of former habitation. (Because remote areas like Nichols cove were beyond the reach of roads, settlers often used horse- or mule-drawn sleds with sourwood runners to transport heavy loads in or out of the woods.) Rock piles and terraces indicate the edges of once-cleared land. At mile 1.6 you reach an obvious junction, usually marked with a sign and always marked with a small, circular, rock-lined burial plot just to the right. There are two headstones, simple and stark, that read:

> *Two sisters of John and Marget Dotson*
> *Born Dec 14, 1914*
> *Died Dec 20, 1914*
> *At rest*

Nichols cove is one of only two areas (the other is the Denton homestead on the southern edge of Joyce Kilmer Memorial Forest) within the boundaries of the Joyce Kilmer–Slickrock Wilderness that were settled, or semisettled, prior to logging and subsequent Forest Service acquisition. According to James Burchfield, formerly with the U.S. Forest Service, the Nichols family were not year-round residents. They ran cattle and grew crops in the cove in summer and left for good not long after logging began in 1915.

The two infants buried in Nichols cove were the daughters of John and Margaret Dotson. The Dotsons, their children, and their grandchildren were and still are well-known residents of the Vonore Community in Monroe County, Tennessee. John Dotson, who never traveled far from the mountains he loved, often herded cattle for people in the highcountry of today's wilderness. At the time of his death, he lived a short distance up a Little Tennessee River tributary, only 7 or 8 line-of-sight miles to the northwest from the mouth of Slickrock Creek.

The gravestone junction is the southwestern end of Yellowhammer Gap Trail. If you continue straight ahead on the sled road, you will be walking on that trail. Nichols Cove Trail bends sharply to the left onto path, follows the gentle slope toward Nichols Cove Branch, then crosses it beyond a prominent campsite. On the bank across the branch, the treadway turns to the right (north) onto a railroad bed and continues downstream. From this first crossing at mile 1.7 to the sixth and final crossing at mile 2.8, the walking follows the wide and easy grade of the former railroad as it parallels and crosses the stream. Just above the fourth rock-step crossing, the brook slides then pours down the middle of a mossy, bank-to-bank, 4-foot-high ledge. The forest along this section is second-growth hemlock and hardwood. Rhododendron and doghobble are abundant in the understory.

After the last crossing the remainder of the trail passes through a rock-wall railroad cut, angles away from the stream, then dips downslope to its end, where it ties into Slickrock Creek Trail above Slickrock Creek. Below the cut the branch begins its final run with a cascade—a sluicing, twisting, 15-foot drop.

eastern white pine

Nature Notes

Fairly common along several sections of this trail, the eastern white pine occurs in scattered pockets throughout the wilderness in a variety of habitats below 4,500 feet. Mature white pines are not plentiful in the wilderness at present, but the abundance of their understory saplings suggests that they will be within the next 75 to 100 years.

Everything about this conifer—its growth rate, its height, its needles, cones, branches, and bark—is distinctive. There is no mistaking a white pine in the Southern Blue Ridge. Its slender needles, soft bluish green and 3 to 5 inches long, spray out five to a bundle or sheath. It is the only five-needled pine in eastern North America. The narrow, banana-shaped cones are 4 to 8 inches long, tapering, and often slightly curved. The branches spoke from the trunk in definite whorls, one whorl per year, a useful aid in estimating age.

The fast-growing and long-lived white pine is the tallest tree east of the Rockies. It can be recognized from a distance by the graceful, upward sweeping tiers of branches that tower like pagodas above the hardwoods. In America's now-gone virgin forests, many of these giants once ranged from 180 to 220 feet in height. The generally accepted maximum size for this evergreen is 220 feet in height and 6 feet in diameter. On the present site of Dartmouth College in New Hampshire, a specimen 240 feet in height was measured; the current North Carolina state champion (an old-growth tree outside of the wilderness) is 13 feet 10 inches in circumference and 178 feet high. The largest of the second-growth white pines in this wilderness, only 80 or so years old, are already 2 to 3 feet in diameter and 100 to 130 feet in height. Barring the southward spread of an exotic fungal disease, they will grow much more.

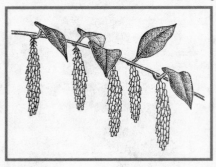

doghobble

A very old white pine has drawn water skyward for 450 to 500 years. No doubt some of the monarchs cut in the early logging days of New England were even older.

The low evergreen shrub abundant near Nichols Cove Branch is doghobble. A Southern Appalachian endemic, this common heath often forms dense thickets in moist, shaded acidic soils next to or near streams. The doghobble's pointed leaves occur alternately along its arching, slightly zigzag branches. New growth is usually a reddish color in the spring. In winter, the uppermost leaves turn reddish purple. Hanging clusters of small, white, urn-shaped flowers bloom beneath the branches from late April through mid-June.

The doghobble plant received its interesting name from mountain bear hunters. The heavy, powerful bears could force their way through the tangles—the dogs couldn't.

Directions

Nichols Cove, an interior trail, has both of its ends connected to the same trail—Slickrock Creek. Starting at the Slickrock Creek Trailhead near Tapoco, the two Nichols Cove junctions are at 4.4 miles (northern, lower elevation) and 8.1 miles (southern, upper elevation). Both junctions are usually signed. (See Slickrock Creek, page 36, in the Slickrock Creek Trailhead section for more information.)

Most people who walk Nichols Cove Trail, especially those who walk Nichols Cove as a quick connector to Slickrock Creek Trail, walk Big Fat Trail first. Big Fat, which provides the shortest-distance access to Nichols Cove, ties into Nichols Cove 0.1 mile from its southern junction with Slickrock Creek Trail. (See Big Fat, page 67, for more information.)

Notes

Wilderness is an anchor to windward. Knowing it is there, we can also know that we are still a rich nation, tending our resources as we should—not a people in despair searching every last nook and cranny of our land for a board of lumber, a barrel of oil, a blade of grass, or a tank of water.

U.S. Senator Clinton P. Anderson
American Forests *(July 1963)*

Joyce Kilmer Forest Trailheads

yellow poplars

Trails

Deep Creek

Haoe Lead

Jenkins Meadow

Joyce Kilmer National
  Recreation

Naked Ground

Stratton Bald

Wolf Laurel

Joyce Kilmer Forest Trailheads
Directions and Map

WITH THE EXCEPTION OF WOLF LAUREL, all of the trailheads in this section are near two important junctions: the four-way intersection at the entrance of FS 416 and the NC 143–FS 81–SR 1127 intersection at Santeetlah Gap.

If you travel from the north on US 129 South, you will reach the Joyce Kilmer approach road, FS 416, first. If you come from Tellico Plains or Robbinsville, you will arrive at the NC 143–FS 81–SR 1127 intersection at Santeetlah Gap first.

Directions from both intersections are provided for each trailhead. Use the directions at the beginning of the book on page 26 to travel to the appropriate intersection, then use the directions given after the trail description to reach the trailhead.

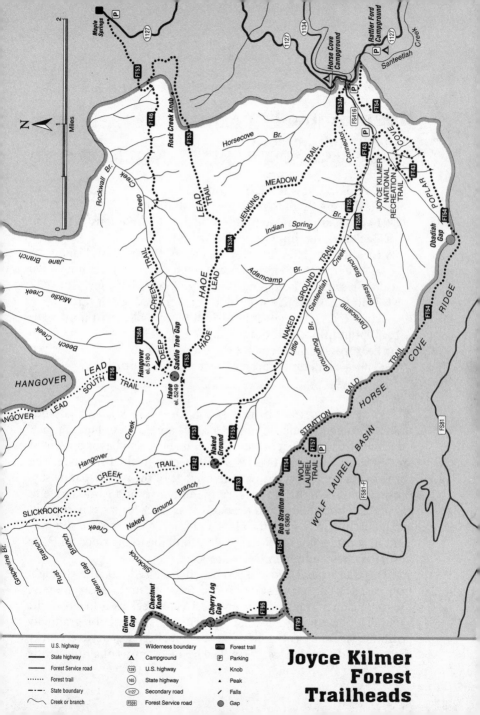

Joyce Kilmer
Forest
Trailheads

Legend:

- ═══ U.S. highway
- ── State highway
- ── Forest Service road
- ⋯⋯ Forest trail
- ─·─ State boundary
- ∿∿ Creek or branch
- ▬▬ Wilderness boundary
- △ Campground
- (129) U.S. highway
- (165) State highway
- (1127) Secondary road
- (FS59) Forest Service road
- (FT98) Forest trail
- (P) Parking
- ◆ Knob
- ▲ Peak
- ╱ Falls
- ● Gap

Deep Creek Trail

Foot Trail 46: 4.0 miles

- **Dayhiking (low to high)** Moderate
- **Dayhiking (high to low)** Easy to Moderate
- **Backpacking (low to high)** Moderate to Strenuous
- **Backpacking (high to low)** Moderate
- **Interior Trail** Eastern (low elevation) terminus on Haoe Lead Trail, 3,640 feet; western (high elevation) terminus on Hangover Lead South side trail (56A), 5,080 feet
- **Trail Junctions** Haoe Lead, Hangover Lead South side trail (56A), Hangover Lead South (see trail description)
- **Topographic Quadrangle** Tapoco NC-TN
- **Features** Winter views of the Hangover; old-growth trees; forest of beech and sugar maple

---

L IKE SEVERAL OTHERS IN THIS GUIDE, Deep Creek is a Jekyll-and-Hyde type of trail. Its first 2.1 miles are easily walked; in fact, they lose nearly 200 feet of elevation. But above and beyond where it crosses Deep Creek, the trail rises 1,600 feet in its final 1.9 miles. The path's overall difficulty rating is an average of the two disparate sections. From low to high, however, the upper section is moderate to strenuous for dayhikers and probably strenuous for most backpackers. If you intend to walk the Haoe Lead–Deep Creek loop, you may want to consider going the easier way, climbing to the ridge on Haoe Lead, then descending on Deep Creek.

This trail is described as it is most often walked, from low to high, from east to west. Starting on the northern slope of Rock Creek Knob, the route slowly angles down toward Deep Creek as it heads up its valley. The beginning 1.5-mile segment, mostly level or gradually downhill, is good, easily followed trail that alternates between rocky path and wide, graded treadway. The first few tenths of a mile gently descend a moist, bouldery slope with a rich understory of herbaceous plants and ferns. After the second large outcrop, the track winds in and out of small, rocky ravines and crosses a series of variable rivulets. In winter and early spring, you can see the ridge across the basin rising to the Hangover's heath bald and rock face.

The north-slope forest is predominantly second-growth, dominated by cove hardwoods. Hemlocks, as usual, are common in the moist ravines and along watercourses. Kitchen Lumber Company logged much of the Deep Creek watershed in the early 1920s. The area traversed by the first half of the trail was, judging by the small number of large or old trees, clear-cut to the quick.

At mile 1.6 the route dips to and crosses a wide, mossy-rocked side branch, permanent but very shallow and unnamed. During April the open, sunny slope above the stream is bright green with the foliage of wildflowers growing by the thousands. Once across the brook, the trail ties into an old roadbed that roughly parallels the branch downstream. Following 0.1 mile on that road, the treadway angles to the left and above it, climbing 0.2 mile by footpath to another old road, which leads to the bridge over cascading Deep Creek at mile 2.1.

After crossing the bridge at approximately 3,440 feet, the course turns left onto the rocky roadbed that closely parallels Deep Creek upstream. The forest along the creek, predominantly yellow poplar and two species of birch, was logged again in the 1950s.

The track rises beside the stream, which pours and pools from one mossy boulder to the next, for 0.3 mile before turning up and away from the creek onto another old roadbed to the right. The road system was still in use until the area was added to the wilderness in 1984. The turns from one former road to another will quickly become more obvious as the wrong-way roads become blocked with deadfalls and return to forest.

Beyond this turn the walking, a steady easy or easy-to-moderate ascent through small hardwoods and hemlock, continues on the wide grade of the roadbed, which switchbacks to the west and swings parallel to Hudson Deaden Branch, barely visible in the ravine below. There is another possibly confusing road-to-road turn at mile 2.9. Here the route veers uphill and to the right onto a narrow side road.

If you miss this turn, you will come to a fork of Hudson Deaden Branch 60 yards beyond where you should have turned.

One-tenth mile past the turn, the trail crosses the rhododendron-edged fork and enters its rich, open cove. It then bends away from the stream and curls sharply up and to the left onto slope before crossing the ridgecrest of a spur. On the other side of the spur, the footpath comes to the end of the old clear-cut. Here the trees—old-growth hemlock, Carolina silverbell, and red maple—are bigger, and the scenery is better (grassy and ferny glades beneath the big trees).

Continuing its zigzag course to the west, the treadway climbs (from mile 3.0 to mile 3.7 it alternates short strenuous pulls with lesser upgrades) near the top of the spur, then slants onto a slope where it crosses seepage springs that feed a last-water rivulet to the left. Shortly after switching to old road, the track turns almost 90 degrees to the right onto path just beyond a rock outcrop to the right.

Deep Creek's uppermost 0.3 mile switchbacks through a forest of beech and sugar maple to its junction with Hangover Lead South's side trail (56A) to the Hangover in Saddle Tree Gap. To the right (north) it is 0.2 mile straight ahead to the look-off at the Hangover. To the left it is slightly more than 0.2 mile straight ahead on the side trail and Hangover Lead South to the tiny clearing on the crown of the Haoe. If you are walking the Deep Creek–Haoe Lead loop, and your first leg was Deep Creek, you will turn left (east) onto Haoe Lead Trail at the clearing.

Nature Notes

Early one morning in mid-May, I came upon a ruffed grouse and her nine or ten chicks smack in the middle of Deep Creek Trail. The instant she saw me, the female grouse shrieked the code-red alarm, then shot directly over my head. Over the years, I had seen this drill four or five times before. And each time the female had distracted me from a good look at her chicks. This time I was ready; I ignored the female and watched the yellow and brown chicks as they broke from their huddle and scattered in different directions. But by concentrating on them as a group, looking at one then another, I immediately lost sight of them all. They simply ran off the edge of my focus and vanished into the forest floor.

After losing the chicks I turned toward the female grouse. She had dropped down behind me and started her crippled-bird theatrics. I took a few steps toward her. She made a series of luring, zigzag rushes, wings dragging, body hunched strangely low to the ground. Her high-pitched whines were a horror-show mix of fear and pain. She was, psychologically at least, a frightened, injured bird.

After watching her antics, I decided to leave them alone and head up the trail. But when I reached the spot where the young had been and stopped for one last look, the big bird flew after me, stopped 7 or 8 feet away—and changed from meek to murderous. She screeched and hissed through her gaping beak. She flared her beautifully patterned, reddish brown tail to full fan, raised her neck feathers into an impressive black ruff. Her eyes, filled with fear only seconds before, were now flashing with rage.

I stood my ground, and the grouse stood hers, pacing back and forth, displaying, hissing—loud like a rattlesnake from hell. I took a step toward her. She fled. And turned back into a crippled bird.

Of the wildlife I observed while hiking in this wilderness, ruffed grouse and red squirrel were by far the most numerous trailside creatures larger than songbirds. The ruffed grouse was also the most common animal on the dirt roads approaching trailheads. They come out on the roads to get grit for their gizzards.

Often mistakenly called partridge or pheasant, the ruffed grouse is the large reddish brown bird that flushes from the edge of the trail with a startling whir. Its 15- to 19-inch length, chickenlike appearance, and a broad black band near the tip of its tail make it unmistakable. Grouse, like northern bobwhite and wild turkey, are ground-nesting gallinaceous birds.

Instead of singing like most birds, male ruffed grouse court females with prancing display patterns and "drumming." During late winter and early spring, usually starting on the first warm days of March, males stand on strategically located logs and beat the air with their cupped wings, creating drumming sounds that can be detected a quarter of a mile or more away. This drumming is most often described as a low, muffled thumping that begins slowly, deliberately and measured, then quickly accelerates into a rapid whir. Bird guides write the sound as *bup...bup...bup...bup... bup.bup.up.r-rrrr.*

Some people say the sound flows over them in waves, that they almost feel it rather than hear it. Others, having just climbed a steep grade, say they think the beginning *bups* are their own heartbeats. Still others claim the drumming is no more than a pulsing sensation, subconscious at first, in their heads. These people tell me they have to become fully aware of the pulsing before they stop walking, listen, and recognize the noise.

The great horned owl, which preys upon grouse, rarely takes a male off its courtship log. The drumming is at such a low frequency, forty cycles a second, that even the keen-eared owl can't hear it. (Guess what happened to the grouse who wooed with higher frequency wing beats?)

Directions

Deep Creek is an interior trail that has its eastern (low elevation) end on Haoe Lead Trail and its western (high elevation) end on Hangover Lead South's side trail (56A) to the Hangover. To reach Deep Creek's eastern end, walk 1.1 miles on Haoe Lead from its beginning near Maple Springs Observation Point. Deep Creek is the right fork at the junction, which is usually signed. (See Haoe Lead, the following trail, for more information.)

To reach Deep Creek's western end, walk Hangover Lead South Trail from its beginning at Big Fat Gap. After walking 2.8 miles, you will come to a three-way intersection atop the main ridge running from the Hangover to the Haoe. Turn left (north) at the junction onto the Hangover Lead South side trail (56A) to the views atop the Hangover. After less than 0.1 mile, you will see the Deep Creek junction, usually signed, to the right opposite a rock outcrop. (See Hangover Lead South, page 62, in the Big Fat Gap Trailhead section, for more information.)

Haoe Lead and Deep Creek Trails, combined with a short segment of Hangover Lead South and the Hangover Lead South side trail near the middle, can be walked as a loop. If you walk Haoe Lead as the first leg of this loop, you will reach a junction on the exact crest of Haoe Mountain after 5.1 miles. To complete the loop, turn right (north) onto Hangover Lead South, walk 0.2 mile straight ahead on Hangover Lead South and the Hangover Lead South side trail (56A), then turn right (northeast) onto Deep Creek Trail.

Notes

Haoe Lead Trail

Foot Trail 53: 6.7 miles

- ■ **Dayhiking In** Moderate
- ■ **Dayhiking Out** Easy to Moderate
- ■ **Backpacking In** Moderate to Strenuous
- ■ **Backpacking Out** Moderate
- ■ **Start** Haoe Lead Trailhead near Maple Springs
  Observation Point, 3,400 feet
- ■ **End** Stratton Bald Trail, 5,280 feet
- ■ **Trail Junctions** Deep Creek, Jenkins Meadow,
  Hangover Lead South, Naked Ground, Slickrock Creek,
  Stratton Bald
- ■ **Topographic Quadrangle** Tapoco NC-TN
- ■ **Features** Winter views and overlook; summer views
  of Slickrock Creek basin and Hangover Lead;
  rock outcrops; good spring wildflower display

THE WORD HAOE (pronounced hay-oh), by all accounts of local legend, is simply an expression of beauty and exhilaration. Everyone I have asked has told me the same story. They all say the name came from Bob Stratton—early settler, hunter, herder, mountain man. When Bob first walked the high ridgeline from what is now Bob Stratton Bald over the Haoe to the Hangover, he was so impressed with the splendor of the landscape that he repeatedly hollered "hey-oh," or something like that. Anthropologists consider this explanation to be a folk etymology, meaning the tale may be absolutely true, or it may simply be a whimsical way to explain the unknown.

Haoe Lead's beginning 3.9 miles, up to its Jenkins Meadow junction, is much newer than the remainder of the trail, which is part of the original Joyce Kilmer Memorial Forest system built with CCC labor in the late 1930s and early 1940s. The more recent segment was constructed in the late 1970s, after the paved road was stopped at what is now Maple Springs Observation Point. The Forest Service trail builders did an excellent job of selecting a scenic and easily walked route. An upper-slope and ridgetop trail that winds east to west, Haoe Lead affords steady winter views through the stick-figure hardwoods.

Haoe Lead is the least strenuous of the long trails that rise to the divide separating the Slickrock Creek and Little Santeetlah drainages. It is easier than the others because it begins at a much higher elevation and ascends gradually for most of the distance to the top of the Haoe. This trail gains only 1,040 feet in its first 3.9 miles to its junction with Jenkins Meadow. By comparison, Jenkins Meadow climbs 2,320 feet in 3.3 miles to the same junction.

The first 0.5 mile of this footpath, wide and graded, angles steadily up a south slope to the ridge of a Rock Creek Knob spur. After continuing on the crest for a short distance, the treadway slants onto the knob's northern slope where the spur rises steeply straight ahead. The next 0.4 mile is easy walking through rugged, scenic terrain, moist and botanically rich. Boulder fields flow down across the route; rock outcrops are common on the upslope. Here the predominantly deciduous, second-growth forest is tall, straight, and diverse.

Following a double-switchback upgrade from a room-sized boulder, the path reaches its first junction, Deep Creek Trail, at mile 1.1. Haoe Lead, doubling back on itself, switchbacks sharply up and to the left at the usually signed junction. It then ascends to and crosses over the same Rock Creek Knob spur before swinging onto the mountain's eastern flank. At mile 1.5 the track comes to a rock outcrop overlook open to the east. Straight out and down are Santeetlah Lake and the settled coves above its far shore. Straight out, the overlapping rows of ridges and peaks become indistinct in the blue distance. (Unfortunately, the blue distance is becoming browner every decade.) The high, wild mountains to the left edge of the view, somewhat blocked by summer leaves, are the Smokies.

Completing the three-quarter loop around Rock Creek Knob, the treadway skirts its south slope, passes below its rocky high point, then rises to the ridge close to the mountain's crown. This ridge is named Haoe Lead. For the next 1.3 miles, from mile 1.9 to mile 3.2, the trail remains on or near the narrow spine of Haoe Lead. This segment undulates with the terrain of the ridge, dipping to the next shallow gap, then ascending to the next low knob.

The sharpness of the ridgecrest is accentuated by the thin layers of rock that break through its backbone. These layers come to a point perpendicular to the ground. From the side they look like long, rounded fins, or the ridged armament of a dinosaur's back. The outcrops are much more evident when the foliage has fallen. Growing between the rock is a forest of small hemlocks and hardwoods dominated by the oaks. Some of the squatty, low-branched oaks and yellow birch are obviously old-growth.

Continuing westward toward the top of the Haoe, the footpath traverses the upper south slope of the lead and soon enters the northern edge of the Joyce Kilmer Memorial Forest. The rest of the trail remains on the forest's perimeter. Here the walking, often downslope from more outcrops, is level or easy up to the junction (approximately 4,440 feet) with Jenkins Meadow at mile 3.9. Beyond this junction, Haoe Lead Trail makes a short, steady upgrade to a wider, level (side to side) section of the ridgeline. This area, where young trees are now abundant, was Jenkins Meadow.

The ascent to Haoe's high point begins in earnest at mile 4.5. This segment rises moderately up to and over a knob, dips to a shallow gap, then climbs progressively harder (from easy to 0.2 mile of moderate to strenuous at the end) to the mountaintop. The final upridge run is on narrow crest, occasionally all rock and Catawba rhododendron. One-tenth mile below Haoe's crown, you come to a usually signed junction. The path that angles slightly up and to the left is the Naked Ground cutoff—a maintained cheater's trail, slightly less than 0.2 mile long, that bypasses the last pull to the Haoe for hikers heading southwest toward Naked Ground. This needless cheater ties back into Haoe Lead Trail 0.1 mile west of the mountaintop.

Haoe Lead reaches its junction with Hangover Lead South Trail in the tiny grassy clearing (not good camping) on the exact cap of the Haoe (5,249 feet) at mile 5.1. Hangover Lead South ends in the opening. To the right (north) from this junction, it is slightly more than 0.4 mile straight ahead on Hangover Lead South and the Hangover Lead South side trail (56A) to the Hangover's views. If you are hiking the Haoe Lead–Deep Creek loop, look for the right (east) turn onto Deep Creek approximately 100 yards before you enter Hangover's heath bald.

Old accounts often referred to the Haoe, the second highest mountain in the combined wilderness, as Haoe Bald. The Haoe was never a true bald. A firetower and free-ranging cattle, which grazed the high, grassy ridges until the late 1960s, kept the crown open. The firetower was flown out by helicopter shortly after the area became wilderness in 1975. As you can see, saplings have recaptured most of the lost ground. There are no views from the top of the Haoe.

Through climbing for awhile, Haoe Lead Trail turns 90 degrees to the left from its junction with Hangover Lead South and descends the highest ridgeline in the wilderness—informally known as the wall—to the west. The upper part of this descent is much sharper than the lower. Here the route hurries down four or five short pitches on rock, through rhododendron at first, as it works its way off the Haoe's roof. Beyond this steep stretch, the treadway rises gently over slight knobs between the long, gradual downgrades. There are occasional summer views of the upper Slickrock Creek basin and its eastern rim, Hangover Lead, to the north.

The path undulates easily to Naked Ground at mile 6.1. After seeing its name on topo sheets and wilderness maps, people tend to think that Naked Ground is something other than what it is today. They are frequently disappointed. I have heard more than one hiker say, "What's so special about Naked Ground?" Indeed, there is nothing special about Naked Ground as a destination, other than convenient, level camping and water. But there is something important about its location. Naked Ground is a gap: it is the lowest point (4,860 feet) on its ridge coming from all four cardinal directions. East to west, it is the deepest gap along the crest between the two highest mountains in the wilderness, the Haoe and Bob Stratton Bald. North to south, Naked Ground is the lowest land on the divide that separates the watersheds of Little Santeetlah and Slickrock Creeks.

Because of its location, this gap is the most important high-elevation junction in the wilderness. Slickrock Creek (north) and Naked Ground (south) Trails end at the wooded gap, forming a four-way intersection with Haoe Lead. Today's hikers, especially those walking up either of the creeks, use Naked Ground in the same way the Cherokee and early settlers did—as a level loafing or camping spot after a hard climb.

Like Jenkins Meadow and the Haoe, Naked Ground was once more open than it is at present. But the ground is still naked in places, from overused fire rings and campsites. The gap has a year-round view from its south side.

Haoe Lead's final 0.6 mile ascends steadily (easy to moderate) through a deciduous forest dominated by beech and yellow birch. The track frequently runs beside a broken line of large outcrops. The very end of the trail curves sharply upward on rock to the exact ridgecrest. Here, at 5,280 feet, Haoe Lead stops at its usually signed junction with Stratton Bald Trail. Stratton Bald Trail rises from the southeast, hits the high ridge at its junction with Haoe Lead, then turns 90 degrees to the left (west) and continues on the ridge straight ahead from Haoe Lead's end. The bald area on Bob Stratton Bald lies 0.8 mile to the west from the junction.

From the Haoe to its western end, Haoe Lead Trail follows the highest and most beautiful ridge in the wilderness. The nearly continuous rock outcrops, though larger, are not as sharp and finlike as those on Haoe Lead (the ridge). Some are room-sized and blocky; others resemble long, gray whale backs. There are wintertime views seven months of the year and occasional clear vistas during the short summer. The trailside is often open and grassy. Short sections of the path are briery, but the Forest Service and hikers keep them whacked back enough to push through.

The variable springs beside the first few miles of this trail are usually no more than wet rock by June of a drought year. Beyond these, there are no more springs all the way to the top of the Haoe. (See Hangover Lead South, page 62, in the Big Fat Gap Trailhead section, for water sources along that trail north of the Haoe.) If you continue on the Haoe Lead Trail from the high point of the Haoe toward Bob Stratton Bald, you will find a fairly reliable spring to the right (north) of the gap at Naked Ground. Walk 70 paces or so down the upper end of Slickrock Creek Trail, then angle left onto the prominent side path that leads to the source spring of Naked

Ground Branch. If there isn't any water flowing, or dripping, out of the grooved wood spigot, head down the bed until you find some.

Most of Haoe Lead's first 2.0 miles are outside of the wilderness. Its ridgeline route, however, probably ensures the corridor with de facto protection.

Nature Notes

This trail has a good spring wildflower display. The herbaceous plants begin blooming in early April at the lower elevations, and continue through most of May on the lofty ridge. During the last half of May the rich carmine color of Vasey's trillium is conspicuous along the higher reaches of the lead. The shrubs—flame azalea, mountain laurel, Catawba rhododendron—blossom from mid-May through early June.

Galax, one of the most abundant wildflowers in the wilderness, is common beside the beginning south-slope sections of this trail. Chiefly a Southern Appalachian species, the galax is often one of the first evergreen plants mountain hikers learn. The

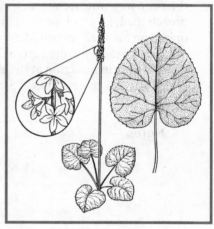

galax

leathery, shiny green leaves (coppery-bronze in winter), round with heart-shaped bases, are easily recognized. And so are the single flowering stems, wands of tiny white blossoms up to 2 feet high, that appear at this elevation in early June.

You can often detect galax colonies by their scent—a peculiar, sweet, skunky fragrance—even before you can see them.

Directions

From the four-way intersection at the entrance of the Joyce Kilmer approach road, FS 416, travel north on SR 1127, also known as Wagon Train Road (a right turn if you have just come through

Horse Cove Campground, entrance marked with a Maple Springs Observation Point sign), approximately 4.5 miles to the parking area and trailhead bulletin board to the right. The trail starts at the end of the guardrail, across the road from the bulletin board. Maple Springs Observation Point, at the end of Wagon Train Road only slightly more than 0.1 mile beyond the trailhead, affords good views of the Great Smoky Mountains National Park to the northeast.

From the NC 143–FS 81–SR 1127 junction at Santeetlah Gap, travel SR 1127 downhill to the northwest approximately 2.2 miles to the four-way intersection at the entrance of the Joyce Kilmer approach road, FS 416. From this intersection, continue straight ahead, uphill, on SR 1127 toward Maple Springs Observation Point.

(See page 26 for the various routes, mileages, and directions to the four-way intersection at the entrance of FS 416 and the NC 143–FS 81–SR 1127 intersection at Santeetlah Gap.)

Notes

Jenkins Meadow Trail

Foot Trail 53A: 3.3 miles

- ■ **Dayhiking In** Moderate to Strenuous
- ■ **Dayhiking Out** Easy to Moderate
- ■ **Backpacking In** Strenuous
- ■ **Backpacking Out** Moderate
- ■ **Start** Jenkins Meadow Trailhead, 2,120 feet
- ■ **End** Haoe Lead Trail, 4,440 feet
- ■ **Trail Junctions** Naked Ground Connector (see trail description), Haoe Lead
- ■ **Topographic Quadrangles** Santeetlah Creek NC, Tapoco NC-TN
- ■ **Features** Boulders and rock outcrops; winter views; old-growth oaks

J ENKINS MEADOW HAS A CONVOLUTED EVOLUTION. Its uppermost 2.0 miles once belonged to the old Haoe Trail, part of the original Joyce Kilmer Memorial Forest system. Shortly after Joyce Kilmer–Slickrock became wilderness in 1975, the Forest Service moved the Naked Ground and Haoe Trailheads away from the Joyce Kilmer parking area. Naked Ground was rerouted out to the entrance of FS 416, the Joyce Kilmer approach road. The Haoe Trailhead was moved over 4 miles away to its present location near Maple Springs Observation Point. From there a new trail, Haoe Lead, was constructed to the west until it tied in with the original Haoe (where Jenkins Meadow joins Haoe Lead today).

All this trail building left the old Haoe as a connector between the new Haoe Lead and Naked Ground treadways. After some further rerouting, that segment connecting the two trails was officially renamed Jenkins Meadow. At that time, before the 1984 wilderness addition, Jenkins Meadow Trail ran along the wilderness boundary, which was then the same boundary as for Joyce Kilmer Memorial Forest. To make an already long story slightly longer, the Forest Service relocated the beginning of Naked Ground back into the memorial forest in 1989 and gave its bulletin board trailhead and former first 0.9 mile to Jenkins Meadow.

Jenkins Meadow is a scenic, easily followed trail. Its first 1.3 miles, the segment built in the 1970s, is wide and graded into the slope. Starting at the wooden railing and steps, the footpath quickly settles into a winding, switchbacking, easy-to-moderate ascent to 0.4 mile, where it curls onto the crest of a Haoe Lead spur. The second-growth forest is oak-pine, numerically dominated by red maple and three species of oak. Tall white pine tower close beside the walkway.

After remaining on the ridgeline for a short distance, the route angles onto south slope and soon passes the first of the boulders and rock outcrops. At 0.9 mile the trail reaches its only junction between its beginning and end. To the left, across the step-over rivulet, the Naked Ground connector leads 0.9 mile to the Naked Ground Trail.

From the junction, Jenkins Meadow quickly curves onto the Haoe Lead spur again, follows it for a short distance again, then slants onto its southern flank where the ridge rises fast. Alternating easy with easy-to-moderate upgrades though a predominantly hardwood forest, the treadway reaches a small bare spot on the backbone of a secondary spur 0.4 mile beyond the connector. The path turns right (north) at the bare spot and rises moderately up the pitch-pine spur before winding around the high point of a knob. The route regains the top of the Haoe Lead spur in a shallow gap at mile 1.7. Here there are winter views of ridges and valleys to either side. To the left (southwest) across the Little Santeetlah Creek basin, Horse Cove Ridge roller-coasters higher and higher toward Bob Stratton Bald. To the right Horse Cove is wedged between Haoe Lead and its spur.

For the next 0.7 mile the grade remains on or near the keel of the narrow ridgeline. After the short, steep ascent from the gap, the walking is easy then progressively harder, scaling the difficulty range from moderate to strenuous. The never-cut hardwood forest is typical of Jenkins Meadow once the trail gains the perimeter of the Joyce Kilmer Memorial Forest.

At mile 2.4 the footpath slants onto the left (southwest) side of the crest and stays there. The remainder of the trail, which makes a diagonal cut up the slope, angles steadily away from the spur. Here the hiking, through open virgin stands of oak on the periphery of the memorial forest, alternates tough pulls with easier upgrades. The final 50 yards climb strenuously to the Haoe Lead junction. To the left (west) it is 1.2 miles to Haoe's crown.

During the times I hiked Jenkins Meadow and Haoe Lead Trails, I met two groups of backpackers who asked the same question: "Do you know where Jenkins Meadow is?" Both groups had hiked its namesake trail so they could camp in the clearing, lounge in lush grass, delight in distant vistas, revel in Orion overhead. And throw the frisbee. But they were having considerable trouble finding the elusive meadow, even though it is marked on wilderness maps and topo sheets. The confused backpackers wondered aloud how they could have missed a large clearing on Haoe Lead's ridge. And they wondered if they had misread the map or if things had changed somehow. Well, they were partially right. They were not lost but things sure had changed: the meadow was gone, grown over. One group was standing in it—in the shade.

Prior to Forest Service acquisition in 1935, the meadow was a man-made (tree girdling and fire) summer pasture for cattle. The 1940 Tapoco topo sheet, the earliest map of its kind for this area, labeled the cleared patches of land "Jenkins Meadow." The name has been retained on every map since. The meadow probably remained partially open until the late 1960s, when free-ranging cattle were no longer allowed on the Nantahala National Forest. Since then, the land has done what it wants. And this land wants to grow trees.

Two regularly used routes lead to the Haoe from the Joyce Kilmer area: the Haoe Lead Trail and the Jenkins Meadow–Haoe Lead combination. There is a substantial elevation difference between the two. Haoe Lead rises a relatively mild 1,040 feet within the 3.9 miles to its Jenkins Meadow junction. By comparison, Jenkins Meadow climbs 2,320 feet in 3.3 miles to the same junction.

The rivulet to the left at 0.9 mile is the only reliable water source along this entire trail. The oozing spring up high near Haoe Lead is variable, which means it may run dry during drought. There is no water beside the Haoe Lead Trail from its junction with Jenkins Meadow to the high point of the Haoe.

Nature Notes

Beyond its first 1.3 miles, Jenkins Meadow remains on or just inside of the ridgetop boundary of the Joyce Kilmer Memorial Forest. Although most of this ridge and south-slope trail passes through what is considered an oak-pine forest, the pines—white and pitch—are minor components. The largely deciduous forest is thoroughly controlled in number and size by the oaks—white, black, northern red, scarlet, and chestnut.

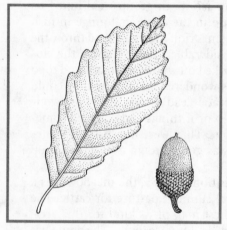

chestnut oak

Joyce Kilmer is a fine virgin forest. But that does not mean there is a uniform sea of giant trees everywhere you look. Dry, rocky ridges, windy and thin soiled, are harsh environments that do not support big boles in great numbers. While there are occasional thick-trunked trees, primarily chestnut oaks, on the ridge, the forest does not fulfill high expectations until the trail slants onto moister slope. Most of the final mile leads through an open stand of black, chestnut, and northern red oak, many in the 9- to 13-foot circumference range. In winter you can see their massive crowns well away from the trail.

The chestnut oak—mainly a mountain tree of the Appalachians—is one of the most common ridge and dry-slope broadleafs in the wilderness below 4,200 feet. This oak received its name because its leaves resemble those of the American chestnut. No longer able to survive in most of its range larger than sapling size because of the chestnut blight, the chestnut has noticeably pointed teeth on the margins of its leaves. The leaves of the chestnut oak—4 to 9 inches long—have margins with noticeably rounded, wavy lobes, no points and no bristles. No other large, common Southern Appalachian hardwood has this leaf.

The mature chestnut oak has a distinctive, deeply furrowed, dark gray or brownish gray bark. Horizontal notches break the deep vertical furrows into ridged, rectangular blocks of various lengths. The bark is a source of tannin, once used to tan hides.

This oak, often the thickest tree on low- and middle-elevation ridges, averages 60 to 85 feet in height and 2 to 4 feet in diameter. Its maximum size—130 feet in height and 7 feet in diameter—represents the record, or near record, for both dimensions. Like many other trees in eastern North America, the chestnut oak attains its largest dimensions in the South, in the highlands of Tennessee and North Carolina. Slow-growing even on good sites, this member of the white oak group is also long-lived—up to half of a millenium.

As usual, the oak-pine forest is too shady, too dry, and too acidic for the ephemeral wildflowers of early spring. But as always in this type of habitat, the next layer up, the shrub layer, more than makes up for this lack. Flame azalea and mountain laurel are abundant in the understory along Jenkins Meadow. The azalea ordinarily reaches its peak on some section of this trail during the first half of May.

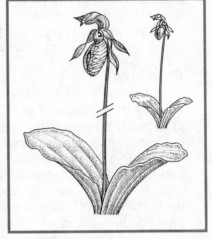

pink lady's-slipper

Jenkins Meadow bisects a scattered colony of pink lady's-slipper that blooms at approximately the same time as the azalea. This orchid, also known as pink moccasin flower, was partridge moccasin to the Cherokee. But no matter what it's called, there is no mistaking this wildflower: the pink lady's-slipper is remarkable even for an orchid. The two oval-shaped, ribbed leaves are large and flaring. The leafless flowering stalk normally rises well above the basal leaves and bears a solitary blossom. The lower petal, or lip, of this flower forms an inflated, deeply cleft, pink pouch that hangs below the hood of the other petals. This pouch, the slipper, is 1$^1/_2$ to 2$^1/_2$ inches long, rough textured and red veined. Georgia O'Keeffe would have enjoyed painting this wildflower.

Pink lady's-slippers occur occasionally on public land throughout the mountains of the South. They often grow, however, in easily exploitable colonies, the kind that are tempting to economic botanists: flower poachers. To pick or dig up even one of these plants is an illegal and contemptible act. It is also a waste of time. These wildflowers have a symbiotic relationship with mycorrhizal fungi in the soil. If you dig them up and take them home, they will die—simple as that. Fungi-independent varieties are commercially available.

Directions

From the NC 143–FS 81–SR 1127 junction at Santeetlah Gap, travel SR 1127 (Wagon Train Road) downhill to the northwest approximately 2.2 miles to the four-way intersection at the entrance of the Joyce KiImer approach road, FS 416. Immediately after turning left onto FS 416, you will notice the trailhead bulletin board, signed Little Santeetlah, to the left of the road. Jenkins Meadow starts at the conspicuous gap—wooden steps and railing—across the road from the bulletin board. There is overflow parking to the right straight across the four-way intersection from the Jenkins Meadow Trailhead.

If you are traveling from the north, heading south on US 129 and taking the dirt-road shortcut (see page 30), you will reach the four-way intersection after passing through Horse Cove Campground. The Joyce Kilmer approach road, FS 416, is straight ahead through the intersection.

(See page 26 for the various routes, mileages, and directions to the four-way intersection at the entrance of FS 416 and the NC 143–FS 81–SR 1127 intersection at Santeetlah Gap.)

Notes

Joyce Kilmer National Recreation

Foot Trail 43: lower loop, 1.2 miles; upper loop, 0.8 mile

- **Dayhiking** Easy
- **Backpacking** Prohibited
- **Loop Trail** Two interconnected loops; lower loop begins and ends at Joyce Kilmer parking and picnicking area, 2,240 feet
- **Trail Junction** Naked Ground
- **Topographic Quadrangle** Santeetlah Creek NC
- **Features** Virgin forest with mammoth yellow poplars; Little Santeetlah Creek; exceptional spring wildflower display

THE JOYCE KILMER NATIONAL RECREATION TRAIL is synonymous with living towers of trees—spiring hemlock and gray columns of yellow poplar rising straight as plumb lines. The upper loop leads through Poplar Cove—where there are more trees over 130 feet high and 15 feet around than along any other 0.8-mile trail, or section of trail, in eastern North America. People come to this cove, as on a pilgrimage, year after year. One man I met called the upper loop the miracle mile.

These trees survive as living monuments to the once great eastern forest that is gone. Poplar Cove is one of the few places that prove pioneer journals were not fairy tales, that can still show us something of what our land once was. Here is a place where the forest has a special dignity and spirit—where people are usually reverent, awed, and some even humbled a bit.

This trail is composed of two interconnected loops; the lower loop is 1.2 miles long, the upper, 0.8 mile. These loops are described as they are most often walked—clockwise from the information shelter to the second plaque, where the loops connect, counterclockwise around the upper loop, then back to the shelter on the remainder of the lower loop.

The wide walkway immediately passes the first commemorative plaque, enters the wilderness, and crosses the bridge over the memorial forest's main stream—Little Santeetlah Creek—flowing clear and cold from an undisturbed watershed. The trail gradually rises away from the creek through a never-cut forest of hemlock and hardwoods. (Storms, including a hurricane and a blizzard, took a heavy toll on the hemlocks in the early and mid-1990s.) But as big as these trees are, they are mere striplings compared to the behemoths ahead. A short distance before the second plaque, the first of the large yellow poplars, a modest mammoth over 16 feet around, stands to the right of the path.

At 0.5 mile the lower loop reaches the second plaque and the North Carolina state record hemlock, listed as 15 feet 1 inch in circumference and 169 feet in height when it was nominated in 1981. This old eastern hemlock is seemingly healthy and is still slowly growing; by the fall of 1997 it measured 14 feet 4 inches around from its high side and 17 feet 3 inches in circumference from its low side, measured at 4^1/$_2$ feet from the ground. Hemlocks are slow-growing, long-living trees. This magnificent conifer is estimated to be 400 to 450 years old.

Poplar Cove Loop, the upper loop, begins and ends along the wooden railing around the hemlock. Here the walking continues through an incredible forest of beech, basswood, yellow birch, Carolina silverbell, sugar maple, northern red oak, cucumbertree, and, of course, yellow poplar and hemlock. As its name implies, the cove is famous for its hundreds of large yellow poplars, each a thick gray pillar rising with little taper. Most of these giants have girths ranging from 14 to 18 feet and heights from 110 to 150 feet. Several trees appear to be over 160 feet tall.

Most of the larger yellow poplars have been storm-topped. After this happens the lateral branches sweep upward, reaching for the sun. In winter, when you can see their silhouettes a long way off, the cove looks like a collection of enormous candelabras.

After slightly more than 0.2 mile (walked counterclockwise), you will come to an immense yellow poplar, the former circumference champ, now runner-up at 20 feet 4 inches. The rules for tree measuring state that you must tape a tree's circumference 4^1/$_2$ feet above the ground. If a tree has a low and high side, as this one does, you must measure from the high side. A few tenths of a mile farther, to the left of the trail like the first giant, stands the former runner-up, now the champ, with a girth of 20 feet 7 inches. This yellow poplar is perhaps 140 to 150 feet tall and 325 to 375 years old.

Poplar Cove is a moist, rich, north-facing slope; in places, especially near the rivulets, the forest floor is green with moss and fern even in winter. The upper loop gradually ascends to its high point, approximately 2,640 feet, before descending back to its beginning. On the way down the trail passes the frequently photographed twin yellow poplars.

From the plaque the lower loop winds gently downhill to the Little Santeetlah, which it crosses on a single split-log bridge with rails. Just beyond the bridge, the Naked Ground Trail begins to the left. (See Naked Ground, the next trail, for more information concerning additional hiking options in the general vicinity of the Joyce Kilmer Picnic Area.) The rest of the wide treadway, with occasional glimpses of the creek, quickly works its way back down to the shelter.

Please, except at the few biggest trees, stay on the main trail even when it's muddy. This is a place of beauty and joy. Children cannot be expected to walk like reverential zombies. However, all parents should teach their children to stay on the main trail so they will not unwittingly tromp wildflowers all the way across a shortcut.

Nature Notes

Because the yellow poplar is an extremely successful pioneer on suitable, disturbed sites, it is very likely that this grove of poplars started after fire, disease, or storm opened the canopy of the cove. Although it is intolerant of shade, the yellow poplar often persists in climax stands. But as you will notice, this tree is not regenerating itself in the cove. When more of the giants fall, the canopy may be opened enough for reproduction. One thing is certain: the cove will not have poplars like this again until several hundred years after the next major disturbance.

The obvious has already begun; there are fewer enormous trees than there were 20 years ago. And there will be even fewer 20 years hence. Over the next 75 to 125 years, most of the huge poplars will be dead and down.

The yellow poplar, also known as tulip poplar and tuliptree, is not a poplar at all; it is in the magnolia family. Only two species of its *Liriodendron* genus remain; the other is found in central China.

This broadleaf occurs in all but the driest situations from the lowest altitudes to approximately 4,200 feet. It is most successful and obtains its best growth, however, in the moist habitats of coves and north-facing slopes below 3,600 feet. Everything about this tree—its leaf, flower, fruit, form, and bark—is distinctive. The uniquely shaped leaves quiver in the slightest wind. In years when drought doesn't brown it early, the fall foliage is bright yellow.

yellow poplar

The erect, cup-shaped blossom, roughly 2 inches deep and 1½ to 2 inches across, resembles a tulip. The six greenish yellow petals often have a splash of orange at their base. You rarely see the flowers of a forest-grown yellow poplar up close unless a storm has knocked them to the ground.

The yellow poplar attains the greatest height of any eastern hardwood. Naturalists generally rank it as the second most massive tree in the eastern forest; they rank the sycamore as the most massive. Without a doubt, these magnificent giants are the most imposing trees in the Southern Blue Ridge. In the coves of the southern mountains, mature yellow poplars are commonly 110 to 150 feet in height and 10 to 15 feet in circumference. Larger trees, like those along this trail, are not unusual in old-growth forests. Their maximum size is approximately 190 to 200 feet in height and 30 to 32 feet in circumference. The current North Carolina state record is 22 feet 7 inches around and 151 feet high. The former North Carolina champ was 181 feet tall. A recent national record was slightly more than 30 feet around. (If you want to see an immense yellow poplar, a living monument of a tree, walk to the Wasilik Poplar—over 28 feet around and long since topped out—not far from Standing Indian Campground on the lower north slope of North Carolina's Standing Indian Mountain.)

Although the trees alone are worth the visit, there is much more to the Joyce Kilmer National Recreation Trail. This area, specifically the Poplar Cove Loop, has an exceptional spring wildflower display. The slope is so rich that you need to walk the loop twice, the first time around to gawk at the trees and the second lap to look at the wildflowers. During the spring I first hiked the trails in this guide, I had the pleasure of walking the Poplar Cove Loop once a week from mid-March through the end of May. On those walks I counted thirty-eight species of blooming wildflowers and saw the leaves of many more that would open later.

large-flowered trillium

It would take a ten-page pamphlet to describe the spring wild-flowers alongside this trail. The best I can do here is to provide general dates and information. The prime blooming season usually lasts a month, from March 25 through April 25. After May 1 the canopy closes and the color wanes quickly. The herbaceous plants blossom in two waves: the first, numerically dominated by spring beauty and hepatica, usually peaks between March 20 and April 5. While it is not as diverse as the second, the first wave is much more profuse. When spring beauty, hepatica, and trout lily reach peak, the cove rivals a western meadow in sheer numbers of corollas. If you are too early for this initial burst at Joyce Kilmer Memorial Forest, you might try the beginning segment of Slickrock Creek Trail.

The second surge, usually climaxing from April 7 to 21, features many species, including four types of trillium and a particularly abundant and beautiful phlox. It is during this time that thousands of large-flowered trillium whiten (before they turn pink) the hill beside and above the higher segment of the upper loop.

Directions

From the NC 143–FS 81–SR 1127 junction at Santeetlah Gap, travel SR 1127 (Wagon Train Road) downhill to the northwest approximately 2.2 miles to the four-way intersection at the entrance of the Joyce Kilmer approach road, FS 416. At this intersection, turn left onto paved FS 416 and follow it for 0.6 mile to its dead-end trailhead and picnic area parking lot (bathrooms and water in season).

For those traveling from the north, heading south on US 129 and taking the dirt-road shortcut, you will reach the four-way intersection after passing through Horse Cove Campground. Forest Service 416, the Joyce Kilmer approach road, is straight ahead through the intersection.

The Forest Service does not allow overnight parking in the Joyce Kilmer lot. If you plan to backpack (camping prohibited along the Joyce Kilmer National Recreation Trail), park your vehicle beside the Jenkins Meadow Trailhead bulletin board at the entrance of FS 416. There is overflow parking to the right straight across the four-way intersection from the trailhead.

(See page 26 for the various routes, mileages, and directions to the four-way intersection at the entrance of FS 416 and the NC 143–FS 81–SR 1127 intersection at Santeetlah Gap.)

Notes

Naked Ground Trail

Foot Trail 55: 4.3 miles

- **Dayhiking (low to high)** Moderate to Strenuous
- **Dayhiking (high to low)** Easy to Moderate
- **Backpacking (low to high)** Strenuous
- **Backpacking (high to low)** Moderate
- **Interior Trail** Southeastern (low elevation) terminus on the lower loop of the Joyce Kilmer National Recreation Trail, 2,300 feet; northwestern (high elevation) terminus on Haoe Lead Trail at Naked Ground, 4,860 feet
- **Trail Junctions** Lower Joyce Kilmer loop, Jenkins Meadow Connector (see trail description), Haoe Lead, Slickrock Creek
- **Topographic Quadrangles** Santeetlah Creek NC, Tapoco NC-TN
- **Features** Virgin forest; Little Santeetlah Creek; early spring wildflower display

NAKED GROUND BEGAN AS A CHEROKEE TRADING PATH, up the Little Santeetlah Creek basin, through the gap at Naked Ground, then down the Slickrock Creek basin to the Little Tennessee River. In fact, the level ground on the north side of Little Santeetlah Creek, about halfway up to the gap, was a traditional campsite noted in Cherokee legend: *Tsunda nilti yi* —"where they demanded the debt from him." To this camp a Cherokee hunter brought back a deer, which the others of the party demanded in payment of a debt due them. The Cherokee say they do not recognize or understand the word *Santeetlah* (the second *t* is silent); they say the name came from the settlers. The Cherokee name for the creek was, and probably still is, the same as their name for the legend.

After the Cherokee were forced out, early homesteaders drove their livestock on the existing track up and over the gap. Today, Naked Ground Trail, paralleling Little Santeetlah Creek, bisects the length of the big-toe–shaped Joyce Kilmer Memorial Forest. The Little Santeetlah Creek basin is the 3,840-acre memorial forest and vice versa. Naked Ground is now the only long trail entirely within the virgin forest and the only trail that traverses the forest's center. All of the other Joyce Kilmer trails, except the two short loops, remain on or near the forest's perimeter ridges.

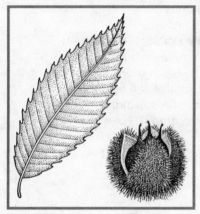

American chestnut

In the summer of 1989, the Forest Service officially moved Naked Ground's lower-elevation end to the lower loop of the Joyce Kilmer National Recreation Trail. Before this change, Naked Ground's length was 5.8 miles. The first 0.9 mile of the old Naked Ground now belongs to Jenkins Meadow Trail, and its former second 0.9-mile section is now a connector between Jenkins Meadow and the new Naked Ground.

Many people who have just walked Poplar Cove Loop are somewhat disappointed by the size of the trees beside Naked Ground. This is to be expected. As far as I know, no other 0.8-mile trail or segment of trail anywhere else in eastern North America winds past so many enormous trees as does Poplar Cove Loop. The trees anywhere else in the East, including those elsewhere in the same forest, can be anticlimactic.

There are several facts you might want to keep in mind as you walk the Naked Ground Trail. The first is still hard to believe. Even though it was never cut, Joyce Kilmer is not the primeval forest the Cherokee saw when they camped next to Little Santeetlah Creek. That forest no longer exists. The mature American chestnut, once the Southern Appalachian's thickest and most abundant tree (it attained a maximum of 9 to 11 feet in diameter and occasionally covered up to 40 percent of the forest in its favored habitat), is gone, wiped out by the accidentally imported chestnut blight.

Oleta Nelms, the naturalist who worked at the Joyce Kilmer picnic area when I walked these trails, told me that when she was young the chestnuts, not the yellow poplars, were the thickest trees in what was to become the memorial forest. The fungus arrived in these mountains in the late 1920s. By 1940, most of the chestnuts were gray snags. The forest and the wildlife it supports have never been the same since.

The second fact is that the original forest, even in the rainy Southern Blue Ridge, was never an unbroken canopy of uniformly huge trees. The trees were, of course, on average much larger than they are now. But they were never the monoculture of thick, foreboding columns depicted by some of our early novelists such as James Fenimore Cooper. In prelogging Southern Appalachia only two trees, the yellow poplar and the chestnut, regularly reached girths over 20 feet. (By today's diminished standards, an eastern tree of that size now seems implausibly large.) And truly giant specimens, those over 25 feet in circumference, over 8 feet in diameter, were scarce even then.

With the mature chestnut gone, only the yellow poplar possesses the genetic potential to reach massive proportions. But even this giant requires exactly the right environmental conditions to gain its maximum, huge size. The Naked Ground Trail remains on the north side of the creek, on the south-facing slope, for its entire length. The south slope, the driest slope, does not have those "exactly right" conditions. You will notice that the other side of the creek, which is facing north, has bigger trees and a greener forest floor. If you walk the Naked Ground Alternate or the Poplar Cove Loop, you will notice the difference. The grass really is always greener on the north-facing slope.

Even though they are in a south-slope forest without the chestnut, Naked Ground's trailside trees are hardly disappointing, especially by today's standards. There are numerous oaks—northern red, white, chestnut—from 9 to 13 feet around. One white pine is approximately 160 feet tall. Hemlocks 110 to 140 feet tall and 9 to 12 feet in circumference flank the stream. Many yellow poplars, while not as large as those along the "miracle mile" of Joyce Kilmer National Recreation Trail, range from 11 to 15 feet in girth. A few, like the one on Naked Ground Alternate, are larger still. There are also some sizable yellow buckeye, red maple, and sugar maple.

Naked Ground rises easily up and away from Little Santeetlah to its first junction at 0.3 mile. Here you will find an unusual trail configuration—a backward fork 40 feet before a forward fork. The path, usually signed, leading to the right and uphill back behind you is the 0.9-mile Jenkins Meadow Connector. At the next fork, the path continuing to the right is the main Naked Ground Trail. The treadway, again usually signed, heading down and to the left is the Naked Ground Alternate (Trail 55A on the Forest Service wilderness map).

If you are dayhiking in the Joyce Kilmer Memorial Forest and want to walk more than just the two short loops, you can make a third loop by taking the Naked Ground Alternate. On your way back, you can further extend your walk by hiking the connector, Jenkins Meadow, and the road back to your car.

The Naked Ground Alternate dips to and crosses Little Santeetlah Creek (a rock-hop when it's low, a wade through cold water when it's not), then rises up and away from the stream through rhododendron. This section of trail winds through an area with large hemlock and yellow poplar (one 18 feet in circumference measured from its high side and perhaps 150 feet high) and a rich, open wildflower slope, similar to the upper Poplar Cove Loop. Early spring wildflowers, such as squirrel corn and spring beauty, blanket the moist hillside from late March through mid-April. The path crosses the creek again and rejoins the main trail after 0.7 mile. As trail 55A drops to its first creek crossing, you will come to an unofficial junction, an alternate to the alternate, above a prominent campsite to the left. You can proceed straight ahead downhill, or curl up and to the right. Continue ahead, slightly to the left, beside the campsite.

Above the first junction with the alternate route, Naked Ground gradually ascends through a mixed broadleaf-conifer forest—hardwoods with hemlock and a few white pine. The treadway, dipping to rivulets, then rising, remains on the slope within earshot of the creek. It crosses Indian Spring Branch at 1.0 mile. This swift, sliding tributary can be tricky to cross after a heavy rain. One-tenth mile beyond the branch, the alternate ties back into the trail. This is the final junction before the gap. From here on up the basin there is just one good, impossible-to-lose footpath, following a beautiful stream through the heart of a virgin forest.

Past the alternate, the track more closely parallels the Little Santeetlah. Even though it's closer, the creek usually stays just out of sight through the rhododendron. There are occasional good views of the cascading stream, but they never last for long. The reason Naked Ground doesn't afford frequent, close-up views or cross the creek, not even once, is the same reason it still has virgin trees: loggers never blasted a railroad up its banks. Every other streamside trail in the two-state wilderness has numerous views, crossings, old railroad beds—and second-growth forests.

Here the walking, still an easy upgrade overall, is through a moister forest of larger trees. Before leaf-out, or after leaf-off, there are good views of the pillarlike yellow poplar boles across the creek. Before it rock-hops Adamcamp Branch at mile 1.6, the path leads through level ground between rivulets. Perhaps the legendary debt was paid here, where the slowly rotting chestnut trunks are scattered about.

Three-tenths mile beyond the branch, the track passes the main trail's largest tree—a completely hollow yellow poplar approximately 16 feet in circumference. The opening extends almost 6 feet above the ground. You can walk inside and stay dry during a spring shower. Frontier journals often recounted cold, rainy nights when entire families, and sometimes even a horse, kept dry in the hollow of a huge tree, usually a sycamore or yellow poplar. Early in the eighteenth century, John Lawson, surveyor general of North Carolina, reported a tuliptree "wherein a lusty man had his bed and household furniture, and lived in it till his labour got him a more fashionable mansion."

From the hollow poplar, Naked Ground continues to the northwest on the largely hardwood slope above the creek. Here it starts to head up a little harder, mixing some easy-to-moderate grades with the gentler ones. At mile 2.4 the footpath and a rivulet intersect between four big yellow poplars. The guardian poplars form the corners of a small square, two on either side of both the trail and the rivulet. Once across this memorable streamlet, the course climbs more steadily through a forest increasingly dominated by thick northern red oaks with wide-branching crowns.

The route rock-steps a Little Santeetlah fork (approximately 3,800 feet) at mile 3.1. It then turns away from the fork and roughly parallels what's left of the main stream. At mile 3.5, across another of this trail's numerous step-over rivulets, the treadway begins the long, hard pull to the ridge. Two-tenths mile after the ascent starts, the final section switchbacks—repeatedly zigzagging left, then right— steadily up a moderate grade (more difficult if you're walking fast or carrying a pack) to its end at Naked Ground. When the leaves are off the trees, you can see the surrounding ridges, the last trickle of Little Santeetlah Creek, and, from the switchbacks, the basin you just climbed.

Naked Ground is a gap, the deepest gap on the ridge between Bob Stratton Bald and the Hangover. It is also a major trail junction. Two trails, Slickrock Creek and Naked Ground, end in the gap, and a third, Haoe Lead, passes through it on the ridge. From the end of Naked Ground Trail, it is 1.4 miles on the ridge to the right (northeast) to the Hangover, and 1.3 miles on the ridge to the left (southwest) to the grassy area atop Bob Stratton Bald. Slickrock Creek Trail, usually signed, leads downslope to the north, over the gap opposite Naked Ground's end. Because it is an important trail junction, level, and has a nearby spring, the gap at Naked Ground is a popular, often crowded camping area. (See Haoe Lead Trail, also in this section, for more information about the gap and its spring.)

In his land ethic bible, *A Sand County Almanac*, Aldo Leopold wrote:

> What a thousand acres of Silphiums looked like when they tickled the bellies of the buffalo is a question never again to be answered, and perhaps not even asked.

To paraphrase his sentiment: What thousands of acres of chestnuts, covering slopes as far as the eye could see, looked like when their creamy white blossoms waved in the spring wind is a question perhaps never again to be answered, and perhaps not even asked.

Directions

Naked Ground is an interior trail that has its southeastern (low elevation) end on the lower loop of the Joyce Kilmer National Recreation Trail and its northwestern (high elevation) end on the Haoe Lead Trail at Naked Ground. Although it is technically an interior trail, Naked Ground essentially begins at the Joyce Kilmer parking area, which serves as its trailhead.

The directions to Naked Ground's trailhead are exactly the same as those for Joyce Kilmer National Recreation Trail. Starting from the information shelter, walk the lower loop in a counterclockwise direction (opposite the bridge over Little Santeetlah Creek). Walk straight out of the shelter, turn left, and head uphill on the wide pathway. After slightly less than 0.3 mile on the lower loop, the beginning of Naked Ground, usually signed, angles up and to the right just before the loop crosses the bridge over Little Santeetlah Creek. (See Joyce Kilmer, the preceding trail, for traveling directions.)

The Forest Service does not allow backpackers to leave their vehicles overnight in the Joyce Kilmer parking area. If you plan to backpack, park your vehicle beside the trailhead bulletin board at the entrance of FS 416, the Joyce Kilmer approach road.

There is space for overflow parking to the right, straight across the four-way intersection from the Jenkins Meadow Trailhead.

Notes

Stratton Bald Trail

Foot Trail 54: 7.8 miles

- **Dayhiking In** Moderate to Strenuous
- **Dayhiking Out** Easy to Moderate
- **Backpacking In** Strenuous
- **Backpacking Out** Moderate
- **Start** Stratton Bald Trailhead near Rattler Ford Group Campground, 2,080 feet
- **End** Fodderstack Trail, 5,160 feet
- **Trail Junctions** Wolf Laurel, Haoe Lead, Fodderstack
- **Topographic Quadrangles** Santeetlah Creek NC, Big Junction TN-NC
- **Features** Winter views and rock outcrop overlooks; botanically rich hollows; virgin forest; Bob Stratton Bald

THIS TRAIL IS NAMED FOR ITS DESTINATION, Bob Stratton Bald, which was named, quite predictably, after Robert B. Stratton. Bob settled new country; he was a mountain man who hunted, herded, did what pioneers had to, to make ends meet in the high Appalachians. Written sources referring to him are contradictory. The only facts I can state with certainty are that Bob Stratton bought 100 acres of land for $9.40 in 1872, and that he lived at 4,400 feet on the south slope of his bald at Swan Meadows. Bob liked his weather brisk and his neighbors distant.

This path, much of it part of the original Joyce Kilmer trail system, heads northwest on the slopes and crest of Horse Cove Ridge, then turns west across the spine of Bob Stratton Bald. An upper-slope and ridge route, it provides steady views during the bare-tree season. At its highest elevations that season lasts seven and one half months—from mid-October through May.

Stratton Bald's ascents are not among the steepest in the combined wilderness, but the trail does climb long and steady. In fact,
this trail gains 3,300 feet to the high point of the bald by mile 6.9.
This elevation-gain total ranks second highest among the trails in
this guide (13.3-mile Slickrock Creek is first). The upper-elevation
section of Slickrock Creek Trail is well-known for its steepness by
Joyce Kilmer–Slickrock hikers. But Stratton Bald, while it doesn't
have the sharp surges, still rises more than Slickrock Creek's uppermost 7.0 miles.

From its beginning near Santeetlah Creek, this impossible-to-
lose footpath immediately turns right and enters the wilderness,
then gradually swings toward the southwest, to the slope high above
the final run of Little Santeetlah Creek. At first the boles are skinny
second-growth. But as the route draws nearer to the virgin forest,
old-growth—mostly species the loggers left, such as hemlock—
becomes increasingly common. The grades of this segment, when
not dipping slightly or level, are easy or easy to moderate. At mile 1.1
the course, by way of a preview, half-circles around the head of its
first virgin hollow.

Two-tenths mile beyond the hollow, the track passes beside a
foundation corner on the edge of the memorial forest. After hiking
this trail, I asked Oleta Nelms, the naturalist who worked at the Joyce
Kilmer picnic area in the late 1980s, if she knew anything about the
old homeplace. She knew plenty. The homesteaders, the only settlers
to live in what was to become the memorial forest, were her grand-
parents—the Dentons. In 1879 her grandfather found a promising
spot with a spring, a gentle slope (gentle for a mountainside), and a
huge chestnut log. He then hollowed out the log, which was thick
enough for him to stand up in, and built a three-sided lean-to
against it. After the dirt-floor structure was finished, the rest of the
family moved from Tennessee. The Dentons lived in this makeshift
shelter, using the chestnut log as a storage area, until they could con-
struct a proper cabin. Oleta said that she was teased at school
because her grandfather had lived in a log.

The 0.8-mile stretch beyond the homestead is one of the most
memorable sections of trail in the entire wilderness, especially in late
April and early May. Here the walking, angling steadily upward

toward Horse Cove Ridge, winds through a succession of northwest-facing hollows, some wet and some dry. The wet hollows have a veneer of water dribbling down wide shelves of mossy rock. To either side of the path, the incredible array of ferns, flowering herbaceous plants, and virgin hardwoods is about as verdant as the Southern Blue Ridge can be. The giant, jagged leaves of the umbrella-leaf and the Dutchman's-pipe vine twirling 50 feet up in the large-leaved trees—basswood, Fraser magnolia, and cucumbertree—complete the feeling of tropical luxuriance.

Above the notch of the last hollow, the path makes a moderately difficult, 0.5-mile ascent to the crest of Horse Cove Ridge. This higher and drier slope is dominated by the oaks. As soon as it reaches the top of the ridge (3,480 feet) at mile 2.6, the route turns right (northwest) onto the southern flank of the lead almost immediately. This maneuver takes the walkway out of the wilderness and around a 3,800-foot, unnamed knob well below its high point. The treadway rises easily, loses some hard-won elevation through a boulder field, rises again, then dips back to the ridgeline on the south side of Obadiah Gap (3,660 feet).

From the gap at mile 3.3, the trail does a second end run on the southern pitch of another unnamed knob, this one 4,060 feet high. Here the hiking ascends steadily through dry-slope hardwoods. Through openings in the heath there are a few year-round views of the big mountain with three named peaks—Little Huckleberry Knob, Huckleberry Knob, and Hooper Bald—across the Santeetlah Creek basin. Even though it's only a knob, Huckleberry, the middle point, is 5,560 feet high. The footpath regains the crest of Horse Cove Ridge (3,940 feet) at mile 3.8.

For the rest of its length, the route continues on or near the keel of a ridge—Horse Cove, a Bob Stratton Bald spur, then the backbone of the bald itself. From mile 3.8 to the Wolf Laurel connection at mile 5.3, the hardest sustained upgrades are no tougher than moderate. At mile 4.2 and approximately 4,000 feet, you enter a beautiful, open grove of large oaks with wide-branching crowns. These oaks—northern red, black, chestnut—have such broad canopies because their former chief competition, the American chestnut, has not been contending for light for the last 70 years. Most of the logs on the ground are chestnut wrecks, gray ghosts of forests past.

After picking its way through a boulder field at mile 5.1 and passing the Wolf Laurel junction, the track ascends over a low knob before dipping to a shallow gap (4,860 feet) at mile 5.9. From this gap the treadway climbs 420 feet in 0.6 mile to its second junction. Its last ascent, through rhododendron and past rock outcrop, becomes progressively steeper as it switchbacks to Bob Stratton Bald's eastern shoulder. At approximately 5,280 feet above sea level, the path pops up to its connection with the Haoe Lead Trail at mile 6.5. Haoe Lead ends at this intersection; Stratton Bald Trail bends 90 degrees to the left and heads west toward its namesake bald.

Now the walking is through a wind-pruned forest composed of squat, low-branching trees, mostly northern red oak, beech, and yellow birch. Here the grass- and brier-lined trail squiggles from side to side as it runs a slalom course around rock outcrops. Three-tenths mile beyond the junction, you pass over the highest point of Bob Stratton Bald—the tallest mountain in the overall wilderness (at least 5,360 feet on top of several outcrops).

Between the bald's crown and its clearing, there are two short side paths that lead to overlooks open to the north. Straight out the Unicoi ridgeline snakes away, spurs splaying to either side, defining and dividing drainages. The most prominent spur, Pine Ridge, descends to the west of Big Fodderstack just 3¹/₂ miles from the look-offs.

The route breaks out of the Fraser firs (planted in the late 1950s) and enters the bald at mile 7.2. A bench mark states the elevation as 5,261.65 feet, give or take an inch or two. The sunny, grassy part of the opening covers perhaps 3 or 4 acres. This clearing affords year-round, over-the-tree vistas of the mountains spanning the horizon southeast to southwest. Just left of due south, and slightly less than 4 miles in the distance, is Huckleberry Knob. To the right of Huckleberry, at south-southwest, there is another massive mountain with several named peaks, the highest of which is Haw Knob (5,472 feet).

The treadway continues straight across the high, northern side of the clearing, burrows into beech–yellow birch woods, then ends at its junction with Fodderstack Trail. These two trails meet at the southernmost point of the boundary between the two wildernesses.

As you will no doubt notice, the bald has been reclaimed by shrubs and saplings on the north side of the path and is still somewhat grassy on the other side. There is a simple, man-made explanation. The trail and the wilderness boundary are approximately the same across the bald. During 1985 and 1986, the Forest Service restored that part of the bald lying outside of the wilderness south of the trail.

For years now it has been obvious that Southern Appalachian balds like Bob Stratton could not sustain themselves without fire and grazing. It has also become apparent that without management these traditional grassy clearings would soon totally vanish. After consulting with many organizations, including the Appalachian Trail Conference, the Forest Service decided to prevent the disappearance of the historic balds by reclaiming and maintaining them in the southern national forests. The Forest Service based its decision to implement this program on three basic values: wildlife habitat diversity, historical perspective, and human preference—we enjoy the aesthetics of grassy openings that provide vistas. Therefore, the portion of the bald south of the wilderness boundary will be maintained in the future.

Canada mayflower

Once the trail rises to Horse Cove Ridge, it does not cross a water source for the rest of its length. There is, however, a variable spring very near the southeastern edge of the bald. If you enter the opening at its eastern, fir-tree end, continue on the trail just past the elevation bench mark, then turn left and follow one of several converging side paths that lead downhill to the spring.

Nature Notes

This trail's elevation gain allows you to climb back up into spring. Many of the same flowers that bloom along Poplar Cove

Loop in late March and early April bloom on Bob Stratton Bald in late April and early May.

Two segments of this path have particularly good spring wildflower displays. The luxuriant, northwest-facing hollows within the memorial forest bloom from early April through early May. The highcountry section of the route, from the Wolf Laurel junction to its end, flowers from early May through the middle of June. Painted trillium are common in association with rhododendron on uppermost Horse Cove Ridge. This highland area also has flowering shrubs—flame azalea, Catawba rhododendron, and hobblebush.

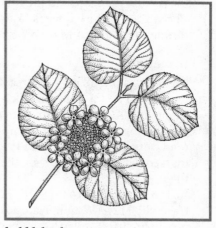

hobblebush

Blooming from mid-May into early June, the unmistakable Canada mayflower occurs in large colonies along Stratton Bald Trail above 4,800 feet. This delicate lily, Joyce Kilmer–Slickrock's version of an alpine wildflower, is found in the wilderness only within one island of high-mountain habitat. And within this small area it is abundant only in the two pockets of land above 5,000 feet.

The hobblebush, also known as moosewood and witchhobble, is another plant that requires northern conditions. This shrub becomes increasingly plentiful in the cool, moist woods of this wilderness above 4,400 feet. Beside the final few tenths mile of this trail, at an elevation of slightly less than 5,200 feet, the hobblebush is the understory.

This member of the honeysuckle family might be more aptly named the footnoose or tripping bush. Its arching branches often take root and create new shoots where they touch the ground. In favorable habitat all these arching branches and new shoots, which make newer shoots, form a tangled growth, hobbling those trying to force their way through.

The hobblebush's large, heart-shaped leaves, usually 4 to 7 inches long, occur in conspicuously opposite pairs along the branches. In September and early October after the berries have turned brilliant red, the foliage becomes strikingly variegated with bronze-red and purple-pink.

This mountain-climbing shrub has flat-topped clusters of blossoms that contain two different types of flowers. The small, densely packed corollas in the middle are encircled by a row of larger flowers—up to 1 inch wide—that are showy but sterile. These fake flowers have no reproductive parts; they serve as sexy clothing to attract the pollinating insects to the drab but fertile blossoms in the center. The disks of white flowers, 3 to 5 inches across the circle, bloom throughout most of May above 5,000 feet.

Directions

Stratton Bald's parking area—a gravel lot to the right with a bulletin board and a split-rail fence—is just inside Rattler Ford Group Campground. The beginning of the trail is less than 0.1 mile from the parking area. Walk the campground road back out to the main road, turn left, and cross the bridge over Santeetlah Creek. Usually marked with a carsonite sign, the trail starts on the left at the end of the guardrail.

From the NC 143–FS 81–SR 1127 junction at Santeetlah Gap, travel SR 1127 (Wagon Train Road) downhill to the northwest approximately 1.9 miles to the paved left turn into the prominently signed Rattler Ford Group Campgound.

From the four-way intersection at the entrance of the Joyce Kilmer approach road, FS 416, follow SR 1127 eastward (immediately cross Little Santeetlah Creek, pass the trail sign for Stratton Bald just before crossing Santeetlah Creek) for slightly more than 0.3 mile to the paved right turn into prominently signed Rattler Ford Group Campground.

(See page 26 for the various routes, mileages, and directions to the four-way intersection at the entrance of FS 416 and the NC 143–FS 81–SR 1127 intersection at Santeetlah Gap.)

Notes

Wolf Laurel Trail

Foot Trail 57: 0.2 mile

- **Dayhiking** Easy
- **Backpacking** Easy
- **Start** Wolf Laurel Trailhead, 4,590 feet
- **End** Stratton Bald Trail, 4,660 feet
- **Trail Junction** Stratton Bald
- **Topographic Quadrangle** Santeetlah Creek NC
- **Features** Short approach trail to Stratton Bald Trail
  and the wilderness

WOLF LAUREL, THE PATH WITH THE WILD, EUPHONIC NAME, has always been a short lead-in trail. Now, because it has been rerouted, it is even shorter—barely long enough to be rounded up to 0.2 mile. Coupled with a 1.2-mile segment of the Stratton Bald Trail, it provides the shortest and easiest route to the ridgecrest between Bob Stratton Bald and the Hangover. Wolf Laurel is not only the shortest trail in this guide but also the only trail completely outside the wilderness.

Wolf Laurel passes through a dark young forest of black cherry, yellow birch, and hemlock before entering an open stand of older hardwoods, predominantly beech and oaks, where ferns are common on the forest floor. It then ends at its T-junction with Stratton Bald Trail on the wilderness boundary.

To the left (northwest) Stratton Bald Trail climbs 1.2 miles to its ridgecrest junction with Haoe Lead Trail. Stratton Bald turns sharply to the left (west) and Haoe Lead ends at this junction. The open, grassy area on Bob Stratton Bald lies 0.7 mile to the west from the Haoe Lead–Stratton Bald junction. To the right (northeast) on Haoe Lead, it is 0.6 mile to Naked Ground, 1.6 miles to the high point of the Haoe and 2.0 miles to the 360-degree view from the Hangover.

The final 0.4 mile along the ridgeline of the wall, from the Haoe to the Hangover, follows the Hangover Lead South Trail and the Hangover Lead South side trail (56A) straight ahead to the open view.

Directions

To reach the Wolf Laurel approach road, FS 81-F, you must travel FS 81 from either its eastern or western end. From the NC 143–FS 81–SR 1127 junction on the southeastern, North Carolina side of the wilderness at Santeetlah Gap, turn west onto the paved entrance of FS 81 (Santeetlah Creek Road). Continue on dirt-gravel FS 81 approximately 6.7 miles (cross bridge over Santeetlah Creek; pass the Stewart Cabin; cross the bridge over Sand Creek) to FS 81-F, Wolf Laurel Road. Turn uphill and to the right onto Wolf Laurel Road, usually marked with one or more signs, and proceed approximately 4.8 miles to the Wolf Laurel Trailhead, where FS 81-F dead-ends at a gate.

From the TN 165–Indian Boundary approach road (FS 345) junction on the southwestern, Tennessee side of the wilderness, travel approximately 11.3 miles on TN 165 East (Overhill Skyway) and NC 143 East (Cherohala Skyway) to the paved left turn onto the western end of FS 81. The FS 81–NC 143 junction is approximately 1.8 miles beyond the TN-NC state line at Beech Gap, where TN 165 becomes NC 143. Proceed downhill on FS 81 (the pavement quickly ends and the road narrows) approximately 4.0 miles, then turn left onto FS 81-F.

Forest Service 81 is a rocky dirt and gravel road. Its steep western section, the section you must drive to reach Wolf Laurel Road from Tennessee, can be muddy and deeply rutted after early spring rains. After the spring grading, usually in late April, this steep section normally becomes passable for conventional passenger vehicles. The condition of FS 81-F, however, often changes from year to year, depending upon what the Forest Service does or does not do to the road. In recent years the road has remained passable for all but the lowest-slung vehicles after spring grading. Small washouts occur after spring and summer thunderstorms, so the wetter the weather, the worse the road.

Forest Service 81 is closed during cold weather, usually from late December through early March. It is not closed on the same date each year; it depends upon the weather. For more information concerning road closings and conditions, call Nantahala National Forest's Cheoah Ranger District.

(See page 26 for the various routes, mileages, and directions to the FS 345–TN 165 intersection and the NC 143–FS 81–SR 1127 intersection at Santeetlah Gap.)

Notes

Citico Creek Wilderness

One hundred years from now when my great-great-grandchildren will be as old as I am today, the main trails of Cherokee National Forest will be at least as populated as are today's trails through the Smoky Mountains. Campsites in the CNF will be crowded. There may even be, perish the thought, paved trails.

What there will not be, one hundred years from now, is still another Cherokee National Forest to explore and save. In Tennessee there are no more high mountains, grassy balds, rushing creeks. All there will be more of one hundred years from now are people and the residue of people.

Lamar Alexander,
from the foreword to
Wilderness Trails of Tennessee's
Cherokee National Forest,
William Skelton, Editor

Sassafras Ridge Trailheads

Unicoi Mountains

Trails

Fodderstack
Cold Spring Gap
Falls Branch
Jeffrey Hell
Grassy Branch
Flats Mountain

Sassafras Ridge Trailheads
Directions and Map

ALL OF THE SASSAFRAS RIDGE TRAILHEADS are located on the north side of the road—NC 143 (Cherohala Skyway)–TN 165 (Overhill Skyway)—that connects Robbinsville, North Carolina, and Tellico Plains, Tennessee. Fodderstack's Sassafras Ridge Trailhead is located at Beech Gap on the Tennessee–North Carolina line, where NC 143 (Cherohala Skyway) becomes TN 165 (Overhill Skyway). All of the other Sassafras Ridge Trailheads are located off TN 165.

All the directions in this section utilize two starting points: one to the west and one to the east.

Approach from the west. All directions originating from the west begin at the TN 165–FS 345 junction at the sign for Indian Boundary Recreation Area. If you are traveling TN 165 East, you will continue straight ahead on TN 165 past this junction.

Approach from the east. All directions originating from the east begin at the NC 143–FS 81–SR 1127 intersection at Santeetlah Gap near the Joyce Kilmer Memorial Forest. If you are traveling NC 143 West from the Robbinsville area, you will curve sharply to the left and remain on NC 143 West at the junction. If you are traveling from the north on US 129 South across Calderwood Lake and take the dirt-road shortcut past Joyce Kilmer Memorial Forest, you will approach this junction on SR 1127. Turn right onto NC 143 West at Santeetlah Gap.

(See page 26 for directions and mileages to the TN 165–FS 345 intersection and the NC 143–FS 81–SR 1127 intersection.)

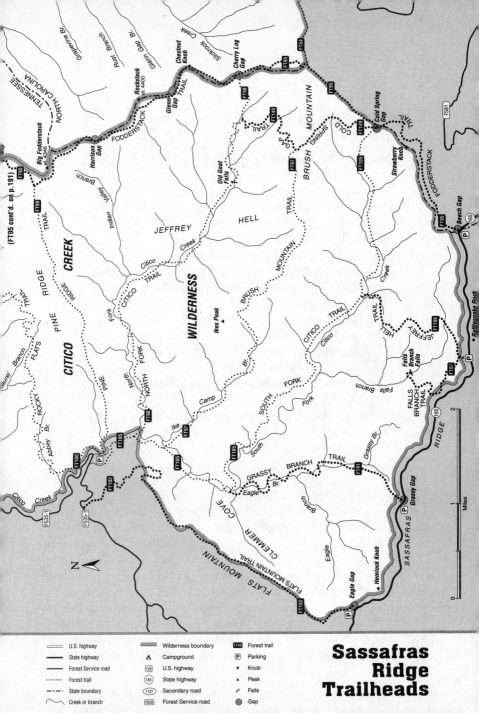

Sassafras
Ridge
Trailheads

Legend		
≡ U.S. highway	▨ Wilderness boundary	FT99 Forest trail
─ State highway	▲ Campground	P Parking
─ Forest Service road	129 U.S. highway	◆ Knob
⋯ Forest trail	165 State highway	▲ Peak
─·─ State boundary	1127 Secondary road	╱ Falls
～ Creek or branch	FS59 Forest Service road	⬤ Gap

TENNESSEE
NORTH CAROLINA

Grapevine Br.
Rust Branch
Glenn Gap Br.
Silltrock Creek
Creek
Cherry Log Gap
F154
FT95
FT95
Chestnut Knob
Rockstack el. 4400
Glenn Gap TRAIL
FT98
FT149
FT149
FT195
Cold Spring Gap
FODDERSTACK
FS81

Big Fodderstack el. 4346
Harrison Gap
FT95
FT105
Branch
Indian Valley
Old Goat Falls
COLD SPRING GAP TRAIL
BRUSH MOUNTAIN
FT191
Strawberry Knob
FODDERSTACK TRAIL
FT195
Beech Gap
P
165

(FT95 cont'd. on p.191)
FT95
FT199
PINE RIDGE TRAIL
CREEK
CITICO
JEFFREY
HELL
Citico Creek
TRAIL
BRUSH MOUNTAIN
FT105
Rattlesnake Rock

Laurel Branch
ROCKY FLATS
CITICO CREEK
Ikes Peak ▲
CITICO TRAIL
Citico
CITICO TRAIL
HELL TRAIL
Creek
JEFFREY
FT196
FT187
P

Abbey Br.
PINE RIDGE
Fork
NORTH FORK
Br.
Camp
SOUTH FORK
Falls Branch Falls
Falls Branch
FALLS BRANCH TRAIL
P

Citico Creek
FS35-1
FS35-1
FT100
P
FT105
FT198
Ike
FT197
FT105
South
Fork
GRASSY BRANCH TRAIL
FT191
Grassy Br.
165
RIDGE

FT102
Eagle Br.
GRASSY Br.
Branch
SASSAFRAS
Grassy Gap
P

CLEMMER COVE
FLATS MOUNTAIN TRAIL
Eagle Branch
Hemlock Knob ◆
Eagle Gap
FT102
P

N ⬐

2
1
Miles
0

Fodderstack Trail

Horse and Foot Trail 95: 12.6 miles

- **Dayhiking (low to high)** Moderate to Strenuous
- **Dayhiking (high to low)** Moderate
- **Backpacking (low to high)** Strenuous
- **Backpacking (high to low)** Moderate
- **Vehicular Access At Either End** Northern (low elevation) terminus at Farr Gap Trailhead, 2,840 feet; southern (high elevation) terminus at Beech Gap Trailhead, 4,490 feet
- **Trail Junctions** Cold Spring Gap, South Fork Citico, Stratton Bald, North Fork Citico, Pine Ridge, Mill Branch, Big Stack Gap Branch, Crowder Branch, Stiffknee (at northern trailhead)
- **Topographic Quadrangles** Whiteoak Flats TN-NC, Big Junction TN-NC
- **Features** Old-growth forest; winter views; series of knobs and peaks known as "the stacks"; diverse spring wildflower display

THE SECOND LONGEST TRAIL in the combined wilderness, Fodderstack is officially designated as a horse route. Despite this designation, it is an easily followed, scenic path that leads through deep woods, as far from a road as is possible in this area. (The steepness of the highways—NC 143 and TN 165—leading to Beech Gap and the lack of trailhead parking for trailers will probably keep horse usage light along the southern end of the trail.) But even if it weren't a good trail, Fodderstack's location would still be crucial to hikers. This north-south track closely follows the main crest of the Unicoi Mountains, which serve as an east-west boundary, separating watersheds, wildernesses, and trail systems. Fodderstack's length and location make it the most important artery in the entire wilderness. It has more junctions—nine—than any other trail in this guide. You cannot hike a walkway from one wilderness to the other without using the Fodderstack.

Fodderstack's length has been increased by 1.8 miles. Its southern trailhead has been relocated from its former trailhead at Cold Spring Gap farther south to Beech Gap. Forest Service 217H, which had been in poor repair prior to its closure, has been gated at Beech Gap and turned into trail.

This trail is described as most hikers start it, from high to low, from south to north. It is most often walked in this direction because the southern end is higher, wilder, steeper, and more scenic than the northern end. There are also several long, interesting loops that begin within a few miles of Fodderstack's southern terminus.

Starting at Beech Gap on the Cherohala Skyway, the trail winds to the northeast on the very gradual grades of the former roadbed. The ridgecrest and upper eastern slopes of Strawberry Knob are dominated by northern hardwoods—beech, sugar maple, yellow buckeye, northern red oak, yellow birch—and hemlock. At mile 1.8 the route reaches its former trailhead, now an important three-way junction. South Fork Citico Trail heads downhill to the left; Cold Spring Gap's southern end is straight ahead. Fodderstack starts its first climb to the right.

Following the wide bed of an old jeep road the treadway gains 740 feet of elevation along the ridge in 1.1 miles. The trail's steepest pull, slightly less than 0.2 mile of moderate to strenuous, is over within the first half-mile. The crestline forest is predominantly northern hardwoods and hemlock. Gnarled old-growth northern red oaks and yellow birches are the thickest trees beside this ascending section. Near the end of the upgrade, the trail bisects a rhododendron slick that, except for the few trees, would be a pure heath bald. The track through the rhododendron is deeply rutted and ordinarily mucky for days after a rain.

The path reaches its high point and second junction at mile 2.9, on the border between the two wildernesses. This connection, on the western shoulder of Bob Stratton Bald at 5,160 feet, is also the highest land in the Citico Creek Wilderness. To the right, it is 0.4 mile on

Stratton Bald Trail to the open meadow.

From its second junction, the route loses 740 feet in 1.1 miles to its third. But instead of continuing straight down the spine, it eases the grade by swinging onto slope and dropping steadily by switchback. This is the only time Fodderstack slips onto the sunrise side, the Joyce Kilmer–Slickrock side, of the ridge. After returning to the crest, the treadway dips to its connection with North Fork Citico Trail in shallow Cherry Log Gap at mile 4.0. This descending segment passes beside the trail's largest trees—old-growth yellow birch, hemlock, black cherry, and Carolina silverbell.

Maintaining its northward course, the wide path rises 0.2 mile to the top of an unnamed knob, then begins a long, predominantly easy downgrade. Here the open forest alternates between hardwoods—dominated by northern red oak and mature, shaggy-barked red maple—and groves of old-growth hemlock. The gradual elevation loss proceeds on the mountainside below the point of Chestnut Knob before regaining the crest and dipping to Glenn Gap (4,100 feet) at mile 5.0.

This trail traverses a ridgeline string of knobs and named peaks—Rockstack, Big Fodderstack, Little Fodderstack—collectively known as the stacks. Beyond Glenn Gap, the route starts a pattern that remains the rule until the very end. Each time the ridge rises sharply toward the top of a stack, the track slants onto its western slope, ascends gradually past the crown, then works its way back to the ridge and down to the next gap.

True to the pattern, the treadway climbs easy-to-moderate grades on Rockstack's (the highest stack at 4,400 feet) sunset side for 0.4 mile before gently descending on or near the rocky keel all the way to Harrison Gap (3,820 feet) at mile 6.4. The forest alongside this section is second-growth hardwoods, largely oak. Once through the saddle of the gap, the walking becomes a steady, easy-to-moderate ascent that switchbacks through more rocky terrain. The dark, thin-layered rock is slate. The upgrade tops out at mile 7.0 high on the western flank of Big Fodderstack, 80 to 120 feet below the mountain's crown (4,346 feet).

Following a 0.3-mile downgrade, the path arrives at its junction with Pine Ridge Trail on the exact backbone of Pine Ridge, a Big

Fodderstack spur. Pine Ridge Trail ties into the main route from the left (west) where Fodderstack curls sharply to the right and down off the crest. Continuing to lose elevation, the track half-loops around a series of moist northwest-facing hollows as it winds down to Big Stack Gap (3,380 feet) at mile 8.1. Mill Branch Trail ends near several large oaks in the gap.

The treadway, proceeding on or close to the ridgetop, rises moderately at first, then more gradually up to and over an unnamed knob (3,640 feet) 0.4 mile beyond the gap. Here you will find leaf-off views of the wall to the southeast, about 3 1/2 miles away as the raven flies. Past the bump after the knob, the grade becomes an easy downhill run through second-growth hardwoods with occasional small pockets of pitch pine. The walking follows the wide corridor of an old road near the end of the descent.

At mile 9.1 the route meets the upper-elevation terminus of Big Stack Gap Branch Trail, marked by a prominent, open campsite to the right (east). From here the former road heads gently down 0.1 mile to a shallow saddle (3,360 feet), where Crowder Branch Trail ends. Across the gap the track rises as usual. This time it alternates easy with easy-to-moderate grades to the point of a knob (3,640 feet) at mile 9.7 before roller-coastering with the ridgeline 0.8 mile to the cap of the next rounded knob (3,640 feet), the one just south of Little Fodderstack.

Over the knob the treadway, which follows the road the rest of the way, descends as always. And as always, it swings onto the western pitch as the ridge steepens toward a stack. With the exception of two short ups, the wide walkway continuously loses elevation as it half-circles Little Fodderstack (3,723 feet) well below its peak. Chunks of quartzite lie strewn along the slope.

Once it regains the crest at mile 11.4, the course rolls with the keel of the ridge—0.2 mile down, 0.2 mile up, 0.2 down, 0.3 up. The final stretch drops off the mountain, then descends in a half-loop to the trail's northern end at Farr Gap.

There are only two springs close beside this entire trail, both on the steep section just north of the Fodderstack–Stratton Bald junction. These springs are variable. By late spring of a drought year, you may have to head downhill to obtain water from the larger one.

There is water down Mill Branch, Big Stack Gap Branch, and Crowder Branch Trails. Crowder Branch is easier and more certain than Big Stack Gap Branch.

Nature Notes

Because of its wide range of elevations and habitats, Fodderstack's diverse spring wildflower display lasts from early April through late May and early June, when the Catawba rhododendron closes out the season. Many segments of the southern, upper-eleva-

Carolina spring beauty

tion half of this trail are sprinkled with first-wave wildflowers. During the last half of April and early May, the trailside north of the Stratton Bald junction—on and off for 3 or 4 miles—is usually dappled with clusters of spring beauty and trout lily. The slope section of the descent from the Stratton Bald junction to Cherry Log Gap has acre upon acre of spring beauties.

Even though it is not the most widespread wildflower in the wilderness, and even though its habitat—rich, open deciduous woods with a herbaceous understory—is limited over large areas of the wilderness, the spring beauty still blossoms in greater numbers than any other spring wildflower. These low (usually less than 6 inches high), sprawling perennials have small underground bulbs. Each bulb may generate from one to many flowering stems, and each stem may produce up to a dozen blooms, though not all at once. These nugget-sized bulbs, once eaten by Native Americans and settlers, have a sweet, chestnutlike taste. They are still eaten by wild boar and black bear.

The delicate, 1/2- to 3/4-inch-wide blossoms have yellow-tinged centers. Their five petals are white or light pink, prominently etched with deep pink or magenta lines. These lines are functional. They are called honey guides because they attract and guide, like little landing strips, the pollinating insects to the nectar sources.

The spring beauty (the Carolina spring beauty to be botanically correct) is one of the earliest bloomers. It begins flowering at the lowest elevations in early March and surges up to the highest mountains by the middle of April. If you hike on a cold, rainy, or snowy day, you might think this member of the purslane family has already finished blooming. But it's just saving energy; when the insects don't fly, the flowers don't open.

Directions

Fodderstack still has either-end vehicular access, but its southern, high-elevation end has been moved further south to Beech Gap. The Beech Gap Trailhead is unmistakable: it is located at the signed boundary between North Carolina and Tennessee, the Cherohala Skyway (NC 143) and the Overhill Skyway (TN 165), and between the Nantahala National Forest and the Cherokee National Forest. A small, brown, carsonite sign marked as #95 usually indicates the exact trailhead at the gated entrance of former FS 217H.

From the Indian Boundary approach road (FS 345)–TN 165 junction on the southwestern, Tennessee side of the wilderness, travel approximately 9.5 miles on TN 165 East to the Beech Gap and Nantahala National Forest signs.

From the NC 143–FS 81–SR 1127 intersection on the southeastern, North Carolina side of the wilderness at Santeetlah Gap, travel NC 143 West approximately 18.0 miles to the Beech Gap Trailhead, which is to the right (north).

To reach the northern, lower-elevation trailhead at Farr Gap, turn from TN 165 onto the paved Indian Boundary approach road, FS 345. If you are traveling from the west on TN 165 East, the turn at this prominent intersection will be to your left. Continue on FS 345 for approximately 1.2 miles to the four-way intersection at the entrance of the recreation area, which is marked by a large Indian Boundary sign. At this intersection, angle to the right onto FS 35-1 (Citico Road, FS 35-1 on the wilderness map, FS 35 on the road sign) and follow that dirt-gravel road for approximately 4.0 miles to its junction with FS 59. Immediately after crossing Citico Creek and entering Doublecamp Campground, turn right onto FS 59 (Doublecamp Road). Proceed on that dirt-gravel road for approximately

6.4 miles to the gap, where the road curves sharply up and to the left as the land drops away from the ridge straight ahead. Opposite the curve, to the right, an old road (now blocked to vehicular traffic) leads a short distance to the trailhead. Stiffknee is the trail that angles down and to the left. Fodderstack Trail is the old road that continues past the bulletin board. There are several turn-in parking areas to the right just before FS 59 turns left at the gap.

(See page 26 for directions and mileages to the TN 165–FS 345 intersection and the NC 143–FS 81–SR 1127 intersection.)

Notes

Cold Spring Gap Trail

Foot Trail 149: 3.2 miles

■ **Dayhiking** Easy in either direction
■ **Backpacking** Easy in either direction
■ **Interior Trail** Southern (high elevation) terminus
   on Fodderstack Trail at Cold Spring Gap, 4,420 feet;
   northern (low elevation) terminus on North Fork
   Citico Trail, 3,840 feet.
■ **Trail Junctions** Fodderstack, South Fork Citico,
   Brush Mountain, North Fork Citico
■ **Topographic Quadrangles** Big Junction TN-NC,
   Whiteoak Flats TN-NC
■ **Features** Lush high-elevation slopes with spring
   wildflowers and old-growth trees; North Fork
   Citico Creek

WHILE THE TRAIL ITSELF IS STILL THE SAME, its access and designation have changed, and both changes are good for hikers seeking a little more solitude. Cold Spring Gap is now an interior trail; you must walk 1.8 miles on the Fodderstack Trail from its southern (high elevation) trailhead at Beech Gap to reach the former trailhead at this trail's namesake gap (Cold Spring). And Cold Spring Gap is no longer a horse trail; it is now designated as hiker only. Because Fodderstack is designated as a horse trail, a few people will no doubt continue to ride on Cold Spring Gap. But as the word gets out and as suitable clearance disappears, there will be fewer and fewer riders. The steepness of the highways (NC 143 and TN 165) leading to Beech Gap is a deterrent to trail riders who do not have heavy-duty diesel rigs. Most riders who use the Fodderstack Trail start at its northern end at Farr Gap.

With the lone exception of the double loop in the Joyce Kilmer

Memorial Forest, Cold Spring Gap is the flattest trail in the combined wilderness. The 1.8-mile Fodderstack approach, which loses 70 feet in elevation, is even easier; it is the easiest trail segment over a mile long in this guide. Cold Spring Gap is a good, easily followed trail, especially for hikers with limited experience or endurance. Its high elevation, lush slopes, spring wildflowers, and old-growth trees make it a good choice for a leisurely nature walk.

Cold Spring Gap, a former logging road, winds northward around a succession of steep-sided hollows. For most of its first half, the walkway remains high, closely following the 4,400-foot contour not far below the main backbone ridge of the Unicoi Mountains. Rich slopes, an open, predominantly broadleaf forest, and long views down hollows plunging farther into Jeffrey Hell characterize the opening mile. The springs along this section are boar-wallowed and variable.

At mile 1.5 in a slight saddle along the crest of Brush Mountain, Cold Spring Gap reaches its junction with Brush Mountain Trail. Brush Mountain follows the ridge to the left; Cold Spring Gap curves to the right and down, dropping to the other (north) side of the mountain. For now, until the canopy closes over the former road, this junction is at the edge of a brier and shrub patch. If you want to turn onto Brush Mountain Trail, watch for the cut-bark blazes and narrow treadway through the vegetation to the left (northwest) in the shallow gap.

After crossing the ridge, the route gradually loses elevation through a thick succession forest coming back from a cut made in the early 1970s. Pin cherry and yellow birch are abundant. Most of the pin cherry, a short-lived succession species also known as fire cherry, will die and fall in the next 50 years.

The track passes over a headwater branch of North Fork Citico Creek at mile 2.4, then again enters forest with old-growth trees. Here the walking leads you through an open stand of hemlock, spiring above the hardwoods upslope and down. These slow-growing conifers, many with girths of 10 to 12 feet and heights of 115 to 140 feet, are by far the largest trees beside this trail. This high-elevation area of the Citico Creek Wilderness was not clear-cut during the logging days of the 1920s. Instead, it was high-graded—selectively cut for valuable species. The hemlock, abundant at lower elevations and considered poor timber, was spared. Today these hemlocks are lingering vestiges of another era, of the primeval forest that existed before the Trail of Tears.

To the left, not far beyond the stream, stands a hemlock that measures 12 feet 8 inches in circumference. A short distance farther along the trail, an even larger one 25 yards to the left measures 14 feet 5 inches around. Like most big trees, it is not that impressive until you stick your nose right up to it. This giant, at least 325 to 375 years old, seemingly healthy and not lightning topped, is the second largest hemlock beside the trails in this guide and the largest overall trailside tree in the Citico Creek Wilderness.

With slightly less than 0.2 mile remaining, the trail turns to path and angles downslope to its ending junction on the bank of the North Fork Citico Creek. One dip near the end is the only part of the trail that isn't easy hiking. To the right, upstream and uphill, it is 0.6 mile on the North Fork Citico Trail to its junction with the Fodderstack Trail.

The sunnier portions of this trail may have briers until the canopy closes over the road. They become worse as the growing season progresses. But usually they are no more than a minor nuisance, and not nearly as bad as a whining companion. Take a hiking stick to keep the briers at bay. And remember, brier whacking is considered trail maintenance.

Nature Notes

The mixed deciduous-evergreen forest along Cold Spring Gap is typical of high, moist Southern Appalachian slopes in that there are very few pines or yellow poplars. The forest is hemlock and those hardwoods—basswood, yellow birch, yellow buckeye, Carolina silverbell, black cherry, beech, northern red oak, Fraser magnolia, red and sugar maple—that prefer or can tolerate cool, moist conditions. In addition to the hemlocks, the loggers left, for one reason or another, what are now the largest and oldest of the hardwoods. Yellow buckeye, some in the 8- to 10-foot circumference range, are the largest broadleafs.

The eastern hemlock is one of two trees (the other is the red maple) that can be found along every mile of trail in the adjacent wildernesses, at all elevations and in nearly every habitat. This grace-ful conifer is most numerous and reaches its largest size on north-facing ridges, moist slopes, and stream margins. The size of its nee-dles and cones makes the hemlock one of the easiest of all trees to identify throughout the year. Its flattened needles are $1/3$ to $2/3$ of an inch long, with two whitish stripes on the undersides. Its roughly oval cones, averaging $3/4$ of an inch in length, are much smaller than any native Southern Appalachian pine, fir, or spruce. With the one exception of the planted Fraser firs on Bob Stratton Bald, the hem-

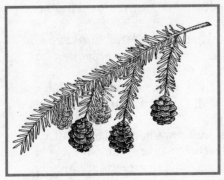

eastern hemlock

lock is the only small-needled evergreen along the trails cov-ered in this guide.

In most parts of its range the hemlock is a medium-sized tree—60 to 80 feet in height and 2 to 3 feet in diameter. But in the mountains of West Virginia, North Carolina, and Tennessee they grow much larger, up to 175 feet in height and 5 to 6 feet in diameter. These giant hem-locks are the oldest trees in the mountain forests of the eastern United States; they live 600 years or more. The oldest of the old can live for a millenium. Be sure to pay your respects.

The first half of Cold Spring Gap has a good spring wildflower display, beginning in the last half of April and continuing through most of May. The season starts with spring beauty, squirrel corn, Dutchman's-breeches, trout lily, wakerobin, and large-flowered tril-lium, among others. By mid-May the color wanes with the final wave of spring wildflowers; foamflower, umbrella-leaf, sweet cicely, and mayapple now dominate the forest floor.

Not long after the color returns, so too does the birdsong. Day after day, as I hiked these trails, I heard the songs of the same three birds—the dark-eyed junco, the winter wren, the veery—over and over again. These three birds sing and breed high up in islands of habitat where it's cool and moist. I never heard the distinctive voices of all three until I was above approximately 3,600 feet.

The dark-eyed junco, also known as the snowbird, calls a musical, telephone-ring trill on one pitch. The winter wren, known as the "short bird with the long song," pours out a long liquid run—a rapid series of high, startlingly clear warbles and trills lasting up to 8 or 9 seconds. You'll know it when you hear it; it's beautiful enough to stop you in your tracks. The veery, a member of the thrush family along with the robin and the bluebird, has the most mysterious and ethereal song you will hear in this wilderness. The veery's call is a downward-spiraling slide-whistle song, a ventriloquial *vee-ur vee-ur veer veer* that rolls down the scale. Again, you'll know it when you hear it, especially if you hear it for the first time during a foggy dawn, when it floats through the gray as though coming from a hole in the ground, somewhere, 20 or 100 yards away seemingly from several different directions. The veery's call note—*peer*—is heard often throughout the day.

Directions

Cold Spring Gap is an interior trail. To reach its southern (higher elevation) end, which is much closer to a trailhead, walk 1.8 very easy miles on the Fodderstack Trail, starting from that trail's southern (high elevation) end at Beech Gap. After walking the former road from Beech Gap, you will arrive at Cold Spring Gap, the site of the former trailhead. Here South Fork Citico Trail heads downhill to the left (northwest); Fodderstack Trail continues uphill to the right (northeast), and Cold Spring Gap Trail starts straight ahead (north) on the old roadbed. (See Fodderstack, the preceding trail, for directions to Beech Gap.)

Cold Spring Gap's northern (lower elevation) junction is on the North Fork Citico Trail, which is also an interior trail. (See North Fork Citico, page 174, in the Citico Creek Trailheads section for more information.)

Notes

Falls Branch Trail

Foot Trail 87: 1.3 miles

- **Dayhiking** Easy to Moderate
- **Backpacking** Moderate
- **Start** Rattlesnake Rock Trailhead, 4,000 feet
- **End** Falls Branch Falls, 3,520 feet
- **Trail Junction** Jeffrey Hell (see trail description)
- **Topographic Quadrangle** Big Junction TN-NC
- **Features** Falls Branch Falls; virgin forest;
  good early spring wildflower display

FALLS BRANCH, THE SECOND SHORTEST TRAIL in this guide, leads to
the tallest waterfall in the combined wilderness. It also enters
one of the two largest pockets of virgin forest in the Citico Creek
Wilderness—perhaps as much as 200 acres—that survived both the
saw and the great fire of 1925. Before wilderness designation, most of
this tract was preserved within the Falls Branch Scenic Area.

Falls Branch shares its trailhead and beginning treadway with
Jeffrey Hell Trail. After 75 yards the trails split apart; Jeffrey Hell curls
to the right and down; Falls Branch bends to the left and heads generally northwestward on the wide walkway of a rocky, old road. This
road was part of the original Tellico Plains–Robbinsville Road used
prior to the construction of Highway 165. The walking, level or an
easy descent while on the roadbed, is on the moist north slope of
Sassafras Ridge for the first few tenths of a mile. In spring the open
downslope is a rich carpet of wildflowers. The forest, with occasional
old-growth right from the start of the trail, is mixed evergreen and
deciduous—hemlock and hardwoods, primarily cove or northern
hardwoods.

The route winds around the heads of hollows, swings close to
the highway at 0.5 mile, then gradually descends to and crosses over

the headwaters of Laurel Branch. Beyond its turn away from the highway, the trail's remaining distance travels through virgin forest. The largest trees, eastern hemlocks, are near Laurel Branch. Here an open grove of these 200- to 300-year-old conifers, with girths of 9 to 12 feet and heights over 120 feet, add their special beauty and dignity to the forest.

At 0.9 mile the track turns 90 degrees to the right (north), off the road onto path. After the turn the trail quickly descends, steeply in places, down a hollow dominated by tall, straight sugar maple, black cherry, and yellow buckeye. It then crosses Falls Branch, rises through the split of a wide fat man's squeeze, and makes a bank-skirting scramble to the waterfall. The footpath ends before the base of the falls. To get the full view, you must walk up the jumble of wet, moss-slick rock in the stream bed.

Falls Branch, a South Fork Citico Creek tributary, is a small volume stream. During autumn of a drought year the waterfall is all but gone. But in winter or spring after a heavy rainfall, it is in wild form, free-falling beyond the bottom lip of rock, sending a shower of mist and white noise downstream. Falls Branch Falls is about 75 to 80 feet high. The water slides over the ledge of a wide, solid-wall rock face in a narrow curtain, then sideslips and widens toward its splash pool. Below the slide, where the rock is cut straight down, the final 50 feet leaps free in an arc—when there's water.

This trail's difficulty is hard to rate. Its first 0.9 mile, though rocky, is a street-shoe stroll. Its final 0.4 mile, however, has steep grades and rough footing in the hollow and rougher rock scrambling for a short distance along the stream. When Falls Branch is running full and the waterfall is at its spray-throwing best, the crossing is considerably more difficult than at normal summer water levels.

Nature Notes

The largest broadleaf trees in the Falls Branch forest are sugar maples. There are half a dozen or more with 11- to 12-foot circumferences fairly near the old road. The sugar maple leaf is distinctive—its silhouette graces the Canadian flag. It has long, pointed lobes and smooth margins, whereas the red maple has much shorter lobes and toothed, serrated margins. Generally recognized as the most brilliant leaf display in North America, the fall foliage is multi-colored—red, yellow, and orange often occur on the same tree, on the same branch.

This maple is one of the largest hardwoods of the eastern forest. In the Southern Appalachians, mature, forest-grown trees have clear, straight boles and average 75 to 100 feet in height and 2 to 4 feet in diameter. The maximum size of this species is 135 feet in height and 7 feet in diameter. Mature trunks have moderately furrowed, light-gray bark that often has a flaky or shaggy appearance. The sugar maple is long-lived, from 300 to 400 years. Wolves once chased elk past the old-timers along this trail.

sugar maple

It is not the slightest bit anthropomorphic to say that the sugar maple is a chemically sentient being. This tree has evolved a strategy to cope with the problem of monoculture—the monoculture of like-tasting leaves. It employs the same strategy that many agricultural experts advise farmers to use: diversification. When insects attack, the sugar maple creates diversity by varying the chemistry, and thus, the palatability of its leaves. This chemical maneuver forces the insects to move in search of good forage, which may become undesirable shortly after they arrive. The defense system is both internal and external. When attacked, these trees get on the horn and send airborne chemical signals to neighboring maples, thereby triggering their defense systems.

Common throughout the southern mountains, brightly colored millipedes, shiny black with yellow or red edging, have a more obvious chemical defense mechanism. Lightly stroke the back of one of these curling arthropods until you get the scent of cherry almond—hydrogen cyanide. Meant to discourage millipede predators, it's harmless to humans.

The beginning of Falls Branch has a good early spring wildflower display. (See Jeffrey Hell, the following trail, for details and description.)

Directions

From the Indian Boundary approach road (FS 345)–TN 165 junction on the southwestern, Tennessee side of the wilderness, travel slightly more than 8.0 miles on TN 165 East (Overhill Skyway) to the prominent, paved trailhead parking area on the left (north) side of the highway. A numbered trail sign usually marks the gap in the rock wall at the far left corner of the parking area.

From the NC 143–FS 81–SR 1127 intersection on the southeastern, North Carolina side of the wilderness at Santeetlah Gap, travel NC 143 West (Cherohala Skyway) and TN 165 West slightly over 19.0 miles to the trailhead parking area on the right. The Falls Branch Trailhead is approximately 1.4 miles beyond the NC-TN state line at Beech Gap, where NC 143 West ends and TN 165 West begins.

(See page 26 for directions and mileages to the TN 165–FS 345 intersection and the NC 143–FS 81–SR 1127 intersection.)

Notes

Jeffrey Hell Trail

Foot Trail 196: 2.2 miles

- ■ **Dayhiking In** Easy
- ■ **Dayhiking Out** Easy to Moderate
- ■ **Backpacking In** Easy to Moderate
- ■ **Backpacking Out** Moderate
- ■ **Start** Rattlesnake Rock Trailhead, 4,000 feet
- ■ **End** South Fork Citico Trail, 3,320 feet
- ■ **Trail Junctions** Falls Branch (see trail description), South Fork Citico
- ■ **Topographic Quadrangle** Big Junction TN-NC
- ■ **Features** South Fork Citico Creek; good spring wildflower display

THE SOUTHERN APPALACHIANS ARE WELL-KNOWN for their breaks or roughs—areas cut up with ridges and creeks and the steep slopes between them. On topographic maps, the contours form tightly bunched, wavy patterns, the brown lines alternately fingering up streams and pointing down the dividing spurs. And randomly spaced throughout this rough terrain, especially where you have decided to drop down off a ridge, are extensive undergrowth tangles of evergreen heath. These heaths are mostly mountain laurel, rhododendron, and, close to water, doghobble. Mountain people call these thickets slicks or hells—bear slicks, laurel slicks, ivy hells, laurel hells, or just plain hells. You crawl through the worst of them down a boar or bear path, on your hands and knees or sliding on your backside, or you don't go at all. Can't go.

It was in such a place, some years before the great Citico Creek fire of 1925, that a man named Jeffrey went bear hunting with several other mountaineers. As the story goes—different in the particulars from teller to teller, but always the same general plot—the hounds jumped a bear and the bawling chase was on. After the bear tired some, he came to bay and fought, broke off and ran some more, then fought, then ran some more. The men followed the running battle from the ridges and spurs as the hounds pursued the bear through the roughs. But there were fewer baying voices than before. The men knew the dogs were taking a beating.

Like the good, rugged hunter he must have been, Jeffrey decided he was going down in there to get his hounds. His hunting companions told him that he was crazy. They told him that going down there in all that ivy would be just like going to hell. But like a character from the pages of a Horace Kephart book, Jeffrey replied that he was going to get his hounds or go to hell—one or the other.

Jeffrey went to hell. Neither he nor his hounds ever came out. Some said he probably had a heart attack; others, wanting a better story, said the bear killed him. No one knows. His body was never found. And ever since, the area where he died has been known as Jeffrey Hell, both in local legend and on federal map.

The sweep of land known as Jeffrey Hell encompasses the Citico Creek watershed south of Pine Ridge. Its namesake hiking trail ventures into its southernmost section. Despite the foreboding story and ominous name, the Jeffrey Hell Trail is safe and easily followed. In fact, its first 1.7-mile segment, which winds northward on the gentle grades of a former logging road, is an easy dayhike stroll. This section ranks among the least rigorous lengths of trail described in this guide.

Seventy-five yards into the woods, Jeffrey Hell swings to the right and down, splitting away from Falls Branch Trail at the fork. Beyond this junction the treadway enters a maturing north-slope forest, open and predominantly second-growth. The forest is diverse: red and sugar maple, yellow and sweet birch, basswood, yellow buckeye, black cherry, beech, Carolina silverbell, and hemlock are common in or near the canopy. The wide walkway gradually loses elevation to the rock and metal culvert bridge (the road was used until the area was designated wilderness in 1984) over Falls Branch at 0.5 mile. It then slowly angles upslope through a younger forest—a thicker forest of thinner trees—to mile 1.0, where the trail tops a wide ridge not far from the high point.

After crossing the crest, the walking is again a gradual, winding downgrade through an open, north-facing forest—hardwoods and hemlock. Here, as at the beginning, there are good views up and down the slope. At mile 1.4 the route follows the right fork as it curves down and to the northeast. Jeffrey Hell descends steadily, easily to moderately, for 0.3 mile before curling sharply to the right (northeast) and down, from former road to quickly descending footpath.

Following the sharp, 100-yard pitch from the road, the remainder of the trail roughly parallels an unnamed tributary branch on easy or easy-to-moderate downgrades. The path is often rocky and wet (especially in early spring) as it tramps beside and in the bed of the shallow stream. After crossing the branch for the third time, the treadway comes to and crosses South Fork Citico Creek—a rock-hop crossing that can be a ford when the water rises—then quickly reaches its ending junction at South Fork Citico Trail.

Nature Notes

The first time I hiked this trail, in mid-April, I had the good fortune of seeing some wildlife before they saw me. That rarely happens. It was about 10:30 in the morning; I was wheel-measuring down the trail in a steady sleet. All of a sudden I saw dark movement ahead. I froze, then slowly eased behind a big buckeye. Two wild boar were roto-rooting their way up the trail, tusking spring beauty tubers. I watched with binoculars. Snouts still down in the dirt, the boars kept raking up the road, moving right toward me. They raised their heads, tested the wind, went back to grubbing. I stood still and wondered how close they would come, how close I would let them come. They kept moving and eating, becoming bigger and bigger in my field of view. The lead boar, the larger of the two at 150 to 175 pounds, raised its head a second time, snorted, then tensed and quivered like a deer before the leap. I could plainly see soil and roots dangling from the upward curling lower tusks. Its shoulders bristled into a hump, its nostrils flared for another sniff. It leapt two or three strides straight toward me before veering up the steep bank and bolting up the mountainside with amazing speed and power. The second followed, a bit slower, but still with surprising power and agility.

Although this trail passes through a predominantly second-growth forest, you will see occasional old-growth—yellow birch, yellow buckeye, eastern hemlock, Carolina silverbell—scattered among the thinner trees. The largest trees along the trail (until the yellow poplars in the cove catch up) are yellow buckeyes, a few in the 8- to 9-foot circumference range. Mature Carolina silverbell and black cherry are especially common. On average, the silverbell's peak bloom occurs sometime between late April and mid-May at this elevation. When you see the white, bell-shaped blossoms waving by the thousands all over the woods, you will know the tree.

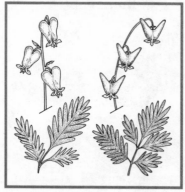

Jeffrey Hell has a good spring wildflower display. If you go early, between April 5 and April 20 when the weather is still often cold, you might see two of the most unusual wildflowers in the Southern Highlands blooming side by side in abundance. Before the taller herbaceous plants sprout and shade them, squirrel corn and Dutchman's-breeches blanket the trail's beginning north slope with dark green. These low, native perennials are closely related; they share the same genus—*Dicentra*. Both have finely divided, deeply cut, dark green leaves. And both have creamy white flowers, approximately 3/4 of an inch in height, that resemble man-made forms. Dutchman's-breeches have two inflated spurs that form the V-shaped legs of tiny pantaloons, cuffs up, waist down. The squirrel corn's shape is the Valentine's Day heart. It is so named because squirrels are fond of its yellow, kernel-like tubers.

Trout lily, wakerobin trillium, and mayapple closely follow the

squirrel corn and Dutchman's-breeches

first wave of *Dicentra* and spring beauty. By mid-May evergreen wood ferns and hay-scented ferns are particularly common.

Directions

Jeffrey Hell shares the same trailhead with Falls Branch. (See Falls Branch, the preceding trail, for directions to Rattlesnake Rock Trailhead.)

Notes

Grassy Branch Trail

Foot Trail 91: 2.3 miles

- **Dayhiking In** Easy to Moderate
- **Dayhiking Out** Moderate
- **Backpacking In** Moderate
- **Backpacking Out** Moderate to Strenuous
- **Start** Grassy Gap Trailhead, 3,420 feet
- **End** South Fork Citico Trail, 2,120 feet
- **Trail Junction** South Fork Citico
- **Topographic Quadrangles** Big Junction TN-NC, Whiteoak Flats TN-NC
- **Features** Rich, rocky slopes; low cascades; good spring wildflower display

GRASSY BRANCH—EASILY FOUND AND EASILY FOLLOWED, short and scenic, botanically rich and somewhat challenging—is an ideal first warm-up hike for the springtime.

Heading northward down a north-facing cove, this Citico Creek lead-in quickly enters the rhododendron and tramps close beside or down the middle of the beginning rivulet. After the first few tenths of a mile, the trail breaks out of the rhododendron and angles onto an open slope as the gathering stream slides out of sight down its V-notched chute. Here the path drops steadily down a rich, rocky slope. Most of the grades range from easy to moderate. The forest is mixed broadleaf-conifer, predominantly cove hardwoods with a broken line of hemlocks bordering the stream. As usual at lower to middle elevations, second-growth cove forests are dominated by tall, straight stands of yellow poplar.

The route crosses Grassy Branch at 0.9 mile—the first of eight crossings, three on Grassy Branch and five on Eagle Branch. Below the first rock-hop crossing, it closely parallels the brook. Unlike many streamside trails which have a 30-foot-wide thicket-growth of rhododendron blocking clear view, this trail is frequently right above the bank and often has little or no rhododendron screening the view. Beyond the third crossing, the treadway becomes an old railroad bed beside a long series of low cascades. Here the branch falls, sluices, and slides over, around, and between massive boulders and slabs of bedrock, 5 to 10 feet a clip.

After the third crossing, the walkway progressively steepens to a moderate downgrade as it keeps pace with the stream. This descending section affords wintertime views of a long ridgeline to the northwest—Flats Mountain. Where Grassy Branch makes its final run, the path pulls away from the water, then curls down and to the left, back to stream level. Only now the stream is Eagle Branch. Grassy Branch lost its name, on the map at least, where the two flowed together a short distance upstream from the route's first crossing of Eagle Branch at 1.6 miles.

Although it switches streams, the walking follows the same general pattern as before. It closely parallels the stream on the gradual downgrade of a railroad bed, crosses it, then parallels it again. Fast-moving Eagle Branch, a major tributary of the South Fork Citico Creek, has slightly more than double the volume of Grassy Branch. It too has big boulders, pouring sluices, and sliding spills. Nothing great you understand, just another average Southern Appalachian wilderness stream: cool air, cold water, mossy rock, soothing sound—sunsparkle white where it flies into foam, lucid green where it pools, crystal clear where it flows shallow.

With slightly more than 0.1 mile remaining, the course suddenly swerves to the left and down, crossing Eagle Branch about 40 yards from where it flows into the South Fork Citico. The rest of the route climbs the opposite bank, levels out on a slope overlooking the creek, then dips to and crosses a small, unnamed stream coming out of Clemmer Cove before dropping sharply down and to the right to its end beside South Fork Citico Creek. Grassy Branch Trail meets the South Fork Citico Trail on a bank above an upstream ford. If you want to continue upstream along the creek, you must immediately make the obvious ford. If you want to continue downstream along the creek, simply turn left and follow the wide walkway.

These branches, like all the others in the mountains, run their deepest during winter and spring before leaf-out. Drought in late spring and summer drops the water levels dramatically; exhilarating cascades become tranquil slides.

Nature Notes

Near Grassy Branch, as in similar habitats throughout the wilderness, the striped maple is common in cool, moist soils beneath a largely hardwood canopy. Well-known in New England as moosewood, this small, widespread maple is also called goosefoot where its range fingers down the mountains of the Southern Blue Ridge. This aptly named tree is easily identified even in winter by its conspicuously striped bark. The bark of a young trunk is yellowish olive green and is streaked with chalky white to pale green vertical lines. As the tree matures the lower trunk loses its distinctive coloration, but the white-on-green striping remains higher up. Small and medium-sized branches are also green lined with white.

striped maple

The striped maple is a small tree, from shrub-size to 30 or 40 feet in height. Its large, three-lobed leaves are 4 to 6 inches long and 3 to 5 inches wide. The margins are doubly saw-toothed.

Grassy Branch has a good spring wildflower display. Once the trail breaks out of the beginning rhododendron, it descends through an open fern and wildflower garden for several tenths of a mile. Sprays of two-foot-high evergreen wood fern are abundant on the rocky slope. Blooming begins in late March and early April. By mid-April you can see five species of trillium—wakerobin, large-flowered, sessile, Catesby's, and painted—some fresher than others. By late May the number of blooming wildflowers dwindles to two—foamflower and common wood sorrel, the one with the cloverlike leaves.

A member of the barberry family along with umbrella-leaf and mayapple, the blue cohosh is common beside Grassy Branch Trail. This large herbaceous perennial blooms quickly after its leaves unfold, usually from early to mid-April here. The small, inconspicuous blossoms, occurring in loosely branched clusters, are greenish purple with six petal-like sepals. The flowers are replaced later by more conspicuous clusters of blue, spherical berries. These berries (which are poisonous) are the reason for one of this plant's other names—electric light bulb plant.

blue cohosh

The blue cohosh inhabits the rich, moist woods of slopes, hollows, and coves, usually below 3,500 feet. It is easily recognized by its height, 18 to 30 inches, and its distinctively shaped leaflets.

Directions

From the Indian Boundary approach road (FS 345)–TN 165 junction on the southwestern, Tennessee side of the wilderness, travel approximately 6.0 miles on TN 165 East (Overhill Skyway) to signed Grassy Gap, then turn left onto the paved road leading downhill to the large trailhead parking area with a split-rail fence.

From the NC 143–FS 81–SR 1127 junction on the southeastern, North Carolina side of the wilderness at Santeetlah Gap, travel NC 143 West (Cherohala Skyway) and TN 165 West a little less than 21.5 miles to the Grassy Gap sign and paved right turn to the trailhead. The Grassy Branch Trailhead is approximately 3.5 miles beyond NC-TN state line at Beech Gap, where NC 143 West ends and TN 165 West begins.

(See page 26 for directions and mileages to the TN 165–FS 345 intersection and the NC 143–FS 81–SR 1127 intersection.)

Flats Mountain Trail

Foot Trail 102: 6.0 miles

- **Dayhiking (low to high)** Moderate
- **Dayhiking (high to low)** Easy to Moderate
- **Backpacking (low to high)** Moderate
- **Backpacking (high to low)** Easy to Moderate
- **Vehicular Access At Either End** Northern (low elevation) terminus on FS 35-1 at Beehouse Gap, 1,960 feet; southern (high elevation) terminus off TN 165 at Eagle Gap, 3,680 feet
- **Trail Junctions** None
- **Topographic Quadrangles** Big Junction TN-NC, Whiteoak Flats TN-NC
- **Features** Good winter views and rock outcrop overlook; late spring flowering shrub display

FLATS MOUNTAIN IS THE ONLY PERIMETER TRAIL in Tennessee's portion of the combined wilderness. But unlike the wilderness-edge trails on the North Carolina side, Flats Mountain Trail runs atop a much larger, earth-made perimeter: the edge of the Blue Ridge Mountains. The wide, mesalike ridgecrest of Flats Mountain is the western escarpment of the Blue Ridge physiographic province. To the west and northwest the land drops away dramatically, 2,000 feet in just over a mile. And that's the end of the mountains, the high ridges that ripple one after the other, to the west. There are no more.

The area around Indian Boundary Lake, down the western slope of Flats Mountain, was once known as Whiteoak Flats; the nearest town to the west is Tellico Plains. Due west the land does not again reach the elevation of Flats Mountain—an unimpressive 3,880 feet by Southern Highland standards—until it rises toward the Rockies near the Oklahoma–New Mexico border.

Flats Mountain is different from every other trail in this guide in yet another way: it skirts two wildlife openings within its first mile, walked south to north. (I saw a striped skunk in the second opening during my first hike of this trail in mid-April.) The Forest Service will continue to maintain these two openings, which are just outside the wilderness boundary. Backpackers will be allowed to camp in these clearings under the following conditions: no fires in the openings and only one group per night. If these man-made meadows are abused, they will no doubt be posted in the future. The gate barring the trail and wildlife openings from vehicular access remains closed year-round.

This trail is described as it is most often hiked, from high to low, from south to north. Walked this way, it has only one sharp downgrade and only one upgrade more difficult than easy. Walked this way, Flats Mountain joins the beginning 8.0 miles of Slickrock Creek and the lowermost 7.0 miles of South Fork Citico as the three easiest long stretches of trail described in this book.

From the gate where the trail starts, the old road rises easily to the exact ridgetop of Flats Mountain. The forest is predominantly hardwood with pitch and white pine and a few hemlock mixed in with the short, low-branching oaks. Soon-to-die chestnut saplings, some 20 to 30 feet tall, are common. Following the northward curve of the ridgecrest, at 0.3 mile the route turns 90 degrees to the right after entering the first grassy clearing. After the turn, the treadway gently undulates with the wide mountaintop for 0.3 mile to the second opening. Along the way there are good winter views of Strawberry Knob, Bob Stratton Bald, and Rockstack to the east.

In spring these wildlife openings are good birding areas. On my second walk through, in late May, I saw some of the mountain's most colorful birds—indigo bunting; scarlet tanager; rose-breasted grosbeak; rufous-sided towhee; great crested flycatcher; and black-and-white, Canada, and chestnut-sided warblers.

The trail turns to path beyond the second opening. At 0.8 mile a side path, just before a rocky high point, leads a short distance to a rock outcrop overlook open to the west. This is the edge of the western escarpment; the precipitous drop begins at your feet. Down below, where the steep slope stops, you will see Indian Boundary Lake and low, forested hills flecked with logging cuts. To the west and northwest across the lake, a patchwork quilt of farms, forests, towns, and big lakes fades into the haze. They are all part of the Ridge and Valley province, which lies in a band between the Blue Ridge and the Cumberland Plateau.

A few yards beyond the side path, the trail tops a slight knob. This knob and the second opening are the high points of the mountain, both about 3,880 feet. A short distance beyond the knob, the track bends sharply back to the left off the ridge onto upper slope, then switchbacks to the right and continues in the same direction of travel. Here the walking begins a pattern that lasts until it reaches a prominent gap at mile 3.2. Each time the ridge rises or dips, the treadway curls backward onto the sunset side of the mountain, switchbacks, and levels out the grade—a trail builder's version of locks. Only once, where it drops down and half-circles a hollow or two, does the treadway remain off the ridge for very long.

Continuing to the northeast from the gap (3,180 feet), the route makes its first climb worth mentioning, moderate at the start, then easier, to the top of a low knob before beginning its first steep descent. Along the way, there are more winter and through-the-pines views of the ridgeline string of knobs and peaks—collectively known as the stacks—to the east. Pockets of pitch and Table Mountain pine become more extensive. The long downgrade, only a short distance of it steep, follows the much narrowed crest to mile 3.9, where the footpath curls sharply off the ridge to the right (the southeastern side) for the first time. After this turn you can see Bob Stratton Bald, Haoe, and Hangover—this area's high lonesome—through gaps in the pines. The treadway continues to lose elevation, winding gently down the piney slope on long, looping switchbacks, into, then back out of, the wilderness.

At mile 4.4 the track crosses over a Flats Mountain spur, the first of many fingering toward Citico Creek. From here the remainder of the route is easy walking as it follows the familiar pattern of lower-slope trail. It tops a spur, continues on the slope, winds above or half-circles around the head of a hollow or two, then follows the slope to the next spur. All this winding over spurs and around hollows means the trailside forest is almost constantly changing exposure. This, in turn, means the forest is almost constantly changing composition, sometimes changing from maidenhair fern and striped maple to galax and pitch pine and back again, within two minutes walk. Near its end Flats Mountain Trail follows a low ridge that leads to the road at Beehouse Gap.

Most of the final 1.5 miles are entirely outside the wilderness. As of now, however, the Forest Service has no plans to cut in the trail corridor.

There is no water on or near this entire trail.

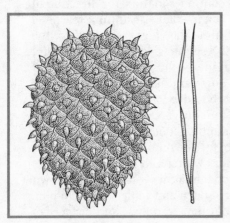

Table Mountain pine

Nature Notes

Except where it heads around hollows, Flats Mountain passes through a forest that is predominantly second-growth oak-pine. The canopy becomes increasingly piney as the trail progresses from south to north, from higher and wetter to lower and drier. But even near its northern end, where the pitch pine is often the dominant tree, you will notice that the pines are not reseeding themselves in the understory. And you will notice the abundance of oak saplings growing beneath the maturing pines. The major reason for this change, this succession, is shade tolerance. Most pines are what foresters call intolerant; they cannot tolerate heavy shade, even the heavy shade from their own kind. The oaks are more tolerant of shade than the pines. Thus if rainfall remains normal, and there is neither logging nor fire, this forest will slowly, but perceptibly from decade to decade, succeed to hardwood. This change is the typical succession following fire or logging, in this case both, in the drier range of the oak-pine forest. (The exception, and there almost always is one, to the pine-to-oak succession is the white pine, which is tolerant enough to come in beneath the oaks.)

The Table Mountain pine, more common along this trail than along any other in this guide, is a minor component of the Southern

Appalachian oak-pine forest. Also known as mountain pine, this conifer grows on dry, rocky slopes and ridges, usually between 2,500 to
4,000 feet of elevation in the wilderness. The Table Mountain's
trademark is its cone; there is no mistaking its look or feel. These
abundant cones, which often persist for years on the tree, are 2½ to
3½ inches long and usually occur in whorls of three or four around
the branch. They have a lopsided base and are thickly spined with
stout, upwardly curving spurs. If a branch were to end at a whorl of
cones, it would resemble a macelike weapon. Its dark bluish green
needles are 1½ to 3 inches long
and occur in stiff, twisted bun-
dles of two.

This small tree, the only
pine restricted to the Appalachian Mountains, is usually only
25 to 40 feet in height and 1 to
2 feet in diameter. Its poor form
is often picturesque. The trunks
are often crooked or leaning; the
thick branches are frequently
gnarled and low to the ground.

Because this trail remains
on dry ridges and slopes for the
most part, it has a relatively
poor spring wildflower display.
But this lack is more than made
up for from mid-May through

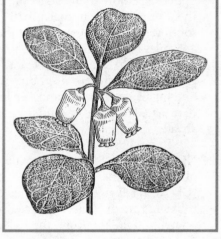

teaberry

early June, when the heath shrubs—first the flame azalea and then
the mountain laurel—flower in colorful clumps.

Conspicuous beds of teaberry, another heath sometimes called
wintergreen, are common beside Flats Mountain Trail. This tiny shrub
—6 to 7 inches tall at most, usually no more than 4 or 5 inches—is
frequently found in the dry, acidic soils of oak-pine ridges. The
teaberry is a creeper; it grows horizontally. The main stem remains
hidden under the leaf litter. What you see above the forest floor are the
vertical branches.

The evergreen leaves of teaberry, leathery and shiny, range from
1 to 2 inches long, usually closer to 1 than 2. Occurring nearly on the

same plane, the small rounded leaves give off a strong wintergreen fragrance when split or crushed. Before the days of synthetics, teaberry leaves were a source of wintergreen flavoring.

The white, waxy, bell-shaped blossoms dangle singly or in groups of two or three beneath the leaves. The 1/3-inch-long flowers bloom from mid- to late June through early August.

Directions

Flats Mountain has either-end vehicular access. Its southern, upper-elevation trailhead is off TN 165 at Eagle Gap. From the Indian Boundary approach road (FS 345)–TN 165 junction on the southwestern, Tennessee side of the wilderness, travel approximately 4.7 miles on TN 165 East (Overhill Skyway), then turn left onto a paved road that leads up and away from the highway to the trailhead parking area. The paved left turn is usually marked with two signs— one for Eagle Gap and another for foot trail #102. The trail is the road, gated 80 yards beyond the parking area, that continues straight ahead.

To reach this trail's southern, upper-elevation trailhead from the NC 143–FS 81–SR 1127 junction on the southeastern, North Carolina side of the wilderness at Santeetlah Gap, travel NC 143 West (Cherohala Skyway) and TN 165 West for slightly over 22.5 miles to the right turn at Eagle Gap. The Flats Mountain Trailhead is approximately 5.0 miles beyond the NC-TN state line at Beech Gap, where NC 143 becomes TN 165.

To reach the northern, lower-elevation trailhead at Beehouse Gap, turn northeast (left if you are traveling TN 165 East from Tellico Plains) from TN 165 onto the paved Indian Boundary approach road, FS 345. Continue on FS 345 for approximately 1.2 miles to the four-way intersection at the Indian Boundary Recreation Area entrance, marked by a large sign. Turn right onto FS 35-1 (Citico Road, FS 35-1 on the wilderness map, FS 35 on the road sign) and proceed on this dirt-gravel road for approximately 1.5 miles to the gravel trailhead parking area, which is to the left across the road from the trail. The trailhead is usually marked with two signs—one for Beehouse Gap and another for foot trail #102.

(See page 26 for directions and mileages to the TN 165–FS 345 intersection and the NC 143–FS 81–SR 1127 intersection.)

The clearest way into the Universe is through a forest wilderness.

John Muir (1890)
quoted in John Muir, John of the Wilderness *(1938)*
L.M. Wolfe, editor

In God's wildness lies the hope of the world—the great fresh unblighted, unredeemed wilderness.

John Muir
Alaska Fragment *(1840)*

Citico Creek Trailheads

South Fork Citico Creek

Trails

South Fork Citico
North Fork Citico
Brush Mountain
Pine Ridge

Citico Creek Trailheads
Directions and Map

BOTH OF THIS SECTION'S TRAILS that have vehicular access—South Fork Citico and Pine Ridge—begin off FS 35-1 (Citico Road).

From the TN 165 (Overhill Skyway)–FS 345 junction, turn onto the paved, prominently signed, Indian Boundary approach road, FS 345. If you are traveling TN 165 East, the turn onto FS 345 will be to the left. Continue on FS 345 for approximately 1.2 miles to the four-way intersection at the Indian Boundary Recreation Area entrance, marked by a large sign. Turn right onto FS 35-1 (FS 35-1 on the wilderness map, FS 35 on the road sign) and proceed.

Forest Service 35-1 is a good dirt-gravel road, wide and level. It remains open throughout the winter except after heavy snows or ice storms. For more information concerning road conditions and possible closings, call Cherokee National Forest's Tellico Ranger District.

(See page 26 for directions and mileages to the TN 165–FS 345 intersection.)

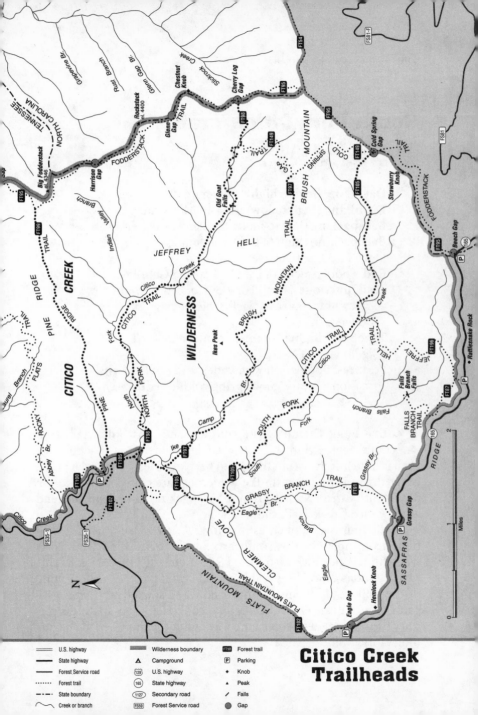

Citico Creek
Trailheads

═══ U.S. highway	▬▬▬ Wilderness boundary	**FT19** Forest trail
─── State highway	▲ Campground	**P** Parking
─── Forest Service road	129 U.S. highway	◆ Knob
······ Forest trail	165 State highway	▲ Peak
─·─ State boundary	1127 Secondary road	╱ Falls
∿∿ Creek or branch	FS59 Forest Service road	● Gap

South Fork Citico Trail

Foot Trail 105: 8.0 miles

- **Dayhiking (low to high)** Moderate
- **Dayhiking (high to low)** Easy to Moderate
- **Backpacking (low to high)** Moderate to Strenuous
- **Backpacking (high to low)** Moderate
- **Start** FS 35-1, 1,700 feet
- **End** Fodderstack Trail at Cold Spring Gap, 4,420 feet
- **Trail Junctions** North Fork Citico, Brush Mountain, Grassy Branch, Jeffrey Hell, Cold Spring Gap, Fodderstack
- **Topographic Quadrangles** Whiteoak Flats TN-NC, Big Junction TN-NC
- **Features** Boulders, low cascades, and pools; occasional bluffs; good spring wildflower display

SOUTH FORK CITICO IS THE LONGEST and most important trail completely within the Citico Creek Wilderness. (Fodderstack Trail is not entirely within the Citico Creek Wilderness.) Seven of the other thirteen trails within the wilderness are closely linked to the South Fork Citico. Numerous long backpacking loops begin and end at the Citico Creek Trailhead.

This trail is described as it is most often walked, from low to high, from northwest to southeast. South Fork Citico Trail starts where the single-track road from FS 35-1 ends at a turnaround. This turnaround is a local beer drinking and parking spot. The beginning of the trail would be much improved if the single-track road were gated at its entrance, grassed in, then converted to footpath. As it is now, the road invites people, one way or another, to trash the beginning of the trail.

After passing through a former wildlife opening that has reverted to forest, the treadway angles down to the old railroad bed beside the creek at 0.4 mile. The railroad grade was used as a road until wilderness designation. The wide walkway parallels South Fork Citico Creek, alternating between bankside and out of sight of the stream. The first time it pulls away from the shoaling water, the track passes through a rich, rocky area that has a good wildflower display from late March through mid-April.

At 0.7 mile, a few yards beyond the roofless remains of a concrete building to the right, the lower-elevation end of the North Fork Citico Trail angles to the left and quickly crosses a bridge over the South Fork just above its confluence with the North Fork. (The view from the bridge is more than worth the very short walk.) That concrete building and the foundations scattered along the beginning of this trail mark the site of a former community, basically a logging camp, that was named Jeffrey. As far as I know, the story of Jeffrey Hell predates the tiny settlement.

While camping near the Citico Creek Wilderness, I met a minister who was born in the concrete building, the camp commissary and powder magazine, in 1923. He told me that single men lived in wooden bunkhouses resembling small army barracks. Married people, like his mom and dad, had it good; they had the privacy of a railroad car all to themselves and their children. He also said that the idea for the mobile home came from the various temporary communities—logging, mining, bridge- and railroad-building camps—where many people once lived in railroad cars.

Beyond its junction with the North Fork Citico, the route continues to the south, following the creek into the wilderness. Here the South Fork is a typically beautiful stream—swift and white where it cascades through boulder jumbles or slides over swirlhole ledges, slow and green where it eddies into small catch pools between runs. The trail arrives at its second junction 0.4 mile past its first. (See Brush Mountain, also in this section, for more information.)

The walking, level or easy up and usually fairly close to the creek, proceeds upstream under the canopy of a second-growth forest. The trees are predominantly hardwoods and hemlock, with an occasional white pine. The one-two punch of cut-everything logging and fire didn't leave a single old-growth bole for miles up the South Fork.

Where the bank pinches in at mile 1.9, you reach an obvious ford, the first of three usually shallow, wet-feet fords along the lower creek. The third ford is 0.3 mile beyond the first. Immediately before this ford Grassy Branch Trail, the path that drops down to the bank from the right, ties into the South Fork Citico.

The easy walking continues as the railroad-bed trail swings to the southeast after the third ford. Boulders, low cascades, and pools remain a common sight. Where the rocks are small, the stream is often wide and shallow and shiny in the sun. But even where shallow, its clarity—like wilderness rivers out West—gives the water the illusion of being shallower than it really is. The opposite bank has occasional small bluffs. The highest, broken and full of vegetation in the cracks, rises 60 or 70 feet above the South Fork.

At mile 3.1, where the railroad once crossed the stream, the treadway turns to the left onto path, up and away from the creek. This grade, the first worth mentioning, climbs a slaty spur for 0.1 mile, angles to the right into a ravine, then quickly crosses a rivulet. After crossing the rivulet, the footpath ascends a dry slope to mile 3.5, where it meets an old road—a horse cut. (See North Fork Citico, the following trail, for an explanation of the cut.)

Many people, especially those fishing the creek, proceed straight up the stream where the trail turns away from it. This is both good and bad. The good is solitude; the bad is briers. Because it is infrequently walked, the segment high above the South Fork tends to become briery in a few spots. The Forest Service brushes out the trail periodically, but the briers always come back. If you wear long pants and carry a creek-fording, brier-bashing hiking stick, you should have no problem.

Remaining level or slightly uphill, the old road winds to the southeast on a sunny, south-facing slope. The cut is occasionally 35 to 40 feet high where it was blasted through rock. The route often snakes back and forth, dodging rocks and trees in the bed. At mile 4.0 you reach a step-over rivulet. As it draws near the South Fork, the track passes above a series of cascades; the most conspicuous one, 10 feet high and 15 feet long, pours over a bank-to-bank ledge. The walking finally comes back to creek level at mile 5.1.

The trail parallels the stream again beyond the horse cut. Now the rhododendron is denser and the treadway stays slightly farther away from the creek. You will hear more cascades than you will see. The fork to the right at mile 5.7 is the end of Jeffrey Hell Trail. Above this connection the South Fork is narrow, more mossy boulder and rosebay rhododendron than water. At mile 6.5 the route rock-steps what's left of the stream, then follows the gentle grade of the former railroad onto a moist, north-facing slope.

After it breaks out of the heath thicket, the walkway enters a second-growth forest where the trees, especially the yellow poplar and black cherry, are much larger than those along the lower end of the creek. Farther up, past a seepage area of headwater springs, the track angles to the right onto path at mile 7.4. Here the trail's only tough ascent begins. The final grunt to its upper-elevation end at Cold Spring Gap, strenuous pulls mixed with respites, gains 600 feet in the last 0.6 mile. And it really doesn't start to climb until almost 0.2 mile past the turn onto path. This ending pitch raised the South Fork Citico's difficulty rating a notch. Before its last mile, which gains approximately 800 feet, this trail's first 7.0 miles average an easy 275 feet of elevation gain per mile—a 5 percent grade.

The forest beside the final 0.4 mile has some old-growth yellow birch, yellow buckeye, and hemlock. The same area has a good wildflower display during late April and early May.

South Fork Citico Creek is the second largest stream in the combined wilderness. It is wide enough, often 20 to 45 feet at its lower end, and deep enough for the usual paradox to apply. When the creek is at its exhilarating best, running full and fast, the fords are at their worst. At normal or slightly above normal water levels, the fords should pose no problem. However, after heavy rain in the right season, primarily winter and spring, the wide lower fords can become dangerous when the water is up and running. During periods of drought, these same fords can be crossed dry-shod.

Nature Notes

The yellow birch, common beside this and many other trails in this guide, is classified as a northern hardwood. Its north-south range runs from southeastern Canada all the way down to northern-most Georgia. Like the many other trees that require a cool, moist habitat, the yellow birch enters the South only within the narrow corridor of the mountains. And within this restricted range, it seeks the coolest, moistest conditions—streamsides at low elevations, north-facing slopes at middle elevations, and upper slopes and ridges at high elevations.

The peeling bark of the yellow birch identifies it from sapling size to maturity. The bark, yellowish silver to yellowish bronze, curls

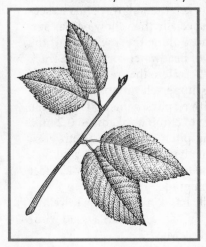

yellow birch

into long, vertical strips. No other tree above 2,000 feet in the Southern Blue Ridge has similar bark. Maturing yellow birches, those over the century mark, lose their youthful, curling hide except on their upper branches. The papery, thin-layered bark is flammable even when wet.

The leaves of the yellow birch, paired at the end of short branchlets, turn bright yellow in autumn. The cracked twigs are aromatic with the scent of wintergreen, though not as strong as those of the sweet birch.

Yellow birch seedlings often germinate on mossy logs. If the fallen log is moist enough, the seedling continues to grow, sending strad-dling roots downward over the log. Eventually, its "nurse log" decays, leaving the tree, like a rider without a horse, propped up on the stilts of its own roots.

Directions

South Fork Citico no longer has either-end vehicular access. Its only trailhead is now at its lower-elevation, northwestern end off FS 35-1.

From the FS 345–FS 35-1 junction at the entrance to the Indian Boundary Recreation Area, turn right onto FS 35-1 and proceed on this dirt-gravel road for approximately 2.3 miles to the entrance of a single-track dirt road leading uphill to the right. A carsonite trail sign usually marks the entrance of this road. South Fork Citico Trail begins where the narrow road ends at a turnaround after slightly more than 0.1 mile.

The turnaround area at the end of the road is trashy and probably a bad place to leave your vehicle. You may want to park out at the entrance along FS 35-1 (very limited). Or you may want to continue a little more than 0.1 mile further on FS 35-1, turn right onto the road (FS 29 on the wilderness map) that crosses Citico Creek on a low, concrete bridge and park in campsite #13. (See the beginning of this trailhead section, page 165, for directions to the FS 345–FS 35-1 intersection.)

To reach South Fork Citico's southeastern, upper-elevation end, start at Fodderstack Trail's upper-elevation, southern end at Beech Gap. Walk the 1.8 very easy miles on Fodderstack to the former trailhead at Cold Spring Gap. Fodderstack continues up and to the right; Cold Spring Gap Trail leads straight ahead from the gap, and South Fork Citico leads downhill to the left. (See Fodderstack, page 132, in the Sassafras Ridge Trailheads section for directions to Beech Gap.)

Notes

North Fork Citico Trail

Foot Trail 98: 5.4 miles

- **Dayhiking (low to high)** Moderate
- **Dayhiking (high to low)** Easy to Moderate
- **Backpacking (low to high)** Moderate to Strenuous
- **Backpacking (high to low)** Moderate
- **Interior Trail** Western (low elevation) terminus on South Fork Citico Trail, 1,800 feet; eastern (high elevation) terminus on Fodderstack Trail at Cherry Log Gap, 4,420 feet
- **Trail Junctions** South Fork Citico, Cold Spring Gap, Fodderstack
- **Topographic Quadrangle** Whiteoak Flats TN-NC
- **Features** Boulders, swirlholes, and low cascades; Old Goat Falls

LIGHTLY USED, ESPECIALLY ON ITS ROUGH UPPER REACHES, this trail follows North Fork Citico Creek from its exact end all the way to and beyond its beginning spring. The first 3 miles are a railroad bed cakewalk, albeit a rocky and wet one, level or easy up. This section frequently is very close to the creek's sluices, slides, swirlholes, and low cascades; very close to the pools, dining-room–sized boulders, occasional small bluffs on the north bank and wilderness water— cold, clear where it shallows and lucid green where it deepens.

Despite the fact that its first 3.0 miles are easy walking, this trail still manages to gain 2,620 feet of elevation. That should tell you something about its final 2.4 miles. The trail earns its difficulty ratings on this stretch. Rising nearly 1,000 feet, the last mile steadily ascends, the hard grades ranging from moderate to strenuous.

This trail is described the way it is most often walked, from low to high, from bridge to gap. After crossing the bridge over South

Fork Citico Creek at its confluence with North Fork Citico Creek, the route enters the wilderness and quickly parallels the North Fork on the long aisle of a former railroad bed. The low dam is an old TVA water gauging station. At 0.4 mile the wide walkway fords the stream, the first of seven obvious fords before Old Goat Falls, then fords again 0.1 mile farther up.

The treadway continues close beside the creek at the bottom of its V-shaped valley—the shape geographers classify as a "youthful valley." Here the forest is tall, straight, second-growth, predominantly hardwoods and hemlock. Sweetgum and sycamore, both low-elevation species in the southern mountains, are fairly common along the trail until it rises above their upper elevation limits.

The third ford comes at mile 1.4; the fourth, 0.1 mile farther. Three-tenths mile beyond the fourth ford, a short distance after the route skirts the rocky bank, a side path leads a few paces to a small variable waterfall. On the far bank of the North Fork, a rivulet tributary slides down rock face before free-falling the last few of its 15 feet.

This waterfall, like thousands of others in the Southern Appalachians, was created by differing rates of erosion. Main streams cut down into their beds faster than tributaries erode theirs. Over time, the difference leaves the tributaries hanging above the main stream. This phenomenon explains why so many waterfalls and cascades occur at or near a tributary's end. Out West where this geological pattern is much more pronounced, the valleys of these tributaries are called hanging side canyons.

The trail changes beyond the sixth ford at mile 2.9. Here the walking, now alternating path with railroad grade, is rockier, steeper (easy to moderate at first), and often farther up and away from the creek. At mile 3.3 the treadway turns abruptly to the left, rises sharply for a short distance, then proceeds on a horse cut. Where the streamside terrain was particularly rugged—all steep slopes and boulder jumbles—the loggers built the railroad up on trestle. And where they built the trestle, they also had to build a road so the horses could walk around the trestled section of track.

Continuing from the horse cut, the route quickly works its way back to creek level, where it winds through a particularly rocky area on path. The stream turkey-tails into three rocky channels at mile 3.5.

The one straight ahead and to the left is a tributary branch; the two on the right are braids of the North Fork. The trail crosses the tributary a few feet below a big boulder, then climbs up the middle ground between a bigger boulder to the left and the upstream braid to the right.

After crossing the side branch, the footpath rises through a changing forest, a cooler, moister forest of larger trees. The sweetgum and sycamore are gone. The second-growth yellow poplars are noticeably larger. Black cherry, Carolina silverbell, basswood, Fraser magnolia, and yellow buckeye are all larger and more common than they were a few miles back. The red maple, plentiful along the lower stretches of the North Fork, gradually becomes less common as the sugar maple increases in number.

Past the long trough of a steep-walled cascade and beyond a house-sized rock outcrop, you finally reach, at mile 4.0, a ledge the creek hasn't cut through. Not yet anyway. A short scramble leads to the base of a waterfall—Old Goat Falls.

What is there to say about Old Goat Falls? It isn't particularly high or powerful, but its double-ledge drop, ricocheting from rock to rock, squirming out of sight in the middle, is beautiful nevertheless. And it has a wonderful, 15-foot watchtower crag, narrow and cleft into two identical faces, standing upright, ready to fall. And it's lit and alive with sunsparkle.

Beyond the falls the trail, repeatedly crossing the branch-sized stream, works its way up what's left of the watershed. These crossings, or rather the original crossings, are not always obvious. Horse riders coming from Fodderstack and Cold Spring Gap Trails use the upper North Fork Citico Trail, and they cross where it's most suitable for the horses. This should become less of a problem now that Cold Spring Gap has been designated for foot travel only.

At mile 4.6 the path crosses the stream 5 feet back from the brink of a 20-foot falls. The ribbon of water slides, then free-falls, over the solid wall of a scarcely eroded ledge. If the trail hasn't been rerouted farther up through the rhododendron, this crossing is potentially dangerous, especially for kids who are running ahead.

Two-tenths mile and one crossing beyond the second falls, you will come to the Cold Spring Gap Trail junction on the right (south) side of the stream. The opening, more than 90 degrees back to the right, is 20 to 25 yards past where the North Fork Citico Trail skirts in and alongside the stream. From this junction the path crosses what's left of the creek one last time, stays left or straight at the fork (the right fork is an old route), then follows a rocky and usually flowing headwater rivulet flanked by rhododendron. The final 0.3 mile climbs progressively harder up the broad V of the uppermost cove through an open forest of mature trees. The route reaches its upper-elevation end and junction with Fodderstack Trail at Cherry Log Gap.

North Fork Citico Creek is the third largest stream in the combined wilderness. At normal or slightly above normal water levels, the fords on this creek should pose no problem. However, after heavy rain in the right season, primarily winter and spring, the lower fords can become dangerous. During periods of drought the upper fords to Old Goat Falls can become rock-hop crossings.

Nature Notes

The forest along the last mile of this trail, like much of the high-elevation forest in the southeastern corner of the Citico Creek Wilderness, was selectively cut rather than clear-cut. This type of forest defies easy categorization. It is neither second-growth nor old-growth. It has occasional old-growth trees, numerous trees approaching maturity, and a diversity of bole shapes, sizes, and textures. Many of the largest trees—yellow birch, hemlock, and yellow buckeye—were commercially undesirable during the logging days. Today some of them have girths of 9 to 11 feet. Most of the mature black cherry and sugar maple in the uppermost cove, too thin for cutting in the early 1920s, are now 90 to 130 years old.

The red maple, abundant along North Fork Citico Creek and common to abundant along every other trail in the wilderness, is the most numerous and widespread tree in eastern North America. Its north-south range—from Newfoundland to southern Florida—is the greatest of any tree in the eastern forest. It grows westward to the Great Plains; nearly everywhere trees grow east of the Mississippi, there are red maples. In the South, it ranges in elevation from sea level to slightly over 6,000 feet in the high mountains. Because of its incredible adaptability, the red maple is also the most widespread tree species in the wilderness, occurring at all elevations and in nearly every habitat. Below 4,500 feet, it is seldom out of sight.

This broadleaf is easily identified, often from a distance, throughout much of the year. In late winter and early spring, its numerous red flowers appear before the leaves break bud. The red blush of its blooms sweeps up to the high slopes from early to mid-April. Where these trees are dense and sunlit, the color is almost as dazzling as in fall.

The foliage of this maple is usually readily identifiable, even

red maple

though the leaves vary somewhat in size and shape. The opposite leaves, which have three prominent, short-pointed lobes and coarsely toothed margins (the sugar maple has a smooth margin), are most often $2^{1}/_{2}$ to $5^{1}/_{2}$ inches long and nearly as wide. There are often two more small lobes (for a total of five) near the base. The leaves turn bright red in fall. Twigs, fruit, and leafstalks are also red.

Like other trees that inhabit a wide range of sites, the red maple's size depends upon where it is rooted. On dry, thin-soiled ridges, where many hardwoods don't grow at all, the red maple remains a

stunted understory tree beneath the pitch pines. But in coves and along stream corridors, where its growth is best, the red maple is a canopy tree, tall and straight. In good habitat many second-growth trees are already 70 to 90 feet in height and 2 to 3 feet in diameter. The maximum size for a Southern Appalachian red maple is approximately 120 feet in height and 5 feet in diameter.

North Fork Citico has a fair spring wildflower display. Pink lady's-slipper, lousewort, showy orchis, and crested dwarf iris, among others, bloom from early April through early May.

If you walk North Fork Citico Creek, or any of the other streamside trails in the wilderness, from mid-April through mid-July, you will probably hear an emphatic squeak-it—the two-noted song of the Acadian flycatcher. The second syllable, the it, is higher in pitch and inflection. The Acadian is small, 5$^{1}/_{2}$ inches long, and well camouflaged with an olive-green back. Unless you are patient and make the effort, you probably won't see this secretive bird, but you won't mistake its comical, squeeze-toy song.

Directions

North Fork Citico is an interior trail that has its western (low elevation) end on South Fork Citico Trail and its eastern (high elevation) end on Fodderstack Trail. To reach North Fork Citico Trail's western end, walk 0.7 mile on the South Fork Citico starting from that trail's northwestern (low elevation) trailhead. Twenty yards beyond the ruins of a large cement building (to the right of the South Fork Citico Trail), angle to the left onto another old road where South Fork Citico Trail turns to the right and rises. This left fork, which quickly crosses a bridge over South Fork Citico Creek, is North Fork Citico Trail. (See South Fork Citico, the preceding trail, for more information.)

To reach North Fork Citico Trail's eastern end, walk 4.0 miles on the Fodderstack starting from that trail's southern (high elevation) end at Beech Gap. Turn left (west) onto North Fork Citico Trail at Cherry Log Gap. Because Cherry Log is not a well-defined gap, this junction may be difficult to find. Three-tenths mile before the junction, there is a flat, rhododendron-flanked campsite to the right. The North Fork Citico Trail junction is to the left opposite another campsite. (See Fodderstack, page 132, in the Sassafras Ridge Trailheads section for more information.)

Notes

Brush Mountain Trail

Foot Trail 97: 4.4 miles

- **Dayhiking (low to high)** Moderate to Strenuous
- **Dayhiking (high to low)** Moderate
- **Backpacking (low to high)** Strenuous
- **Backpacking (high to low)** Moderate
- **Interior Trail** Northwestern (low elevation) terminus on South Fork Citico Trail, 1,880 feet; southeastern (high elevation) terminus on Cold Spring Gap Trail, 4,360 feet
- **Trail Junctions** South Fork Citico, Cold Spring Gap
- **Topographic Quadrangles** Whiteoak Flats TN-NC, Big Junction TN-NC
- **Features** Winter views of Sassafras Ridge and Pine Ridge; Ike Camp Branch

---

BRUSH MOUNTAIN IS A TRAIL WITH CHARACTER—one to remember, should you ever hike it. This primitive path, which traverses the big woods of Jeffrey Hell country, is the least traveled in the combined wilderness. I walked it twice during the spring, and the only tracks I saw, other than those of boar, bear, deer, and turkey, were my own from the previous time. When you walk it by yourself, the isolation is deep enough to induce the "what ifs." What if this happens, what if that happens, what if…thoughts essential to wilderness.

This trail could use a few more feet to help the Forest Service keep it open. But I hope it doesn't become new and improved. I hope it remains just like it is—ungraded, rocky, wet, often narrow and sometimes hard to follow, even with the cut-bark blazes.

Brush Mountain is described as it is occasionally walked, from low to high, from northwest to southeast. The trail begins by fording South Fork Citico Creek. Once across, it quickly turns left, rises, then swings onto the railroad grade that parallels Ike Camp Branch. From here the track follows the branch—a lively, cascading brook when there's water—upstream to the southeast. The route crosses Ike Camp Branch, the first of five times, at 0.4 mile.

From the first dry-shod crossing to the fifth at mile 1.6, the treadway roughly parallels the branch as it rises up its valley. Here the walking, often rocky or muddy or both, alternates between former railroad and narrow path, between bank level and slope out of sight of the stream. The grades are predominantly easy or easy to moderate to mile 1.3, where they become moderate until the fifth crossing. Upper Ike Camp Branch is a small, spilling stream occasionally flanked with large boulders. Like most watercourses in the combined wilderness, it has quartzite boulders in its bed.

The primarily deciduous forest beside the branch is surprisingly open for second-growth. The trees—hemlock, northern red oak, basswood, black cherry, white ash, witch-hazel, red maple, yellow poplar, yellow and sweet birch—are typical of streamside Southern Appalachia below 3,000 feet. As always, species composition changes with elevation. Yellow buckeye, sugar maple, and Carolina silverbell, which need a cool, moist habitat to compete for the canopy, do not become substantial trees until the trail climbs nearly 1,000 feet up the watershed.

Beyond the fifth crossing, Brush Mountain steps over the shallow northeast fork of Ike Camp Branch, then slogs straight up a washed-out railroad bed. The railroad bed is eroded because it was built, where suitable, above the stream bed. Today, these two beds and the trail are often the same. This 0.4-mile stretch, a steady easy or easy-to-moderate upgrade, is the wettest, rockiest piece of trail in the entire wilderness. It is particularly fun to walk in the spring right after a heavy rainfall.

Finished with its roughest footing, the path narrows and ascends sharply to a slight gap (3,580 feet) at mile 2.2. This gap is on the ridge between Ikes Peak (3,800 feet), which is to the left (northwest), and a Brush Mountain spur. Beyond this first gap the route becomes unpredictable—it often goes where you think it won't or shouldn't.

The 0.5 mile from the first gap to the second gap pinballs through the woods. After turning 90 degrees to the right (southeast) at the first gap, the treadway rises with the ridge, slants down off the ridge to the left, descends to and crosses the head of a hollow, then climbs up and over another ridge. Next it drops steeply to and crosses a boar-wallowed seepage area and climbs progressively harder past the high point of a knob before gently dipping to the second gap at mile 2.7.

The remainder of the trail stays on the upper slopes or the winding, broken crest of Brush Mountain—a western spur off the ridge that runs across Bob Stratton Bald. Although it follows a general pattern, the route still occasionally dives off the mountaintop where you least expect it. The path usually leaves the ridge onto the northern slope to the left. The final 1.7 miles have numerous short, steep grades.

Brush Mountain Trail passes through a prominent gap with tall yellow poplars at mile 3.1, then angles onto the northern slope (logging road at first) and gradually rises 0.3 mile to the next gap. Starting at mile 3.6, the deep-forest footpath follows the narrow, rocky ridgecrest (winter views of Sassafras Ridge to the south and Pine Ridge to the north) for 0.1 mile before dropping off to the left. Following a short, strenuous pitch, the treadway turns 90 degrees to the right (where it once continued straight ahead) with 0.1 mile remaining. Brush Mountain's high-elevation end ties into Cold Spring Gap Trail, a former road.

Nature Notes

The ridge and slope section of this trail ranges through a predominantly second-growth hardwood forest with surprisingly few oaks. The timber along the last mile of the path was being selectively cut for valuable species when the Citico Creek fire stopped operations in 1925. As a result, there are many old-growth trees from 4,000 to 4,400 feet. Given time, the loggers would have cut the commercially valuable sugar maple. The hemlock, yellow buckeye, Carolina silverbell, and poor-form yellow birch were spared because they weren't worth the trouble. The thickest Carolina silverbell beside the trails in this guide—8 feet 6 inches in circumference—stands near the treadway at mile 3.8.

The witch-hazel, an understory tree usually 10 to 30 feet high, is common beside Ike Camp Branch. Found below 4,500 feet throughout the wilderness, this slightly aromatic broadleaf is most common and noticeable on moist, shaded slopes and along stream banks free from rhododendron. Many features of this tree are unique, unusual, or distinctive. Its easily recognized alternate leaves—3 to 5 inches long and 2 to 3 inches wide, wavy-edged, and widest beyond mid-point—have lopsided bases and round-toothed margins.

The witch-hazel blooms later than any other tree, perhaps even any other plant, in the Southern Appalachians. It flowers in fall after it loses its leaves, usually from late October through November. Each small, bright yellow blossom has four twisted, hairlike petals. When the flowers are in clusters, as they often are, they resemble tufts of teased yellow hair.

About the same time it blooms, the seedpods fire their black, shiny seeds (those that developed from last fall's flowers) up to 30 feet from the tree.

Aromatic oils extracted from leaves, twigs, and bark are still used in some shaving lotions and patent medicines. And diviners still use a forked branch of the witch-hazel to dowse for water.

witch-hazel

Directions

Brush Mountain is an interior trail that has its northwestern (low elevation) end on South Fork Citico Trail and its southeastern (high elevation) end on Cold Spring Gap Trail.

To reach Brush Mountain's northwestern end, walk 1.1 miles on South Fork Citico starting from that trail's northwestern (low elevation) end. After walking slightly more than 1.0 mile on the South Fork Citico Trail, you will see Ike Camp Branch as it cascades into the South Fork on the far bank. One hundred yards beyond Ike Camp Branch, you will notice a boulder on your side of the creek and a line of rocks (some piled) leading to another boulder on the far side of the creek. Those two boulders mark the beginning of Brush Mountain Trail, which immediately fords South Fork Citico Creek. (See South Fork Citico Trail, page 168, for more information.)

To reach Brush Mountain's southeastern end, you must walk segments of two trails—Fodderstack and Cold Spring Gap. Starting at Fodderstack's southern (high elevation) Beech Gap Trailhead, walk 1.8 miles on the Fodderstack Trail to its junction with Cold Spring Gap, then follow Cold Spring Gap Trail for 1.5 miles. Look for Brush Mountain Trail to the left in a slight saddle where Cold Spring Gap crosses the ridge of Brush Mountain, then curves down and to the right. (See Fodderstack, page 132, and Cold Spring Gap, page 139, in the Sassafras Ridge Trailheads section for more information.)

Notes

Pine Ridge Trail

Horse and Foot Trail 99: 3.5 miles

- ■ **Dayhiking In** Moderate
- ■ **Dayhiking Out** Easy to Moderate
- ■ **Backpacking In** Moderate to Strenuous
- ■ **Backpacking Out** Moderate
- ■ **Start** Pine Ridge Trailhead, 1,720 feet
- ■ **End** Fodderstack Trail, 4,000 feet
- ■ **Trail Junction** Fodderstack
- ■ **Topographic Quadrangle** Whiteoak Flats TN-NC
- ■ **Features** Excellent winter views of North Fork Citico's upper basin and surrounding mountains

PINE RIDGE IS A DESIGNATED HORSE TRAIL, although you can walk it if you want to. I didn't particularly want to and did so only for the sake of completeness. Perhaps low expectations boosted my opinion of this trail; except for some unauthorized, homemade blazing, I enjoyed it and think that under similar conditions most other walkers would too.

Except for the obvious, I don't know what the trail conditions would be like after heavy horse usage, especially after rain. However, since most of the trail runs along the dry southern slopes of Pine Ridge, the footing will probably be fairly good under normal conditions. When I walked Pine Ridge on a weekday in mid-April, well after hunting season and before horse riding picks up again in May, the trail was utterly deserted—except for a pair of gobblers—and in good shape. The few horse tracks were old, and there wasn't a boot print anywhere.

Pine Ridge, though a horse trail, is the only ridge and upper-slope trail that runs west to east through the Citico Creek Wilderness. And by virtue of that fact, it is the only trail that provides numerous bare-branch views of the wide, rugged southern half of the wilderness: Jeffrey Hell. Those views to the south give you a good feeling of isolation, of elbowroom and wildness of big woods. If you want to try this trail, I recommend you do so in March or April, after it has had some time to rest after hunting season and before leaf-out (before May 1). In mid-April warm weather, birdsong, blooming red maples, and serviceberries come with the views.

Pine Ridge gains its elevation—all 2,280 feet of it—as gently as possible in 3.5 miles. It doesn't undulate up and down with the ridgecrest like some trails, nor does it gain half of its elevation all at once like others. It rises steadily all along the way. The grades are predominantly easy or easy to moderate. There are no long, sustained moderate grades, and no strenuous gradients at all. I gave this trail its difficulty rating for the sake of consistency, because of the number of feet gained per mile and the cumulative effect of the steady climb. It does rank, however, at the lower, easier range of its ratings.

Immediately after entering the forest, the trail turns right and follows an old road away from FS 29. It quickly reaches a slope above a bend in Citico Creek, then dips to and crosses an unnamed tributary branch. That dip is the last downgrade, and that branch is the last reliable source of water. Beyond the stream the trail—now an open path brushed out for the high clearance required by horseback riders—begins its remarkably steady ascent. The treadway switchbacks onto the top of a Pine Ridge spur at 0.6 mile. Pine Ridge is the sharply rising ridge less than a mile to the north. The route slowly angles over and up to the crest of Pine Ridge, which it finally reaches at its exact ending point.

For the next mile the aislelike trail remains on or near the keel of the spur. At mile 1.6 it angles onto the southern slope of Pine Ridge, continuing its slow climb through a largely hardwood forest dominated by the oaks. Here the walking winds around or passes above the heads of steep hollows that plunge into Jeffrey Hell country.

The trail ends as soon as it gains the narrow backbone of Pine Ridge, at a cleared campsite that marks its junction with the Fodderstack Trail. If you want to walk on the Fodderstack Trail to the south (low to high) toward Bob Stratton Bald, angle slightly to the right and follow the crest up toward the rounded crown of Big Fodderstack (4,346 feet). If you want to walk on the Fodderstack Trail to the north toward Farr Gap, cross over the ridgecrest and follow the trail as it curls sharply to the right and down.

Nature Notes

This trail passes through a second-growth oak-pine forest. In general the pines—pitch, Table Mountain, Virginia, and white—dominate the lower ridges and the hardwoods dominate the slopes and higher ridges. When the leaves are gone, there are views of hollows and spurs and basins and long ridges floating in the hazy distance. Looking off the southern slopes of Pine Ridge, you will see three striking, easily recognized features. The first is North Fork Citico Creek's troughlike upper basin—remote, wild, big enough for a bear or two. The second is the dividing line ridge of the Unicoi Mountains, roller-coastering away from Big Fodderstack to Bob Stratton Bald—from nearly east to south-southeast—dividing drainages, wildernesses, counties, national forests, and states. And last, but never least, is the long, high-flung, seemingly level wall of Bob Stratton Bald.

Directions

From the FS 345–FS 35-1 junction at the entrance of the Indian Boundary Recreation Area, turn right onto FS 35-1 and continue on this dirt-gravel road for approximately 2.4 miles to a sharp downhill curve to the left. Near the middle of the curve, turn right onto the road (FS 29 on the wilderness map, unmarked at its entrance) that almost immediately crosses Citico Creek on a low concrete bridge. Follow that road across the bridge to campsite #13.

The Pine Ridge Trailhead is easily found. Walk the one-track road (FS 29) 65 yards past campsite #13 to the three vehicle-blocking boulders to the left. Usually marked with a horse-rider trail sign, the route begins behind the boulders. (See the beginning of this trailhead section, page 165, for directions to the FS 345–FS 35-1 intersection.)

Notes

The wilderness and the idea of the wilderness is one of the permanent homes of the human spirit.... If we do not preserve it, then we shall have diminished by just that much the unique privilege of being an American.

Joseph Wood Krutch
Today and All Its Yesterdays *(1958)*

Doublecamp Creek Trailheads

Crowder Branch

Trails

Rocky Flats
Mill Branch
Crowder Branch
Big Stack Gap Branch
Stiffknee

Doublecamp Creek Trailheads
Directions and Map

ALL OF THE TRAILS IN THE DOUBLECAMP CREEK section that have vehicular access—with the exception of Rocky Flats, which has one end off FS 35-1 and the other on FS 59—begin on the right (southeastern) side of FS 59.

From the TN 165 (Overhill Skyway)–FS 345 junction, turn onto the paved, prominently signed, Indian Boundary approach road, FS 345. If you are traveling TN 165 East, the turn onto FS 345 will be to the left. Continue on FS 345 for approximately 1.2 miles to the four-way intersection at the Indian Boundary Recreation Area entrance marked by a large sign. Turn right onto FS 35-1 (Citico Road, FS 35-1 on the wilderness map, FS 35 on the road sign) and proceed approximately 4.0 miles to its three-way intersection with FS 59. Immediately after crossing Citico Creek and entering Doublecamp Campground, turn right onto FS 59 (Doublecamp Road).

Because of recurrent flooding, Doublecamp is no longer a formal campground where fees are charged. However, the campground is still labeled on the wilderness map, is still known as Doublecamp, and is still open to the public.

Forest Service 35-1 is a good dirt-gravel road, wide and level. Except for the dodgable potholes, FS 59 is also a fairly good dirt-gravel road, suitable for regular passenger vehicles after the spring grading, usually mid- to late April. Beyond the Crowder Branch Trailhead, FS 59 becomes rougher on the uphill section to Farr Gap. Both roads remain open throughout the winter except after heavy snows or ice storms. For more information concerning road conditions and possible closings, call Cherokee National Forest's Tellico Ranger District. (See page 26 for directions and mileages to the TN 165–FS 345 intersection.)

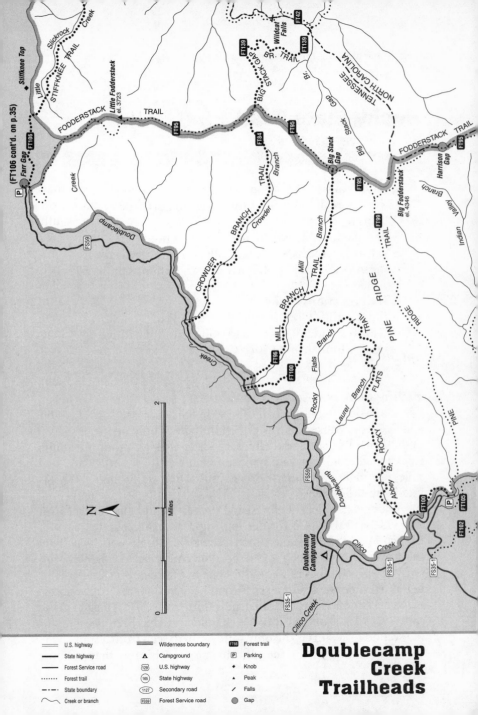

Stiffknee Top

Little Slickrock Creek

STIFFKNEE TRAIL

FODDERSTACK

Little Fodderstack
el. 3723

TRAIL

FT139

Wildcat
Falls

FT42

BIG STACK GAP

BR. TRAIL

FT139

TENNESSEE

NORTH CAROLINA

FT95

FT84

FT95

FODDERSTACK TRAIL

FT95

Big Stack Gap

Big Stack Gap

FT95

Harrison Gap

Indian Valley Branch

Big Fodderstack
el. 4346

FT99

(FT106 cont'd. on p.35)

Farr Gap

FT106

P

Creek

Doublecamp

FS59

CROWDER

BRANCH

Crowder

TRAIL

Branch

MILL

BRANCH

Mill

Branch

TRAIL

PINE

RIDGE

TRAIL

PINE

RIDGE

FT96

FT100

Rocky

Flats

Branch

TRAIL

RIDGE

ROCKY

FLATS

Creek

Laurel

Branch

Doublecamp

Abbey Br.

PINE

FT100

P

FT105

FT102

N

Miles

2

1

0

Doublecamp
Campground

Citico   Creek

FS59

FS35-1

FS35-1

FS35-1

Citico Creek

≡ U.S. highway	▬ Wilderness boundary	FT98 Forest trail
▬ State highway	⬛ Campground	P Parking
— Forest Service road	(129) U.S. highway	◆ Knob
⋯ Forest trail	(165) State highway	▲ Peak
-·- State boundary	(1127) Secondary road	╱ Falls
⌇ Creek or branch	FS59 Forest Service road	⬤ Gap

Doublecamp
Creek
Trailheads

Rocky Flats Trail

Foot Trail 100: 4.5 miles

- **Dayhiking** Easy to Moderate in either direction, but more difficult from southwest to northeast (low to high)
- **Backpacking** Moderate in either direction
- **Vehicular Access At Either End:** Southwestern terminus near FS 29, 1,680 feet; northeastern terminus on FS 59, 1,880 feet
- **Trail Junctions** None
- **Topographic Quadrangle** Whiteoak Flats TN-NC
- **Features** Ridges, slopes, and hollows of Pine Ridge; Abbey Branch and Citico Creek

THIS TRAIL IS DESCRIBED FROM BARELY HIGHER to barely lower, from Doublecamp Road (FS 59) to FS 29 across the bridge over Citico Creek. Walked in this direction there is only one short, steep upgrade as the route gradually ascends to its high point. Although Rocky Flats does not gain or lose much elevation within any one mile, it usually heads up or down, most often gently, and rarely remains level for long.

Rocky Flats enters the forest and rises easily into the wilderness on the wide walkway of a former logging road. After paralleling Mill Branch for a short distance, the treadway angles up and away from the stream, crosses over a low ridge, then continues to gain elevation (easy or easy to moderate) on the slope not far below its crest. Starting at 0.6 mile the trail passes through a stand of small trees dominated by Virginia pine. This area, now third-growth, was logged in the early 1970s. Little of the Citico Creek Wilderness has been clear-cut for the second time; this is the only third-growth seen from a trail.

The route dips from the cut, which is slightly more than 0.2 mile across, to the tall, straight second-growth trees—yellow poplar, yellow buckeye, basswood, sweetgum, red maple, and more—beside the beginning of Rocky Flats Branch. Here the good water, the level land, the piled rocks, and the chimney, still largely intact, mark the site of a homestead abandoned in the early 1920s, while the going was still good before logging and fire. Now a narrow path, the trail angles down to and rock-steps the branch at mile 1.1.

After the crossing, the track closely follows the brook downstream for less than 100 yards before turning 90 degrees to the left (south) and climbing up an open north-facing hollow with large, well-spaced trees. Some of the slow-growing beeches and hemlocks, both often left by early loggers, look thick enough to be old-growth. The 0.1-mile ascent is straight up the hollow and progressively steeper toward the end of the pull. At the end of the grade, the trail turns 90 degrees again, this time to the right (west).

Beyond the second sharp turn, the footpath begins a pattern that lasts for 1.5 miles. Here, on the steep northern slopes of Pine Ridge, the trail rises over the crest of a spur, then slopes to and half-circles one or more hollows before rising up and over the next spur—again and again. The ridges and upper slopes are oak-pine; the slopes above the hollows are largely oak—white and chestnut—and the hollows are dominated by cove hardwoods, especially the yellow poplar. The top of the first spur is the route's high point, approximately 2,900 feet. Although there is a great deal of up and down and over and around, the grades are predominantly easy or easy to moderate. At mile 1.9 the treadway rock-hops Laurel Branch.

At mile 2.7, Rocky Flats follows the pitch pine ridge of a spur for 0.1 mile before curling to the left and dropping easily to the beginning rivulet of Abbey Branch. After crossing the trickle for the first time, the treadway proceeds gently downhill, closely paralleling and rock-stepping the small stream on an old railroad grade. Hemmed-in Abbey Branch, with a miniature pool below a miniature bluff, is scenic in its own small-scale way. Forty yards beyond the seventh and last crossing (the first one or two might be dry), where the railroad bed rises above the stream, the trail cuts sharply back to the left onto path at mile 3.5 as the railroad grade proceeds straight ahead.

Beyond the turn the treadway quickly tops the knife-edged ridge that separates the Abbey Branch and Citico Creek valleys. On the other side the dry, rocky slope plunges, steep as a gorge, 150 to 200 feet to Citico Creek. You can hear the cascades and see the quivering sunsparkle through the pines. Across the creek to the west, an unnamed, sharp-pointed knob towers 400 feet above the Citico.

The well-constructed footpath gradually gains elevation along the precipitous slope before swinging away from the stream. It then heads around hollows and over spurs, through a maturing, predominantly hardwood forest. After cresting the final Pine Ridge spur, the trail descends to its bank-level end. Portions of the last 0.1 mile drop sharply above a horseshoe bend in Citico Creek.

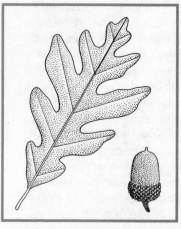

white oak

Nature Notes

The white oak, one of the most widespread trees in the eastern United States, is common in the wilderness. Of the six large oaks frequently found in the wilderness (black, scarlet, southern red, northern red, and chestnut are the others), the white is the easiest to identify. Its light green, distinctively lobed leaves are 5 to 9 inches long and 2 to 4 inches wide.

This oak is most plentiful, and has its best form and growth, below 4,000 feet. It seems to compete best on upland sites—well-drained slopes, flats, and upper hollows—above creeks and the moistest parts of coves. Where conditions for growth are favorable, it can slowly become one of the largest trees in the eastern forest. The usual dimensions for mature white oak are 80 to 100 feet in height and 3 to 4 feet in diameter. But on good sites it once grew much larger—to a maximum size of 150 feet in height and 9 feet in diameter. However, because its wood was in such great demand, and because it was most abundant at the easy-to-reach lower elevations, there are very few massive, good-form white oaks left in the Southern Highlands. Judged by the original standard, there are no large white oaks along the trails of this wilderness. The current North Carolina state record is listed as 124 feet in height and 22 feet 10 inches in circumference.

Quercus alba is slow growing and very long-lived. Estimates of its maximum lifespan range from one-half to three-quarters of a millenium. But no one knows for sure. All the evidence isn't in yet. Some of the white oaks growing in New Jersey and the eastern shore of Maryland that were landmarks in the late 1600s, and that have been open-grown shade trees for the last 300 years, are still holding trunk and soul together today.

Directions

Rocky Flats has either-end vehicular access along the same road system. To reach its southwestern, lower-elevation trailhead, turn right onto FS 29 (marked on the wilderness map but not on the road), cross over Citico Creek, then park in the large primitive campground (signed campsite #13) immediately across the bridge. There is cleared camping area to either side of the road. The trail is to the left of the road (from the way you came in) at the back edge of the clearing farthest from the road. If you're having trouble finding the beginning treadway, walk the road 65 to 70 yards beyond the end of the bridge to the remains of a low cement foundation. From the far left corner of the foundation, angle less than 45 degrees to the left a short distance to the trail in the nearby woods. Because of recurring vandalism, the carsonite trail sign has been tucked in 35 yards down the path. Campsite #13 serves as the parking area for three trails—Pine Ridge, Rocky Flats, and occasionally South Fork Citico. (See Pine Ridge, page 185, in the Citico Creek Trailheads section for directions to FS 29.)

To reach its northeastern, higher-elevation trailhead, continue (past the turn onto FS 29) on FS 35-1 (Citico Road) approximately 1.5 miles to the three-way intersection at Doublecamp Campground. Across the bridge in the campground, turn right onto FS 59 (Doublecamp Road) and follow it for approximately 2.5 miles. The trail, usually signed, is to the right of the road 110 yards beyond the bridge over Doublecamp Creek (the first noticeable bridge over the creek that parallels Doublecamp Road) and before the bridge over nearby Mill Branch.

Mill Branch Trail

Foot Trail 96: 2.5 miles

- **Dayhiking In** Moderate
- **Dayhiking Out** Easy to Moderate
- **Backpacking In** Moderate to Strenuous
- **Backpacking Out** Moderate
- **Start** Mill Branch Trailhead, 1,880 feet
- **End** Fodderstack Trail in Big Stack Gap, 3,380 feet
- **Trail Junction** Fodderstack
- **Topographic Quadrangle** Whiteoak Flats TN-NC
- **Features** Steep-sided cove of a Mill Branch tributary; small pocket of old-growth forest

HEADING SLIGHTLY SOUTH OF DUE EAST, the trail parallels Mill Branch on the wide bed of an old logging railroad. In places the ties are still visible. Even though the treadway remains fairly close to the branch, it wanders far enough away for the screen of hemlock and rhododendron to keep the stream just out of sight. Mill Branch —a series of miniature shoals running through mossy boulders—is a gentle brook by Southern Appalachian standards.

The walking, through a mixed broadleaf-conifer forest, is easy until the route dips to and crosses the branch for the first and only time at mile 1.0. Above this crossing, the trail switches streams and rises up and out of the steep-sided cove of a Mill Branch tributary. The former railroad parallels the rocky notch of the tributary before angling up the slope to mile 1.7, where it passes over a spur ridge through a banked cut. This climb is by far the trail's longest and hardest; most of it is moderate to strenuous.

On the other side of the ridge, the forest changes abruptly as the path enters a moist, north-facing hollow. The second-growth trees here, hemlock and cove hardwoods dominated by yellow poplar, are much taller and thicker than the spindly pole timber below. Most of the trail's remaining distance—an easy walk crossing one spring head after another—traverses a gentle seepage slope. The uppermost flow of Mill Branch is to the left, through the thicket-growth of rhododendron.

With 0.1 mile left, the treadway breaks out of the rhododendron and enters a pocket of old-growth forest that surrounds a prominent camp. Here large sugar maple, yellow buckeye, Carolina silverbell, and northern red oak mark the end of the clear-cutting. One of the old oaks, rotting and almost dead, is the thickest normal-boled northern red oak along the trails of the contiguous wilderness. The tree is too fluted and knotted for accurate measurement; the best I could manage was a circumference of 15 feet 2 inches. The Forest Service believes the logging had advanced to this point when the Citico Creek fire started and burned for months in the summer of 1925.

A short, final pull will lead you to the Fodderstack Trail junction in Big Stack Gap.

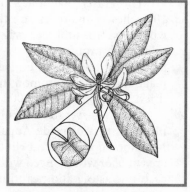

Fraser magnolia

Nature Notes

If you look up the south-facing slope along the first mile of trail, you will notice the trees are often small, seemingly stunted for the 75 years of growing time since logging. This forest, dominated by chestnut oaks in thin, rocky soil, is the direct result of the one-two-three punch of old-style timbering, fire, and erosion. Several old-timers told me that 2 to 4 feet of topsoil, even more in places, were washed away from many steep, exposed slopes by the winter rains that followed the fire of 1925. Stark photos tell the story: pictures of gullies and trees standing on the stilts of their own roots.

The Fraser magnolia, one of three deciduous magnolias within the wilderness, is common beside Mill Branch and its tributary. The Fraser is easy to identify. It is a small to medium-sized tree with smooth, light gray or light gray-brown bark. Its leaves—crowded into whorls at branch ends, usually 6 to 18 inches long and 3 to 8 inches wide—are the second largest among trees found in this wilderness. The richer the habitat, the larger the leaf. Saplings occasionally have jungle-sized leaves 9 to 10 inches wide and 18 to 20 inches long. The conspicuously eared base (auriculate in botanese) of the Fraser magnolia leaf is diagnostic. The tree with the slightly larger, uneared leaf—the umbrella magnolia—is much less common in the wilderness.

The Fraser magnolia's fragrant flowers, pale yellow and 8 to 10 inches in diameter, are the second largest of any plant in the wilderness (the umbrella magnolia has the largest). They bloom from mid-April through most of May, depending upon elevation and the progress of the season. Endemic to the Southern Appalachians, this magnolia is fairly common throughout the wilderness, except in the driest situations, below 5,000 feet.

The large evergreen shrub so abundant beside this trail, synonymous with streamside Appalachia, is the rosebay rhododendron. Also known as the great rhododendron, this heath has flowers that are white or white tinged with pale pink. Clusters of these blossoms, each one as big and beautiful as a corsage, bloom in hot weather, starting in late June and usually reaching peak sometime in July. In cold weather the large, leathery leaves curl and droop, resembling green mop heads.

The rhododendrons were symbolically important to the Cherokee. They never burned them because they believed that doing so would bring on a spate of cold weather and, worse yet, destroy the medicinal properties of the species. The Cherokee think the belief originated because the leaves, when burned, make the hissing sound of a winter snowstorm.

Directions

To reach Mill Branch and its trail, turn right onto FS 59 (Doublecamp Road) immediately after FS 35-1 (Citico Road) crosses Citico Creek and enters Doublecamp Campground. Continue approximately 2.6 miles (the road closely parallels cascading Doublecamp Creek and crosses Doublecamp Creek near Mill Branch) on

FS 59 to the trailhead, which is to the right of the road 50 yards beyond the bridge over Mill Branch. (The trail before the bridge is Rocky Flats.) There is limited pull-off parking near the trailhead, which is usually marked with a sign. (See the beginning of this trailhead section, page 189, for directions to the FS 35-1–FS 59 intersection.)

Notes

Crowder Branch Trail

Foot Trail 84: 2.6 miles

- **Dayhiking In** Moderate
- **Dayhiking Out** Easy to Moderate
- **Backpacking In** Moderate to Strenuous
- **Backpacking Out** Moderate
- **Start** Crowder Branch Trailhead, 1,920 feet
- **End** Fodderstack Trail, 3,360 feet
- **Trail Junctions** Fodderstack, Big Stack Gap Branch (see trail description)
- **Topographic Quadrangle** Whiteoak Flats TN-NC
- **Features** Low, sliding cascades of Crowder Branch; tall, straight second-growth forest

SHORTLY AFTER ENTERING THE FOREST—hemlock and white pine mixed with diverse hardwoods—Crowder Branch Trail turns left, then soon rock-steps its namesake stream, the first of nine easily recognizable crossings. Here the familiar pattern begins. Following an old railroad grade, the treadway crosses then parallels the brook upstream, dipping to cross, rising to parallel again. The branch— cold, clear, mossy, shallow, and 6 to 12 feet wide—is often within eyesight, almost always within earshot.

After the seventh crossing at 0.8 mile, the walkway climbs (moderately for 0.1 mile) for the first time. Where contour lines are close and streamside trails climb, however, there is often a reward for your effort. Crowder Branch, dropping as much as the trail is ascending, sluices through a series of low, sliding cascades, noisy when the water is up.

For the next 0.5 mile the trail, now narrow path often tunneling through rhododendron, works its way up the watershed on an easy upgrade. The forest becomes increasingly hardwood, and the slopes become steeper, a more pronounced V. The footpath's only sustained climb, becoming progressively sharper from easy to moderate-strenuous, begins at mile 1.4 and ends shortly after the ninth crossing at mile 1.9. Near the start of the ascent, there is an old-growth yellow buckeye—over 100 feet in height and 8 to 9 feet in girth—that survived logging and fire. It is the largest tree along the trail and, barring death, should remain so well into the twenty-first century. Farther up, there are frequent views of the narrowed brook as it spills down a boulder-choked trough.

Beyond the ninth crossing the walking, level or gradually up through thin hardwoods and rhododendron, continues beside or in the rocky stream. Here the route repeatedly crosses the braiding branch or slogs straight up its bed.

This pattern continues most of the way to an open, grassy camping area (a spring on the left) at 2.4 miles. From this camping spot the remainder of the trail turns right and follows the old wagon track through Crowder Fields—a former pasture maintained by the Forest Service as a wildlife opening until 1984. The Crowders were the only settlers to live up near the Fodderstack ridge year-round. They lived close to the pasture, at an elevation of almost 3,400 feet, until around the time the Forest Service bought the land in 1935. In the spring of 1997 there were still some gnarled apple trees, a few fallen and nearly dead, in the rapidly disappearing pasture. As part of the biological wilderness, the field won't last long. Beyond 2005, only the new hardwoods and the old apple trees, if you can still find them, will suggest its former presence.

Crowder Branch Trail ends at its T-junction with Fodderstack Trail, at a campsite in a slight saddle on the ridge. To the right (southeast) it is 0.1 mile on the Fodderstack Trail to its junction with Big Stack Gap Branch Trail.

Nature Notes

On the north side of the stream, the trail often appears to be a dividing line, with dry-site species such as chestnut oak and sourwood on the upslope and cove hardwoods such as yellow poplar and basswood on the downslope. The south-facing slope, like the one on Mill Branch Trail, shows evidence of poor growth since logging and fire. Most of the forest beside the stream is tall, straight, second-growth, the trees still competing for the canopy.

Like most heavily shaded streamside trails, Crowder Branch lacks a good spring wildflower display. One wildflower, actually a flowering vine, however, is common on the rich hardwood slopes near the stream. This ropelike woody vine, often twining 40 or more feet up into the trees, is the Dutchman's-pipe. Fairly common throughout the wilderness in coves and hollows, on streambanks and rich slopes, this deciduous vine is characteristic of the moist hardwood forest. Occasionally, in small areas, it becomes abundant enough to resemble a deep wilderness kudzu.

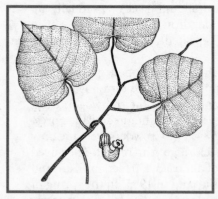

Dutchman's-pipe

The Dutchman's-pipe is easily recognized. Its large alternate leaves are heart-shaped and usually 4 to 8 inches wide. Its uniquely formed flowers have no petals; their sepals form hook-shaped, pipe-like blossoms that are approximately 2 inches in length. The ends of the flowers flare out into three short lobes. The blooms, greenish at first, then turning a brownish purple, last from late April through May.

The Dutchman's-pipe belongs to the birthwort family. Flowers and roots from this group of plants were formerly used as medicinal aids in childbirth. They were selected, primarily, based on the Doctrine of Signatures—a medieval theory stating that if any part of a plant resembled a part of the human body, that part of the plant was divinely created to contain curative properties for the body part. Since the flower of the Dutchman's-pipe supposedly looked like a fetus, it was administered to ease the pain of delivery.

Nearly everyone who has read nature books or watched public television knows about the classic Batesian mimicry involving the monarch and viceroy butterflies. Throughout much of the United States, including the rich hardwood forests of the Southern Highlands, there is another example of this type of mimicry, more interesting and complex but much less televised. The caterpillars of the pipevine swallowtail feed on the leaves of the plants in the birthwort family, such as Dutchman's-pipe, ingesting and storing aristolochic acid as they munch. This acid makes the adult butterflies unpalatable to their predators.

The pipevine swallowtail is black and irridescent blue. And so too are five palatable species, each gaining a measure of protection from their copycat appearance. In the monarch-viceroy model, where the sexes look alike, all the viceroys mimic the coloration of the poisonous monarch. Two pipevine impersonators, however, are half-mimics: only the females imitate the distasteful butterfly. One of these two, the tiger swallowtail, carries the mimicry to an even more complicated level—only some of its females pattern themselves after the pipevine swallowtail. Tiger swallowtails, all the males and a portion of the females, that is, are easy to identify. They are the big, bright yellow butterflies with bold black markings that flutter up and down the open aisles of streams like Crowder Branch. The remaining females are black and bright blue like the pipevine butterfly.

Directions

To reach Crowder Branch and its trail, turn right onto FS 59 (Doublecamp Road) immediately after FS 35-1 (Citico Road) crosses Citico Creek and enters Doublecamp Campground. Continue approximately 3.4 miles (the road closely parallels cascading Doublecamp Creek, crosses Doublecamp Creek, then crosses Mill Branch) on FS 59 to the trailhead, which is to the right of the road 15 yards before the bridge over Crowder Branch. There is limited pull-off parking near the trailhead, which is usually marked with a sign. (See the beginning of this trailhead section, page 189, for directions to the FS 35-1–FS 59 intersection.)

Notes

Big Stack Gap Branch Trail

Foot Trail 139: 1.8 miles

- **Dayhiking (low to high)** Moderate
- **Dayhiking (high to low)** Easy to Moderate
- **Backpacking (low to high)** Moderate to Strenuous
- **Backpacking (high to low)** Moderate
- **Interior Trail** Southeastern (low elevation) terminus on Slickrock Creek Trail, 1,920 feet; northwestern (high elevation) terminus on Fodderstack Trail, 3,400 feet
- **Trail Junctions** Fodderstack, Slickrock Creek, Crowder Branch (see directions, page 208)
- **Topographic Quadrangles** Whiteoak Flats TN-NC, Tapoco NC-TN
- **Features** Winter views of Bob Stratton Bald and the Hangover; rock outcrop overlook; good flowering shrub display in May

---

BIG STACK GAP BRANCH CONNECTS the Citico Creek trail system, via Fodderstack Trail, with Slickrock Creek and its trail system. It is the only trail that connects the combined wildernesses near the middle of their east-west border. Even though this easily followed footpath loses (or gains) 1,480 feet, it does so with a minimum of leg strain for this amount of elevation change over 1.8 miles. There are no long, steep stretches.

Big Stack Gap Branch is described as it is most often walked, from Fodderstack to Slickrock Creek, from high to low. Still occasionally blazed with old bear reserve signs, the route quickly dips from the master ridge of the Unicoi Mountains into a moist hardwood hollow. At 0.2 mile the track crosses the hollow's intermittent rivulet, then descends a spur ridge running to the northeast. Here the hiking, easy to moderate or moderate, is through a low-canopied forest dominated by oaks and pitch pine. During winter, and to a lesser extent during summer, you can see the ridgeline from Bob Stratton Bald over the Haoe to the Hangover to the right (southeast) off the spur. The long, seemingly level summit of the bald is 4 line-of-sight miles away.

At 0.6 mile the treadway curls down and to the right (south) off the spur. Immediately before the turn, a small open knot of rock affords a good look at the double-humped peak of Little Fodderstack Mountain to the north. Once off the spur and onto slope, the narrow footpath loses elevation steadily on long, looping switchbacks for 0.5 mile. On the way down there are occasional between-branch views of the Hangover. These framed vistas have a focusing, magnifying effect. On the clearest days you get a touch of that out-West optical illusion: it looks as if the high lonesome is just a short walk away.

Continuing to lose elevation, the trail descends moderately on the crest of a spur fingering toward Slickrock Creek to mile 1.4, where at a slight saddle, it once again turns sharply down and to the right. This time it drops into a cove and onto the wide walkway of an old skid road. The change in forest composition and tree size is as abrupt as the turn. Here the second-growth forest—hemlock mixed with cove hardwoods—is tall, straight, and diverse. The final section gradually angles down toward Big Stack Gap Branch until, with 0.1 mile remaining, it rock-steps across the stream. The path ends at its usually signed T-junction with Slickrock Creek Trail, next to a campsite overlooking the creek. To the left (downstream) it is two fords and 0.4 mile to Slickrock Creek's Wildcat Falls.

Level campsites are at either end of the trail. Big Stack Gap Branch, and obviously Slickrock Creek, are the only sure year-round water sources.

Nature Notes

With one significant exception, this trail passes through a predominantly second-growth oak-pine forest. Five species of oak and three species of pine—pitch, white, and Table Mountain—account for the majority of the larger boles. The thickest trailside trees (until the yellow poplars catch up) are the occasional old-growth chestnut oaks—low-limbed logger's culls, a few in the 10- to 12-foot circumference range. Stump-sprout saplings of the American chestnut still persist.

The oak-pine forest has a poor early spring wildflower display, especially compared to the higher-elevation, cove hardwood forest. But in May the canopy closes, and understory of the oak-pine forest catches up in color when the flowering shrubs, primarily mountain laurel and flame azalea, bloom. The flame azalea, a tall deciduous heath in the same genus as rhododendron, is abundant on the dry slopes and spur tops of this trail. William Bartram, the eighteenth-century botanist and explorer, described the "fiery" azalea in his book, *Travels*, first published in 1791:

> The epithet fiery, I annex to this most celebrated species of Azalea, as being expressive of the appearance of its flowers, which are in general of the colour of the finest red lead, orange and bright gold, as well as yellow and cream colour; these various splendid colours are not only in separate plants, but frequently all the varieties and shades are seen in separate branches on the same plant; and the clusters of the blossoms cover the shrubs in such incredible profusion of the hill sides, that suddenly opening to view from dark shades, we are alarmed with the apprehension of the hill being set on fire. This is certainly the most gay and brilliant flowering shrub yet known.

Bartram's description of the flame azalea's color is accurate enough—it is splendid. In the flowery style of his day, when real men weren't afraid to gush over beauty, Bartram's "set on fire" image was an acceptable exaggeration from the American frontier. In truth, at the peak of a good year in those places where the flame azalea is abundant, the blossoms do light up the spring green forest with bright orange.

Although most common in low- to middle-elevation oak-pine

forest, the flame azalea flowers at all elevations of this wilderness. The blooming begins at the lowest elevations from mid-to late April and climbs to the grassy area atop Bob Stratton Bald from mid-May to early June, depending on the progress of the season. The blooms usually peak along this trail, again depending on the progress of the season, from May 8 to May 23.

Directions

Big Stack Gap Branch is an interior trail that connects Slickrock Creek Trail with Fodderstack Trail. Its lower-elevation, southeastern terminus is located on Slickrock Creek Trail, 7.4 miles from Slickrock Creek's trailhead near Tapoco and 5.9 miles from Slickrock Creek's upper-elevation terminus at Naked Ground. Its upper-elevation, northwestern terminus is on Fodderstack Trail, 3.5 miles from Fodderstack's lower-elevation, Farr Gap trailhead and 9.1 miles from Fodderstack's upper-elevation, Beech Gap trailhead.

flame azalea

If the junction signs are missing, both ends of Big Stack Gap Branch can be somewhat difficult to find. Both ends, however, have prominent campsites at their exact junctions (this may have something to do with the disappearing signs). Walking south on Fodderstack Trail from Farr Gap, you will find the campsite (to the left on the east side of the trail) and the upper-elevation terminus of Big Stack Gap Branch 0.1 mile beyond Fodderstack's junction with Crowder Branch Trail, which is in a shallow gap. (See Fodderstack, page 132, in the Sassafras Ridge Trailheads section to find more information.)

Walking south on Slickrock Creek from its trailhead, you will find the junction campsite and the lower-elevation terminus of Big Stack Gap Branch just across the creek after the ninth ford. (See

Slickrock Creek, page 36, in the Slickrock Creek Trailhead section, for more information.)

The shortest, though not easiest, route to Big Stack Gap Branch's upper-elevation end is Crowder Branch Trail. Follow Crowder Branch 2.6 miles to its end, then turn right (southeast) onto Fodderstack Trail and continue 0.1 mile to the junction campsite on the left. (See Crowder Branch, the preceding trail, for more information.)

Notes

Stiffknee Trail

- **Dayhiking In** Easy
- **Dayhiking Out** Moderate
- **Backpacking In** Easy to Moderate
- **Backpacking Out** Moderate to Strenuous
- **Start** Farr Gap Trailhead, 2,840 feet
- **End** Slickrock Creek Trail, 1,400 feet
- **Trail Junctions** Fodderstack (at trailhead), Slickrock Creek
- **Topographic Quadrangles** Whiteoak Flats TN-NC, Tapoco NC-TN
- **Features** Winter views of Tallassee and Milligan Creek basins; Little Slickrock Creek

S TIFFKNEE, LIKE TEARBRITCHES TRAIL in the Cohutta Wilderness of north Georgia and the Bustass Trail in western Wyoming, has one of those interesting names that came from the condition of an early hunter or settler. But compared to many of the other trails in this guide, Stiffknee hardly lives up to its name. It is, at most, intermediate in difficulty. In fact, once it drops into Little Slickrock cove, the walking is easy and pleasant, not tough on the knees at all.

Stiffknee is one of only three trails connecting the hiking systems of the two contiguous wildernesses. It is the only Slickrock Creek lead-in trail that originates at a Citico Creek (Tennessee) trailhead.

Stiffknee's first 0.8 mile winds outside of the wilderness boundary. Heading generally eastward, the treadway quickly descends through rhododendron tunnels on graded footpath. Here the hiking follows the familiar slope-hollow-spur pattern of mountainside trail.

And here along the moist north slope, the mature second-growth forest, dominated by oak and pignut hickory on the slope and cove hardwoods in the hollows, is diverse and predominantly deciduous. The route remains on easy-to-moderate downgrades until it switchbacks sharply down a spur for 0.1 mile to Stiffknee Gap (2,340 feet) at mile 0.8. Straight ahead the ridge rises to Stiffknee Top and the long crest of Tallassee Mountain. To the left (north) of the gap there is a winter view of the twin basins of Tallassee and Milligan Creeks and the mountains that define their watersheds.

The path turns right (south) in the gap, enters the wilderness and dips into Little Slickrock Creek's uppermost cove. The forest in the upper cove has rebounded beautifully since it was cut in the 1920s; already some yellow poplar and white pine have extended their reach above 100 feet. In places, the forest has a dense, double-layer canopy—hemlock under hardwood—shady and cool on a warm day.

The track soon crosses a headwater rivulet, then roughly parallels the quickly growing stream, Little Slickrock, to the southeast. The walking, usually level or easy down, is on rocky trail near the creek—a clear, cold brook most often out of sight behind a screen of rhododendron and doghobble. Look for piled-rock terraces, evidence of a former logging camp, where the land becomes gently sloping.

At mile 2.4 the footpath crosses the stream, the first of five times. Below the first crossing the treadway closely parallels the watercourse on the gradually descending, wide walkway of an old railroad bed. This last section presents numerous open views of Slickrock Creek's largest tributary, now 10 to 15 feet wide with shallow, slightly greened pools. Like most streams in the wilderness, Little Slickrock Creek has quartzite boulders in its bed. Near the end of the trail there is a 10-foot section of rail, obviously left when the track was removed during World War II. The U.S. Forest Service considers objects like saw blades, cable, and rail—slowly rusting artifacts from the early logging days—to be cultural resources.

Stiffknee ends at a campsite beside Little Slickrock Creek (35 yards from Slickrock Creek), at its signed junction with Slickrock

Creek Trail. From the end of Stiffknee Trail, it is 1.2 miles and two fords downstream to Slickrock Creek's Lower Falls, 2.7 miles and four fords upstream to Wildcat Falls.

Nature Notes

Stiffknee leads through a succession of habitats that support a typically diverse forest. The second time I hiked this trail, after the canopy had leafed out, I noted thirty-seven tree species without making a special effort for a high count. There are, no doubt, at least ten or fifteen more species near the trail. The reasons for this diversity—glaciation, mountain range orientation, weather, time, evolution—are complex. The result, however, is simple: the richness of the Southern Appalachian forest is unequaled over most of the world's temperate zone. The most diverse area in the Southern Highlands, the Great Smoky Mountains National Park, has more native tree species (101) than does all of northern Europe. There are more kinds of trees within 30 yards of this trail than within all of Yellowstone National Park's 2.2 million acres. The botanical garden abundance of our southern mountains is something to brag about, something to appreciate and protect.

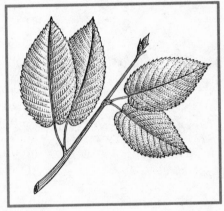

sweet birch

Within its preferred habitat, the sweet birch, also known as black birch, is one of the most common trees in the wilderness. It is especially abundant beside this trail. While this birch is often numerous on rich slopes and in moist coves, it is most plentiful along the once-logged stream corridors. There you can often find stands of sweet birch shooting up through the rhododendron thickets.

Sweet birch bark resembles that of black cherry. On young trunks it is dark brown tinged with red or sometimes nearly black.

Young boles also have prominent horizontal stripes (lenticels) and very small vertical peels, nothing at all like the wide, papery curls of yellow birch. On older trees the dark, almost black bark is fissured into large irregularly scaled plates. In winter, the dark bark and the long, drooping male catkins near the tips of the twigs make this birch easy to identify.

Sweet birch leaves, paired at the end of short branchlets, turn bright yellow in autumn. Its crushed leaves and cracked twigs have the spicy scent of wintergreen. In the past, birch beer was fermented from its sap, and oil of wintergreen was obtained from the bark and wood of saplings. Yellow birch has the same scent, but not as strong.

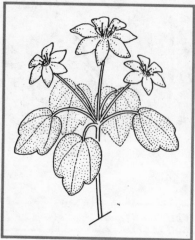

rue anemone

A medium-sized tree, *Betula lenta* is usually 50 to 80 feet in height and 1 to 2½ feet in diameter. Its maximum measurements are 110 feet in height and 5 feet in diameter. This birch reaches maturity in 150 years, and old trees may attain the three-century mark.

Stiffknee has a fair first-wave spring wildflower display, beginning in early April and lasting throughout most of that month. One of the most common wildflowers in the wilderness, the rue anemone, is abundant along the trail above Little Slickrock cove. A member of the buttercup family, the rue anemone is one of the low (4 to 8 inches), ephemeral flowers of early spring. It is so named because of its resemblance to the wood anemone, or windflower. Both species, which often grow in the same habitat, have dainty white blooms that vibrate in the slightest breeze, while neighboring plants remain perfectly still. The rue anemone's delicate white flowers, numerous across a colony, are ½ to 1 inch wide, with five to ten petals (actually sepals). Equally small and delicate, its distinctive leaflets have rounded, three-lobed tips. The rue anemone is found on rich slopes at lower and middle elevations.

Directions

To reach Farr Gap and its two trails—Stiffknee and the northern (low elevation) end of Fodderstack—turn right onto FS 59 (Doublecamp Road) immediately after FS 35-1 (Citico Road) crosses Citico Creek and enters Doublecamp Campground. Follow FS 59 for approximately 6.4 miles to the gap, where the land drops away from the ridge straight ahead and the road curves sharply up and to the left. Opposite the curve, to the right, an old road (now blocked to vehicular traffic) leads a short distance to the trailhead. Stiffknee, usually marked with a sign, is the trail that angles down and to the left, The old road that continues past the bulletin board is the Fodderstack Trail. There are several turn-in parking areas to the right just before FS 59 turns left at the gap. (See the beginning of this trailhead section, page 189, for directions to the FS 35-1–FS 59 intersection.)

Notes

What I want to speak for is not so much the wilderness uses,
valuable as those are, but the wilderness idea, *which is a*
resource in itself....

Something will have gone out of us as a people if we
ever let the remaining wilderness be destroyed....We need
wilderness preserved—as much of it as is still left, and as
many kinds—because it was the challenge against which our
character as a people was formed. The reminder and the
reassurance that it is still there is good for our spiritual health
even if we never once in ten years set foot in it....

That is the reason we need to put into effect, for its
preservation, some other principle than the principles of
exploitation or usefulness or even recreation. We simply need
that wild country available to us, even if we never do more
than drive to its edge and look in. For it can be a means of
reassuring ourselves of our sanity as creatures, a part of the
geography of hope.

Wallace Stegner
"The Wilderness Idea" (1960)

The Idea of Wilderness

WILDERNESS ADVOCATES SEE the Wilderness Act of 1964 as the most foresighted land-ethic legislation since the formation of the National Forest System. The concept of designated wilderness represents a progression of concern, a hard-won belief by the majority that some parcels of the earth should have their own heritage, should be allowed to become what they will, unmanipulated by humans. This act of preservation, a tithing of wildness for ourselves and for the future, is an important but as yet paltry beginning reparation for our abuse and misuse of the land and its life.

Those who oppose the concept of designated wilderness view it as a radical step that locks up resources. Let it be emphatically stated to them, however, that the idea is often a matter of preference—a matter of zoning really. Either we can choose to continue opening large areas of our Southern Appalachian forest to road building and logging in order to satisfy the incessant demands of a world crowded with people chanting "more, more, more," like a mantra. Or we can choose to preserve, to lock up diversity and beauty—clear, unsilted streams, magnificent forests, views into wild and natural land—by designating significant tracts as wilderness. Even though the physical resources of these areas would no longer be available for extraction, we can still use them—recreationally, spiritually, scientifically—in their natural state.

Unlike Alaska and the western states, the central and eastern regions of our country have only three categories of federally owned wild land—national wildlife refuges, national parks, and national forests—where wilderness designation is possible. Within that immense expanse of our country east of the Rockies, from Texas to South Carolina, from Nebraska to Pennsylvania, federal ownership of those three types of wild land constitutes less than 5 percent of the total land mass. Some states within that region, especially those with flat topography and good soil, have little or no opportunity for wilderness.

Within that less than 5 percent, only certain areas—those that are roadless, predominantly publicly owned, and large (usually at least 5,000 acres)—are qualified to be considered for a roadless inventory, the first step toward designation. Once an area is inventoried as roadless, it still has to be sufficiently scenic and undisturbed—and often economically useless—for there to be enough support to continue the qualification process.

Although percentages vary from state to state, congressionally mandated wilderness within that region east of the Rockies is, at best, somewhere between 5 and 10 percent of the federal wildlands. Thus, designated wilderness over much of our country is a small fraction of a small fraction: two to three-tenths of 1 percent of the total land base. Even in our relatively wild South, with its mountains, swamps, and forests, the figure remains below 1 percent.

Unlike large sections of the midwest, the South fortunately still has the opportunity for more wilderness. Our best opportunity lies within the national forests of the Southern Appalachians—the South's largest concentration of publicly owned land.

Especially in the highest and most remote mountains, road building and logging in the steep-sloped Southern Appalachians is destructive and costly. Bulldozing and stabilizing roads in this high-rainfall, mountainous terrain is so expensive that the federal government must subsidize it. The road building and logging damages watersheds, leaves the forest less diverse, harms certain wildlife species, and keeps the land in its ecological infancy. Spending money to subsidize destructive logging that yields little of the national lumber output makes neither ecological nor economic sense. This is especially true where we are further fragmenting the small amount of unprotected public land that remains wild and natural.

We are always faced with difficult land-use choices; designating wilderness is just one among many. But today at a time when the pace of life is increasingly frenetic—when ocean levels, global temperatures, and human populations are rising; when acid rain is falling and ozone layers are disappearing; when our collective actions lead to the daily extinction of species —it makes good sense to spare a few more teaspoons of wildness as havens for life and for human hope and renewal, protected both for and from us.

The Wilderness Act

The Wilderness Act of September 3, 1964, established the National Wilderness Preservation System, the first of its kind in the world. The idea of wilderness means different things to different people. Some describe any patch of woods bigger than their backyard as wilderness. Others won't call an area true wilderness unless it meets rare conditions: that it takes at least a week to walk across the longest part of it, that there is no sign of human habitation even from the vistas, and that all of the original predators are still on patrol. Knowing that the term is nebulous, as much spiritual as physical, the framers of the law attempted to define the qualities and purposes of wilderness. The following are salient ideas from the act.

A wilderness:

■ is an area of undeveloped federal land retaining its primeval character and influence, without permanent improvements or human habitation;

■ has at least 5,000 acres of land or is of sufficient size to make practicable its preservation and use in an unimpaired condition;

■ generally appears to have been affected primarily by forces of nature, with the imprint of man's work substantially unnoticeable;

■ is hereby recognized as an area where the earth and its community of life are untrammeled by man, where man himself is a visitor who does not remain, and which has outstanding opportunities for solitude or a primitive and unconfined type of recreation;

■ is devoted to the public purposes of recreational, scenic, scientific, educational, conservation, and historical use;

■ is preservation that will secure for the American people of present and future generations the benefits of an enduring resource of wilderness—unimpaired for future use and enjoyment.

What is permitted in wilderness?

■ Primitive recreation such as dayhiking, backpacking, and camping

- Hunting and fishing in accordance with state and federal laws
- Collecting berries, nuts, and cones for personal use
- Scientific research compatible with wilderness values
- Primitive facilities, if critical to the protection of the land
- Nonmotorized wheelchairs

What is prohibited in wilderness?
- New road construction
- Timber harvesting
- Structures of any kind, except those primitive facilities deemed necessary to protect the land
- Mechanical transport (bicycles, wagons, carts)
- Public use of any motorized vehicles or equipment
- Removal of plants, stone, or moss for personal or commercial use
- Removal of historical or archeological artifacts by the public

Wilderness Additions

Three parcels of public, national forest land adjacent to the Joyce Kilmer–Slickrock Wilderness have been proposed as additions to the existing core wilderness. These extensions—Yellowhammer Branch, Deep Creek–Avery Creek, and Obadiah Gap—would add approximately 9,000 protected acres if all three were designated as wilderness. The Yellowhammer Branch tract is located along the northeastern corner of the core wilderness. The largest tract, Deep Creek–Avery Creek, would add protected forest to the eastern flank of the wilderness from Horse Cove Campground all the way north to Big Fat Gap. Long east to west and narrow north to south, the Obadiah Gap parcel lies along the high-elevation, southern edge of the wilderness—north of FS 81 and south of Bob Stratton Bald and Stratton Bald Trail.

Yellowhammer Branch and Deep Creek–Avery Creek have already been inventoried as roadless by the Forest Service: the first hurdle toward eventual wilderness designation. However, only 1,271 acres of the Yellowhammer Branch tract were inventoried as roadless, and only 1,896 acres of the approximately 4,500-acre Deep Creek–Avery Creek addition were inventoried as roadless. As of spring 1998, the Obadiah Gap parcel has not been inventoried as roadless by the Forest Service.

Two areas on the Tennessee side of the combined wilderness—Flats Mountain and the Joyce Kilmer–Slickrock Extension—have also been proposed as wilderness additions. The Flats Mountain tract is situated along the southwestern side of the Citico Creek Wilderness, west of Flats Mountain, north of the skyway, and up the east side of FS 345. From the mouth of Slickrock Creek to the east, across Farr Gap in the middle, and widening to the west beyond Salt Spring Mountain, Joyce Kilmer–Slickrock Extension stretches along, then over, the northern perimeter.

The 2,228-acre Flats Mountain area was not considered roadless by the Forest Service in its last management plan and this roadless area has not been inventoried as such in preparation for the next plan. Out of Joyce Kilmer–Slickrock Extension's 5,198 acres, only 1,425 acres are currently inventoried as roadless.

The Forest Service is required to revise its national forest management plan every 10 to 15 years. The Cherokee National Forest's last management plan was completed in 1985, and the Nantahala National Forest's last plan was completed in 1987. Thus, the Cherokee National Forest must complete its next plan by the year 2000, and the Nantahala National Forest must complete its plan by 2002. The first two steps in the designation process—the roadless inventory and the wilderness requirements review—begin with the Forest Service.

On January 22, 1998, the U.S. Forest Service announced a proposal to protect 33 million acres of "roadless areas" in our national forests, while the agency reconsiders its controversial policy of constructing and maintaining logging roads. In the Southern Appalachians of Georgia, Tennessee, Virginia, and the Carolinas, the road-building moratorium protects approximately 500,000 acres in 150 roadless areas from logging. This moratorium is an interim measure that will last only 18 months.

If you want to have your views counted, write the Forest Service and express your thoughts concerning the future of your national forests. And if you want to start on the forest floor of the new plan, enabling you to provide comments to the Forest Service during the crucial early stages, ask the Forest Service to place you on the mailing list for the "Forest Plan Revision." (See page 227 for addresses.)

Environmental and Courtesy Guidelines

THIS SECTION OF THE BOOK offers tips to help you plan a safe and enjoyable hike that will leave little impact on the wilderness trails.

Before the Hike

■ **Limit group size** to no more than six for backpacking and no more than eight for dayhiking.

■ **Split large organized groups** into two or three smaller parties allowing the groups to go to different destinations, travel opposite directions on the same loop, stagger their start, or do whatever it takes to avoid overwhelming everyone and everything in their path.

■ **Plan ahead**—remember that large creeks with waterfalls and swimming holes, open areas with views, and major trail junctions with level ground and water will be heavily used during warm-weather holidays and weekends.

■ **Take a backpacking stove** so you won't have to build fires for cooking.

■ **Repackage food supplies** in sealable bags or plastic bottles so there will be fewer boxes and tinfoil pouches to burn or carry.

On the Trail

■ **Don't litter**—not even the smallest of candy wrappers or cigarette butts. (When we drag our butts up to the Hangover for the view, we don't want to see yours half-twisted in the dirt at our feet.) If you pack it in, pack it out—all of it.

■ **Don't be a hider**—a person whose consciousness is caught between right and wrong. The undersides of rocks should be salamander sanctuaries and tree hollows should be wildlife dens—not beer can repositories.

■ **Remember that organic scraps are definitely litter.** No one wants to see your orange peels or peanut hulls or a campsite compost pile crowned with eggshells. Either burn it or carry it out.

■ **Carry a plastic bag with you.** Help pick up what those unpatriotic louts—those who do not respect the beautiful land of their own country—have left behind.

■ **Take the dump du jour at least 100 feet from the trail** and at least 150 feet from a campsite or water source. Dig a cat hole with boot heel or plastic trowel, then cover everything up well.

■ **Stay on the main trail** (preceding precept is notable exception) no matter how muddy, and do not cut across switchbacks. Cutting across switchbacks tramples vegetation, starts erosion, and encourages more shortcut taking. Feel free to educate the uninformed. Many people have no idea they are doing anything wrong.

■ **Step to the high side** so you don't cave in the lower side of the trail when stepping aside to let other hikers or backpackers pass.

■ **Don't pick, pluck, dig up, or cut up any flowers, plants, or trees,** not even the tiny ones you think no one will miss. Let offenders know of your disapproval, gently and tactfully, at least at first.

No-Trace Camping

■ **Don't use worn out, naked-ground campsites.** Let them heal. Use lightly worn existing campsites, or better yet, move well away from the trail (and from the stream) and make a no-trace campsite that will rarely, if ever, be used again.

■ **Don't cut standing trees** or pull up or beat down vegetation to make room for your tent or tents. Be gentle; think of the wilderness as a friend, and think of yourself as a guest. Fit in, tuck in, don't hack in.

■ **Don't enlarge an existing campsite.** There is no need for large groups to circle the wagons against the night. Fit in and tuck in.

■ **Absolutely no campsite construction**—leave the blueprints and hard hats at home: no boot bulldozing, trenching, or building rock or log furniture or shelves; no hammering nails in trees, digging latrines, or piling rocks to dam or bridge streams, etc.

■ **Use biodegradable soap** and dispose of waste water at least 100 feet from camp and 150 feet from any water source.

■ **Don't wash dirty dishes directly in a spring or stream.** Don't use soap on yourself or your clothes directly in a spring or stream.

■ **Don't spit your toothpaste on the campsite vegetation.** After a month of drought, heavily used sites resemble bird roosts.

■ **Make your campsite look at least as natural as when you found it.** Replace branches, twigs, and leaves cleared for the sleeping area.

■ **Keep length of stay to one or two nights.**

■ **Wear soft-soled shoes in camp.**

■ **Avoid building campfires.** Carry a portable camp stove for cooking. If you do start a fire, keep it small and use only dead and down wood. Leave the chain saws and axes at home.

■ **Erase all evidence of a campfire** built with no fire ring. Scatter the ashes, replace the duff, and camouflage the burned area.

■ **Don't build fire rings—tear them down.**

■ **Never build a fire on a dry, windy day.**

Backcountry Courtesy

The wilderness has been set aside as a haven for solitude, a place where the impact of civilization is scarcely noticeable. You can enhance the wilderness experience by following these guidelines.

■ **Leave radios and tape players at home.**

■ **Don't take a dog into the wilderness unless it is well trained.** Leave behind dogs that may growl or bark at other hikers.

■ **Take consideration**—do nothing that will interfere with someone else's enjoyment. It is considered insensitive to enter the wilderness with a very large group (a van or bus load, for example) that will completely overrun and overwhelm other hikers.

■ **Keep as quiet as possible.** Drunken parties, war whoops, and loud radios are frowned upon, and downright rude.

■ **Remember that campsites are first come, first served.** Don't whine, argue, or try to crowd in if someone already has the camp you really wanted. Move on down the trail.

■ **Help preserve the illusion of solitude, for yourself and others.** Make yourself as unobtrusive, as invisible, as possible. Use earth-tone tents and tarps and, if possible, camp far enough off the trail so that other hikers can't see you and vice versa. When choosing the color of your day or backpack, however, temper the ideal of unobtrusiveness with the reality of hunting—in and out of season.

Tips for Beginning Hikers

THIS IS A WHERE-TO AND WHY-TO BOOK, not a how-to book. There are already plenty of those. And after all the finger-wagging do's and don'ts in the environmental guidelines section, I am ambivalent about including still more. After all, wilderness is a place of freedom, where you make your own decisions and fill out your own report card. The wilderness, however, is also a place where mistakes are magnified. To help beginners avoid some of the mistakes I made when I first started hiking, I feel obligated to mention a few practical points—based on personal experience and years of observation.

Most of the predictable problems that occur while dayhiking or backpacking can be prevented with common sense and good judgment, but inexperience—not knowing what to expect, what to do, or when to do it—often can preclude good judgment. How can you avoid poison ivy if you don't know what it looks like? How do you know to take along moleskin if you've never heard of it? In hiking, as in almost every other endeavor, ignorance and inexperience are liabilities. That is why it is so important for beginning hikers, especially backpackers, to start out slow and easy, then progress from there.

■ **Think of the "what ifs" before you leave home.** What if it rains or snows? What if you can't find a particular junction? What if it turns cold? What if your hiking partner can't handle the climb? And so on. The more of these questions you can answer or solve to your satisfaction, the better your trip will be.

■ **Prepare a reasonable hiking plan.** Match your route and method of travel with your level of experience and fitness. If you are a first-timer, and unsure of your physical capabilities, try car camping and dayhiking first. That way you can learn some camping skills and gauge your mountain fitness level before planning your first backpacking trip.

■ **Protect your possibles—your food, extra clothes, matches, sleeping bag—from becoming wet.** Devise a way to keep your daypack or backpack dry at all times. Backpackers who wear rainsuits rather than ponchos should have a waterproof backpack cover. You may want to further protect your food, clothes, and sleeping bag with waterproof plastic bags. Trash compactor bags are cheap, sturdy, and waterproof. Overprepare to the point just short of ridiculousness.

■ **Take care of your feet.** Moleskin, cushioning shoe pads, arch supports, and Second Skin should prevent or alleviate most foot problems. As soon as you feel chafing, stop and stick some moleskin on your feet. It will protect you from blisters for days and days. If you already have a blister, try Second Skin to ease the pain and cushion the area.

■ **Dress appropriately.** Shorts are fine for wide, promenade trails where you have 5 feet of personal space. But on wilderness paths, where treadways are often narrow, shorts do not always afford adequate protection. They might on some trails, but definitely won't on others. Tight-fitting blue jeans, no matter how good they look on you, are the worst kind of pants to wear hiking, especially when wet. Pick a pair that are lightweight, loose fitting and fast drying.

■ **Take a walking stick.** When considering safety and survival, most people think of maps and compasses and sharp knives. In my experience, however, a hiking stick contributes more to your safety on a hourly and daily basis than almost anything else you can take along. It is especially important if you are dayhiking alone or backpacking. If you haven't fallen in the woods yet, you haven't hiked very much. When you fall while wearing a backpack, you fall fast and hard. A sharp knife may help you cut things to splint a broken bone, but a walking stick will almost always prevent you from falling and breaking a bone, or turning an ankle, in the first place.

■ **Make sure your water supply is safe.** For years, when my canteen ran dry, I took pleasure from drinking cold, clear, presumably pure water straight from springs and high rivulets. But no more. The odds finally caught up with me. While walking the trails described in this book, I suffered an attack of the Mini Watu—what Sioux Indians call water imps. My particular imp was Giardia; and attack is an apt word. Now I'm a born-again water purifier.

I won't go into the nauseous, gaseous details, but I do want to state unequivocally that you do not want these protozoan parasites to set up shop in your stomach. They make the shyest of persons get up and do what must be done. They make you sick; some of the prescribed pills make you sick; and after the parasites are dead and you are cured, they can leave your gut ravaged for months.

There are three general ways to purify water: boiling, filtering, or chemical treatment. Boiling, because of the time and fuel required, is usually considered impractical. In recent years water filters have become lighter and more effective. Before buying one, make sure it will at least remove all particles larger than 0.4 micron. You can also use water purification tablets, available at most backpacking shops. How-to books and magazines recommend tablets that use iodine as their principal purifying agent. The iodine-based tablets are safer and more effective (and retain their potency longer after the bottle is opened) than others. Some people, particularly those who have had water imps, filter first, then treat.

Adopt-a-Trail

THE U.S. FOREST SERVICE HAS INSTITUTED an "Adopt-a-Trail" program, which gives individuals, friends, families, and organizations the opportunity to do something worthwhile: to become Forest Service volunteers. The Forest Service provides a pat on the back and all the equipment—saws, shovels, axes, shin-guards, plastic bags—you could possibly use or carry. Volunteers provide the time, energy, and enthusiasm needed to clean up and trim out their adopted trails.

The Forest Service, and indeed all those who use and respect the wilderness, will greatly appreciate your help.

If you are interested in becoming the foster parent of a wilderness trail or a section of a long wilderness trail, call or write the Tellico Ranger District in the Cherokee National Forest or the Cheoah Ranger District in the Nantahala National Forest. (See the following page for addresses and phone numbers.) Don't worry, there are still plenty of trails to go around.

Addresses

THE NORTHWESTERN PORTION of the Joyce Kilmer–Slickrock Wilderness and the Citico Creek Wilderness are located within the Tellico Ranger District of the Cherokee National Forest. North Carolina's much larger share of the Joyce Kilmer–Slickrock Wilderness is located within the Cheoah Ranger District of the Nantahala National Forest. For more information, call or write:

Cherokee National Forest

Tellico Ranger District
USDA Forest Service
250 Ranger Station Road
Tellico Plains, TN 37385
(423) 253-2520

USDA Forest Service
Supervisor's Office
P.O. Box 2010
Cleveland, TN 37320
(615) 476-9700

Nantahala National Forest

Cheoah Ranger District
USDA Forest Service
Route 1, Box 16-A
Robbinsville, NC 28771
(704) 479-6431

USDA Forest Service
Supervisor's Office
P.O. Box 2750
Asheville, NC 28802
(704) 257-4200

Maps of the Cherokee National Forest, the Nantahala National Forest, and the combined wilderness are available from the Forest Service offices for a small fee. The title of the map of the combined wilderness is *Joyce Kilmer–Slickrock Wilderness and Citico Creek Wilderness.*

Topographic Quadrangles (1:24,000) are available from the United States Geological Survey: USGS Information Service, Box 25286, Denver, CO 80225, (303) 202-4700.

About the Author

TIM HOMAN, experienced hiker and outdoor writer, is the author of *The Hiking Trails of North Georgia* and the editor of *A Yearning for Wildness: Environmental Quotations from the Writings of Henry David Thoreau*. He lives in Colbert, Georgia, with his wife Page Luttrell.